ABOUT THE AUTHOR

Brydon Coverdale appeared on several quiz and game shows as a contestant, winning $300,000 on *Million Dollar Minute* before being cast as 'The Shark' on Channel Seven's *The Chase Australia*, where contestants must beat Brydon to win their cash prize. He has also worked as a writer for pub trivia and currently writes a bylined daily quiz in the *Herald Sun*, the *Daily Telegraph*, *The Courier Mail* and *The Advertiser*, as well as a weekly quiz in one of Australia's biggest rural newspapers, *The Weekly Times*. Away from quizzing, he spent eleven years as a cricket journalist for ESPNcricinfo, the world's leading cricket website, travelling the world to cover Australia's national team. He lives in Melbourne and is married with three children.

THE QUIZ MASTERS

Inside the world of trivia, obsession and million dollar prizes

BRYDON COVERDALE
(aka THE SHARK)

ALLEN&UNWIN
SYDNEY•MELBOURNE•AUCKLAND•LONDON

First published in 2022

pp. 196–198: Grateful acknowledgement is given for permission to quote from *A Thinking Reed* by Barry Jones, copyright © 2006. Used by permission of Allen & Unwin. All rights reserved.

Allen & Unwin
83 Alexander Street
Crows Nest NSW 2065
Australia
Phone: (61 2) 8425 0100
Email: info@allenandunwin.com
Web: www.allenandunwin.com

A catalogue record for this book is available from the National Library of Australia

ISBN 978 1 76106 550 7

Index by Puddingburn Publishing Services
Set in 11.9/20 pt Stempel Garamond LT Std by Bookhouse, Sydney
Printed in Australia by McPherson's Printing Group

10 9 8 7 6 5 4 3 2 1

FOR ZOE, MY CARRY-OVER CHAMPION

AND FOR HEIDI, FLETCHER AND AVERY, OUR THREE MAJOR PRIZES

CONTENTS

WHO AM I?

FOUR QUESTIONS. THIRTEEN SECONDS. FORTY-EIGHT THOUSAND DOLLARS.
I can do this, but I'll have to be bloody fast. Come on, Brydon.
Focus. Listen. Speed. Jump in when I can.

'And your time restarts . . . now.'

'The confectionery name "nougat" is from which—'[1] (*This*
must be about languages, I have to jump in and take the punt.)

'Correct.'

'In which Sydney park is the Archibald Fountain?[2]' (*Ugh,*
I'm from Melbourne; guess whatever Sydney park I can name.)

'Correct.'

---

[1] French
[2] Hyde Park

'The film *Darkest Hour* stars Kristin Scott who?[1]' (*Easy, there's only one actress with those names.*)

'Correct'.

'In which ocean is . . .' (*Two seconds left, do I jump in and guess Pacific, it's the biggest ocean with the most islands? No, I can spare one more second.*) '. . . South Georgia Island?[2]' (*Thank God I waited.*)

'Ooooohhh! He's got it, team! Oh, team, it does not get closer than that! I'm really sorry to say goodbye to that $48,000. You have been a terrific team . . .'

▼

Four good, hard-working people have just seen their cash prize—$12,000 each—vanish before their eyes. Had I stabbed at Centennial Park instead of Hyde Park, the money would have been theirs. If I had jumped in on the percentage guess—the Pacific Ocean—for the final question, they would have been laughing. Instead, their winnings have disappeared on a remote island in the South Atlantic. The contestants are devastated; I have done my job.

Perhaps running those two thoughts together is misleading. My job is not to devastate people, per se, but it's a common side effect. As a 'chaser' on the television quiz show *The Chase Australia*, my task is to stand between contestants and their prize

---

[1] Thomas
[2] Atlantic

money, to either beat them and stop them winning a cent, or to make them really earn their cash if they are good enough to defeat me. The role frequently leaves me with mixed feelings. Viewers may be surprised to learn that chasers even *have* feelings. Much like professional sportspeople, we are fiercely competitive and hate losing, but when we are beaten there is a silver lining: the ecstatic contestants on the winning team have just experienced the highlight of their year. It may even have been a life-changing moment. Good on them, I always think, while simultaneously kicking myself for not knowing what sport Ryan Broekhoff plays[1], or choosing the wrong colour for the left-hand stripe on Mexico's flag[2], or failing under intense time pressure to work out what four-letter word can precede 'file', 'polish' and 'clippers'[3]. The flip side is that, more often than not, the contestants go away disappointed, and I always feel for them. Why? Because I've been there before. Many, many times.

Years ago, well before *The Chase*, I read the popular science book *Outliers*, in which the author Malcolm Gladwell analyses the factors that contribute to success. Gladwell makes frequent references to the '10,000-hour rule', the concept that virtually anyone can reach the elite level in any skill if they put in 10,000 hours of practice. I saw his examples—musicians, sportspeople,

---

[1]   Basketball

[2]   Green

[3]   Nail (I find the answer to this kind of question either comes to mind straight
      away or not at all).

entrepreneurs—and wondered why I had wasted my time doing a bit of this and a bit of that. I was a fairly good cricket writer, having spent a decade as a correspondent for ESPNcricinfo, but anyone who works in the same field for ten years should become an expert. Outside work, I was a jack-of-some-trades and master of none. It never occurred to me that quizzing was a skill that I had spent thousands of hours honing—perhaps not 10,000, but well on the way. If that seems like a remarkable lack of self-awareness, I should explain that much of my quiz practice had taken place organically, over nearly three decades. When professional cricketers bat or bowl in the nets, they are clearly refining specific skills for an identifiable purpose. A pianist is obviously practising when they sit down at the piano. I didn't set out to become a professional quizzer. As far as I knew, no such job existed. But all those hours I came home from school and flicked through atlases and encyclopedias, memorised lists of prime ministers and capital cities, obsessively watched *Sale of the Century* and *Who Wants To Be a Millionaire?*, trained myself to go on those shows and win money, and wrote thousands of my own trivia questions, turned me into one.

I'm often asked what got me so interested in trivia. The glib answer is that, as the youngest of four children, I was always trying to prove that I was just as good as my older siblings whenever we played Trivial Pursuit. There is some truth to that, but the real explanation is that I have always been intensely competitive at games and sports, and deeply curious about the world around me. Combine those two traits and what do you have? An obsession with quizzing, a sport for the brain.

Sometimes I wonder what my grandfather would make of my job. Ned Pollard, my mother's father, was a rugged Aussie bloke who grew up the eldest of eight children with not much money, fought in World War II and drove an Army truck that was blown up by a German mine in the North African desert, came home to a Soldier Settler block, cut down timber and split fence posts and built a dairy farm from scratch, lost a finger in a machinery accident, milked cows twice a day for most of his life and worked his body bloody hard until his heart gave up while he was carting hay in his late seventies. And here is his grandson sitting on his backside in an air-conditioned studio, in a tailored blue suit, hair slicked back like a sleazy Mob lawyer, showing off by recalling what famous singer launched the House of Dereon fashion label[1], or which Marvel character is also known as Power Man[2], or the name of the easternmost Caribbean island[3]. I hardly know what to make of this absurd situation myself.

I shouldn't make assumptions. My grandpa loved reading and learning, and in later years we discovered he was a secret bush poet. When I was fourteen, I read his most poignant poem, about the passage of time, at his funeral, and there wasn't a dry eye in the church. He was also a great raconteur, always ready

---

[1]   Beyoncé
[2]   Luke Cage
[3]   Barbados

with a funny story or a witty aside. He would probably have been proud of the learning involved in my job—and of the need to not take the role too seriously. All four of my grandparents were dairy farmers. Ten of my twelve uncles and aunts were dairy farmers. My parents were dairy farmers. As a child, I had milk flowing through my veins. (Not literally, that would have killed me. Blood is a superior fluid for the human circulation system.)

My father, David Coverdale (who shares his name with the lead singer of which rock band?[1]), dreamed of being a radio presenter, and, as a naturally talkative, curious type, he would have been great at it. But he never got that chance. He was pushed into dairying by his father and made to leave school at fourteen despite having little interest in the farm. He never wanted to impose that on his children; we were encouraged to choose our way in life, and, for all four of us, that meant moving to Melbourne to study at university. Like many family farms of the era, ours was sold when Mum and Dad retired. I studied journalism and travelled the world covering the Australian team's tours in my dream job as a cricket writer. Now, I'm a professional quiz player. How is that even a thing? Here I am, a married father of three, dropping my kids off at school or kinder while the other parents go off to perform valuable, important occupations. Doctors. Police officers. Teachers. But I wouldn't trade this job for the world.

Dictionaries tell us that trivia, by definition, has little value or importance. Dictionaries are wrong. Trivia can bring together

---

[1] There are two acceptable answers: Whitesnake or Deep Purple.

families over a board game. It can unite communities at a fund-raising quiz night. It keeps friends in touch over a pub trivia evening, and in a locked-down world in 2020 and 2021 it maintained vital social connections through quiz events on Zoom. It has turned the loneliest hour, midnight to 1 a.m., into a lively hub on national radio. Trivia can provide an outlet for people who struggle to find their place in life, and gives them something of which they can be proud. And if that is not enough value, it can also lead to cold, hard cash. Just ask Martin Flood, Rob Fulton and Andrew Skarbek, all of whom became millionaires on Australian quiz shows. Just ask the countless other contestants who have earned life-changing money on television quizzes.

Just ask me. At 5 p.m. on weeknights, I sit in judgement on trivia players, hundreds upon hundreds of contestants since *The Chase Australia* began in 2015. I know exactly how they feel. Once upon a time, it was me trying to win big on game shows. Or win small on radio quizzes. Or win bragging rights at Trivial Pursuit. This is the story of my experiences—the triumphs, the hurdles, the failures—and those of others like me. From prime ministers to meatworkers, from comedians to funeral celebrants, Australians love their trivia. Why? That's the million-dollar question.

CHAPTER 1

A LATE-NIGHT INITIATION

IT'S WELL AFTER MIDNIGHT AND THE HOUSE IS DEAD QUIET. I'M THE ONLY one still awake. A long telephone extension cord runs from the hall of our farm homestead, all the way to my bedroom, under the door and into the privacy of my own personal space, an important fortress of solitude for any fifteen-year-old boy. I have the phone clutched to my ear—not for a breathless exchange with a girlfriend, although I am excited. In fact, I'm not even part of the conversation; I'm eavesdropping on two people I've never met. And then, I hear the click. The volume has increased, and so has my adrenaline. Oh god, it's happening. It's actually happening. And a familiar, mellifluous voice is now talking directly to me: 'Brydon from Camperdown, you're next . . .'

▼

You don't get good at something by taking the easy path. Don Bradman honed his skills by throwing a golf ball against a water tank and hitting it with a cricket stump. It was such a difficult task that a cricket ball then seemed like a watermelon to The Don, and he became the greatest batter in cricket history. I practised my cricket by throwing a tennis ball against a big, wooden stable door, and I used a cricket bat. I became a mediocre middle-order player for the Bookaar Pelicans in the Mount Emu Creek Cricket Association, a cricketing MECCA in name only. I didn't push myself at sport, but I did when it came to quizzing. And what better way than by tackling a live, national radio quiz at the age of fifteen? In a small rural town, with all my siblings having moved to the big smoke, and the internet still in its infancy, I didn't have much choice if I wanted a trivia challenge.

Every weeknight, after the midnight news bulletin, ABC radio host Tony Delroy opened the phone lines to callers from all over Australia, and sometimes beyond, for the cult quiz known as The Challenge. It was a 25-question affair, with five categories and five questions in each. The categories varied every day and so did the contestants, depending on who had achieved the perfect timing required to dial in at the precise moment when a space on the switchboard opened up. Since that was a skill all of its own, the same contestants frequently popped up.

And what a mishmash of callers it was. The occasional expert quizzer rang in, but for others The Challenge was first and foremost a valuable social outlet. It was a malleable hour of radio that could go in any direction. For some callers, the appeal was hearing a friendly voice on the other end of the phone, a host who was up for a chat about anything. It was a safe, inclusive space that welcomed all comers and fostered a unique community that built up around the show. For many, the quiz was secondary. Tony frequently gave clues if a caller was struggling with an answer. In theory, the second half of the quiz was conducted in a so-called 'clue-free zone', but Tony was such a softie that he didn't always stick to his own rule.

The format was simple: one contestant at a time would choose from the five categories, and kept playing until they answered a question incorrectly. Whoever was next in the switchboard queue took their place. The winner was the caller who correctly answered question 25. The prize was a random assortment of goodies from the ABC Shop—a book, perhaps, or a CD, maybe the current *Gardening Australia* magazine. The winner was also banned from the quiz for a month, a rule intended to make sure the same people didn't triumph night after night.

I'm not sure how many times I made it through to play The Challenge—probably no more than ten. Half the battle was navigating the nearly constant busy signal on the ABC phone lines. My technique was to pre-dial the phone number during the midnight news bulletin, hang up, and then, the instant the news finished and the 'Lines are now open' announcement was made, to hit redial and hope I had beaten most of the country. Failing that, I would press redial as soon as each contestant gave an incorrect answer and was cut off. Sometimes that was the better outcome, as it meant getting through later in the quiz when I would have to answer fewer questions to win.

Usually, I failed to get through, but twice I won the quiz by answering question 25. I remember my first winning question, from 1997: 'Name either of the countries that will co-host the 2002 soccer World Cup[1]'. I was no soccer fan. But I was fifteen years old; Tony took pity and reluctantly gave me a clue (I think he told me it would be held in Asia), and I guessed correctly. It was an exhilarating moment: I was a Year 10 student in a small country town, and I had won a national quiz! I had won a . . . Tania Kernaghan CD?

I didn't get a lot of mail as a teenager. There were a couple of penfriends who dropped off after introductory letters. There were the magazines I received from the 'M-Team', the dairy industry's attempt at a cool club for children. There was the adult video catalogue from a PO Box in Canberra that I had trouble explaining when I opened it at the dinner table, and which it turned out was retaliation from a mate who was annoyed that I had signed him up to the M-Team. And then there was the package that arrived from the ABC a week or two after my victory. In it was a book I knew I would never read (*Fermat's Last Theorem* by Simon

---

[1] Japan and South Korea

Singh), and the CD, which I barely touched for fear it would give me country music germs. And I couldn't have been happier.

▼

'It's surprising how competitive it got,' Tony Delroy says. 'It was only a fairly modest prize, but everybody was very keen to have the bragging rights.'

Fittingly, I'm interviewing Tony over the phone. Meeting in person a voice I've known for thirty years would be unsettling, like sitting face-to-face with Siri.

'If you gave somebody a nudge in The Challenge and [the audience] thought that it was too big a push, you heard about it.'

Sometimes, though, clues were essential. On one occasion, Tony asked who wrote a series of novels featuring the private detective Cliff Hardy. The answer was Peter Corris, the Sydney author renowned as one of Australia's leading mystery writers. I'm a crime fiction buff, and the Cliff Hardy books are among my favourites. Apparently the same couldn't be said of Tony's radio audience. Gradually, he fed out clues, giving the first name Peter, then the letter *C*. Then *o*. Then *r*. Then another *r*. Then *i*.

'I was down to "Peter C–o–double r–i" and they're still getting it wrong,' Tony says. 'It knocked out about 29 contestants.'

Corris might have been highly respected within his genre, but it wasn't much of a testimonial for his cut-through with the general public. Whether he was listening, and cringing, as caller after caller failed to identify him, remains a mystery, but if he wasn't, someone told him about it.

'He certainly knew about it after a while,' Tony says, 'because I did a literary lecture with him and he said, "You don't have to tell me."'

Still, it was after midnight, so no one was listening, right? Wrong. Tony Delroy's *Nightlife* show became a national institution and the quiz a radio icon. Tony's show started in 1990, originally live to air in New South Wales, Queensland and Victoria. Gradually, it broadened to a national audience.

'What happens with radio is that it almost goes into the reverse of television,' Tony says. 'As television peters out, radio actually lifts up, particularly talk radio. And we were finding that from about 9.30 p.m. eastern [time], the population would start to rise. And quite often on a Friday night, we'd be getting up to probably 30 per cent, 35 per cent of the available audience for that 12.00 to 1.00 hour.'

Calls came from anywhere and everywhere—and not just within Australia. When digital radio took off, contestants rang in from all over the world. There was a regular caller from Edinburgh, another from Los Angeles. London. Italy. Once, a listener who was holidaying on a Caribbean cruise called in from the Turks and Caicos Islands.

'There was one couple who were at the Mawson Station in Antarctica,' Tony says, 'and they rang in on a couple of occasions to play while they were down there on the ice sheet.'

You never knew who would turn up on The Challenge—Tony tells me the former leader of the Australian Democrats, Cheryl Kernot, sometimes called in from her Canberra office. But the heart and soul of the quiz was the long list of regulars who rang in, ostensibly to play, but just as much to have a chat. Some voices became almost as familiar as Tony himself. There was elderly Tom from Toowoomba, a dyed-in-the-wool union man and salt-of-the-earth Aussie. There was Neven from St Kilda, a trivia obsessive who frequently answered huge runs of questions and often deliberately threw question 25, so he wouldn't suffer the month-long ban (we'll encounter Neven again). And there was a woman from the New South Wales town of Bingara who went by the name of Magpie, for whom The Challenge proved life changing. On a trip to Queensland, Magpie met up with another regular caller, and the next thing Tony knew was he had been sent an invitation to their wedding.

As with any community, there were sad moments as well.

'We did lose some people along the path,' Tony says. 'I always remember Eileen from Cairns, who was a lovely old lady, well in her eighties, and everybody used to be drawn to the fact that she was such a nice person by the sound of her voice. When she passed, there were cards, letters and floral tributes sent to the church from listeners around the country.'

It was on The Challenge that my colleague on *The Chase Australia*, the 'Supernerd', Issa Schultz, cut his quizzing teeth as a teenager. Starting around the age of sixteen, Issa became one of the regulars, winning the quiz, by his estimate, 'six or eight times', and collecting a swag of ABC prizes.

'*Delicious* magazine made up most of the bookcase at one point,' Issa jokes.

For four years, Issa called in most nights, and had an outstanding success rate at finding his way through to the switchboard. Like most regulars, he discovered the trick to getting through—a method I never stumbled on myself.

'I had two landlines and there was a trick to it,' Issa says. 'The touchtone phones would redial very quickly, so I would continuously be doing that. But also, they'd often let you sit in the queue before they announced the lines were open. I remember ringing in during the weather, and the guy on the switch would bring you in. I think a lot of regulars knew that, hence it was always Magpie from Bingara or whoever. If I was stuck somewhere with just a mobile phone—and these were old mobiles—I wouldn't get on as it took forever to redial.'

Just as you never knew who would pop up on the quiz, you also had no idea who was listening—and who might find The Challenge life changing without even calling in. The comedian Denise Scott wrote in her memoir, *All That Happened at Number 26*, that when she and her husband John were going through a difficult time in their marriage, Tony Delroy's quiz helped them reconcile. They would lie in bed at night listening to The Challenge, answering the questions. 'Doing something together that wasn't connected to love or pain helped us to reconnect,' Scott told *The Age* in 2010. So, The Challenge generated one marriage and helped save another—let's not delve into whether it ever had the opposite effect.

The midnight quiz thrived for a combination of reasons. One was its accessibility: anyone with a radio could listen, and anyone with a phone could call. You weren't playing for sheep stations but you could call in from a sheep station. The questions were fairly gettable, with the odd tough one thrown in, and the vibe wasn't too serious. It became a community in which listeners felt they knew the familiar callers, from all corners of Australia. And it was guided, with a light touch, by a welcoming host who fostered the community—some of whom he came to regard as friends. If you asked Australians to name the country's most iconic quiz host, many people would jump straight to Tony Barber or Eddie McGuire, the highly visible faces of television quizzing for decades. But there is an argument for the understated, underrated Tony Delroy, who hosted his national radio show for 26 years and, by accompanying listeners as they dozed off, achieved an intimacy that no television host ever could.

'That's the way it was designed,' Tony says. 'It was light, bright, and if you happened to be still awake and functioning, we went into the "Issue of the day" immediately afterwards, because it gave people another outlet to get involved.'

As time passed, new challenges arose. Tony was always happy for his callers to have a 'brains trust', a few friends or family members who could be consulted about an answer. That was part of the community spirit. But the nature of a radio quiz, and not being able to see the callers, meant that when internet search engines became more powerful, some players found it tempting to expand their brains trust to include the worldwide web.

'Nine times out of ten,' Tony says, 'you can pick it because you hear the keys moving in the background. My ears are really attuned to people using other sources to come up with the answers. And the thing that gives it away—they initially have no idea and then miraculously pull an answer straight out of a hat.'

The googling of answers is a constant difficulty for pub quiz hosts these days too, although at least they might spot the telltale player looking suspiciously down at their phone. And it's at pub trivia that Tony nowadays gets most of his exposure to quizzing, having departed from the ABC in 2016. Not surprisingly, after two and a half decades of hosting a nightly quiz, and asking what must have been well over a hundred thousand questions, he has found himself a reasonably good trivia player.

'I'm quite handy at pub trivia these days,' Tony says. 'We do it probably every two or four weeks. Some mates, just for a bit of fun. We do okay. We win more than we lose.'

Still quizzing after all these years.

▼

Tony Delroy might have departed, but the *Nightlife* lives on—and so does the quiz, now known as The Mighty Challenge. I haven't been a regular listener since my days as a teenage caller, but if I ever found myself with the radio on after midnight it was easy to slip back into his quiz, like a favourite blanket. The soothing voice, the chatty contestants, the clue-free zone—the task of wrapping The Challenge up by 1 a.m., which could be its own challenge if the questions were too hard or the callers too rambling. In October 2018, I decided to listen to the quiz for the first time since Tony's departure. The host was Philip Clark, who had succeeded Tony as the *Nightlife* presenter. The names of the callers had changed, but their propensity for conversation had not.

The first contestant, who gave his full name as Mister Barry Byrne, from Mount Isa, describing himself as a passionate constitutional monarchist, welcomed the Duke and Duchess of Sussex to Australia and congratulated them on the impending arrival of their first baby. He chose the category 'Born in Russia', but was unable to name the American composer born Israel Baline in Russia in 1888[1]. (Sadly, Barry Byrne died in 2020 aged 52. An obituary in the *North West Star* newspaper explained that he was a disability pensioner who regularly arranged morning teas at the local library to celebrate the Queen's Birthday and her accession to the throne. A former mayor of Mount Isa described him as 'fascinating and eccentric but loved by everyone'.)

Next was Victoria, from the small town of Jeparit in Victoria's Wimmera district; she spoke about the unexpected rain the town had just had and chatted to Philip about the former Australian prime minister who was born in Jeparit[2], before she too bowed out on the question of the composer. David from Mosman Park in Perth also talked about the weather and picked the correct composer before switching to a category called 'Cops and Robbers'. The question of which animated television series

---

[1] Irving Berlin
[2] Sir Robert Menzies, whose family ran the tiny town's general store.

features Police Chief Wiggum[1] didn't suit him, and he departed, telling Philip: 'I'll speak to you next week'.

Then came the most remarkable caller, Emily, who on *Nightlife* was known as 'The Duchess of Dubbo'. Emily, who sounded ancient yet lively, had a lengthy chat to Philip about what was going on in her life before they finally returned to Chief Wiggum. 'Oooh, I haven't had a TV for over forty years,' she said. 'Okay, is it . . . okay, geez, I'm stumped with that one, darlin'. Can you give me a different one? Hey, Philip, give me an animal one, will ya?' (I later discovered that Emily Lyons was 95 at the time—on her birthday, a month earlier, Philip had spoken to Emily about her extraordinary life that included Native American heritage, travelling with the circus in her youth and living as a ward of the state. She was clearly a beloved member of the *Nightlife* family, despite rarely answering a question correctly.)

The name of the country that produces more than half of the world's hazelnuts[2] proved tricky—a damn hard question. The only Russian tennis player to win a career grand slam[3] tripped a few people up. A caller with a broad Australian accent, on the road between Narrandera and West Wyalong, told Philip of the howling wind: 'I hope everyone's got their dogs on the chain tonight, it'd blow the buggers away. It'd blow the rainwater clean out of the tank, it would.' Asked which Italian company

---

[1] *The Simpsons* (bonus points if you knew Chief Wiggum's first name was Clancy).

[2] Turkey

[3] Maria Sharapova

uses a quarter of the world's hazelnuts[1], he took a good stab at Nestlé but was incorrect. As 1 a.m. approached, some long tangents having taken a chunk out of the hour, Philip moved into speed-quizzing mode to get The Mighty Challenge finished. Finally, he found a winner when a caller named Karen correctly answered question 25, identifying which riddle first appeared in print in an 1847 edition of *The Knickerbocker* magazine[2].

Sometimes, the quiz takes a different path, depending on which callers make it through. I heard in recent years of a contestant who had won big money on television quiz shows calling up one night and answering virtually all the questions himself. Quizzing is not always about cash and prizes. I wonder if The Challenge would have survived for thirty years had it been more serious. I suspect not, because then it would be less fun. A key reason the quiz has worked so well for so long is a counterintuitive one: because the stakes are so low.

---

[1] Ferrero

[2] 'Why did the chicken cross the road? To get to the other side.'

CHAPTER 2

HANDS ON BUZZERS

FIONA: $50

BRYDON: $45

JOHN: $30

It's okay, I'll be fine. The odds are in my favour by 20 to 1. If Fiona answers this question correctly, I'm safe. If I answer correctly, I'm safe. If John answers correctly there's a six-out-of-seven chance I'm safe. There is, statistically, a 95 per cent chance that I will be safe. But it's more than that really, because this is a 'Who am I?' question, my greatest strength. Then why am I so nervous? Because 95 per cent is not 100 per cent. If John answers correctly and picks the $25 from the Fame Game board, I'm eliminated. Sunk. And I can't be sunk yet. There's $270,000 on the line. Win eight episodes and the jackpot is mine. This is

14

episode four. I'm nearly halfway there. It'll be fine. Listen for the birth and death dates. It'll be fine. Oh, god, please let it be fine.

'Who am I? Born in 1890 (*Wait, where's the date of death? They always give a date of death.*), I worked in the US, England and France before becoming a foundation member of the French Communist Party in 1920. (*Okay, it's someone French.*) Founder of the Indochina Communist Party (*Wait, could it be Ho Chi Minh? I need another clue, I need to hear 'Vietnam'.*) in Hong Kong, I returned to my—John?'

'Ho Chi Minh.'

Shit, shit, shit. John has got it. Why didn't I buzz in? Okay, don't panic. There are seven faces on the Fame Game board. Only one can knock me out. Please don't pick the $25, please don't pick the $25.

'So, John, which of our famous faces would you like?'

John, a jovial, white-haired pensioner from Langwarrin on the Mornington Peninsula scans the seven faces on the board. Three questions ago, I had a healthy lead. I was on $60; Fiona, a nurse from Adelaide, was on $50; and John, having answered a few questions right and a few questions wrong, was back on the starting score of $20. As the leader at that point, midway through round three, I had the option to play the 'Cash Card' game, to spend $15 of my score for a one-in-four chance at winning $5000 cash. To play, I would drop behind Fiona and there was a tiny risk in doing so, because the lowest-scoring player at the end of the round would be eliminated. But with two regular questions remaining plus the final 'Who am I?', I felt safe. Could I be eliminated? Yes, if John staged an uncharacteristic late surge, but it was like a team needing 36 off the final over to win a cricket match: statistically possible, but not going to happen. Sure, Sir Garfield Sobers once hit six sixes in an over, but John seemed more Garfield the Cat than Garfield Sobers. It was a risk that I, as a nineteen-year-old first-year university student, was willing to take for a chance at $5000. I played the Cash Card, did not win the $5000 and set my mind back on the game.

The host, Glenn Ridge, continued with the next two questions. 'From his aggressive foreign-policy stance, Germany's Otto von Bismarck was nicknamed the what chancellor?' I didn't know and was disconcerted to hear John buzz in with the correct answer[1].

'Which document invites applications from the public to subscribe for securities of a corporation or proposed corporation?' An arts student, all I knew about finance was how to split a rent bill five ways. But John nailed this answer too[2]. Now he has chimed in with Ho Chi Minh, and I'm sweating. Fiona, on $50, is safe. I'm on $45 and John has $30. John has just completed a hat-trick of questions having trailed virtually all night. He would probably prefer to pick a prize off the board, something he can take home instead of a useless bump to his score. John looks over the famous faces and makes his selection.

'Suzie Wilks.'

---

[1]   Iron
[2]   Prospectus

And my fate, my lifelong quiz show dream, rests on what *Changing Rooms* presenter Suzie Wilks has hidden behind her face.

▼

A church hall in Toorak might have seemed an unusual location for *Sale of the Century* to hold auditions, but to me it made perfect sense. Toorak was Melbourne's wealthiest suburb; *Sale* called itself 'Australia's richest quiz'. A church was a place of worship; *Sale* was my religion. When I moved from the small town of Camperdown to Melbourne at the end of high school, to study journalism at university, my first point of business was not to unpack my belongings or buy my uni books but to call Channel Nine and ask how to become a contestant on *Sale*. I had been obsessed with the show from an early age. Like plenty of Aussie children, I had idolised footy players and cricketers and had their pictures on my wall. Unlike most kids, I put *Sale* champions on the same pedestal.

Cary Young was the best of the best, the Don Bradman of *Sale*. Cary was a diminutive chap with a faint Kiwi accent and a distinctive goatee beard; it was no coincidence that when I made my television debut on *Sale* I had a goatee myself, channelling the great man. Then there was Virginia Noel, Fran Powell, David Poltorak, David Bock, Kate Buckingham. The list goes on. As a child, I would have paid good pocket money to put up a poster of them, if such a thing existed.

On family holidays, if we were still on the road at 5.30 p.m., when *Sale* aired in country regions, my parents wouldn't hear the end of it. Why were we not checked in to our accommodation yet? Did they not understand that holidays were a 9-to-5.30 affair? *Sale of the Century* didn't take a break just because we did. It was a hard sell to dairy-farming parents who understandably wanted to make the most of their annual two weeks off. But to me, missing an episode of *Sale* was like missing the Australian cricket side or my favourite football team, Carlton, playing a game. And while I wasn't hopeless at footy or cricket, I was never going to reach the elite level. *Sale* was another matter. That was something I *could* aim for, a realistic goal that was always in the back of my mind, if not the front.

Within days of moving to the city, I sent off a stamped, self-addressed envelope to a post box in South Melbourne, as advised by the Channel Nine switchboard. Three weeks later, a letter arrived inviting me to audition. I arrived at St John's in Toorak on a March evening in 2000, carrying a clipboard and pen, because, as the letter made clear, 'you will be writing on your knee'. As prospective contestants were checked off a list, ushered in and seated in rows of chairs, I scanned the room to assess the competition. There must have been a hundred of us. Mostly men. Mostly middle-aged or older. The more I looked, the more obvious it became: I was very, very young to be a late middle-aged man. Still, I was hopeful. Back in 1988, a sixteen-year-old named Andrew Werbik had won the lot on *Sale*. I had two years on him.

A fifty-question general knowledge quiz was followed by interviews for those who passed. I don't recall much about the questions except that they were hard. Really hard. When they asked what city was Russia's primary naval base during World War II[1], I knew I was in trouble. There was also something about centrifugal force. Or was it centripetal force? To me they both sounded like challenges Mike Whitney might have refereed on *Gladiators*. The upshot was that I scored in the low twenties, and the pass mark was 27 out of 50. I had spent years dismissing losing *Sale* contestants as unworthy dummies, but I now realised that everyone who made it onto the show deserved respect. If they had failed on camera, it must have been down to other factors: nerves, lack of speed, strong competition. But they had all succeeded where I had not: they had passed this audition.

So I went back to life as a first-year uni student, living in a share-house in West Melbourne with four friends who had also moved from Camperdown. Ours had been such a small year level that this share-house constituted a third of the graduating class. Only fourteen of us had finished Year 12, which took some of the shine off my achievement of being dux. There could hardly have been a smaller puddle in which to be the big fish. Now, the blow of failing the *Sale* audition made me realise how good I wasn't.

The silver lining was that you could audition again, so on a cold winter's night in mid-July, I found myself again in the St John's church hall, hoping for divine intervention. The questions

---

[1] Vladivostok

fell my way and I passed the general knowledge test. I remember
the thrill of nailing an obscure answer—Frank Sinatra's middle
name[1]—and the trepidation of wondering what the producers
would ask me in the interview. I wasn't the outgoing, loquacious
type. But I had one big advantage, though I didn't realise it: I was
a teenager. Anyone who didn't fit the dominant middle-aged bloke
demographic—women and the very young, especially—stood a
better-than-average chance of being selected, to ensure variety
in contestants. In hindsight, I suspect all I had to prove in that
interview was that I could hold a conversation and would not
hide under my chair if the host asked me how I was going.

Three months later, the producers called me: I was in. I had
three days to prepare for the biggest moment of my life. Three
days to get my hands on a suit, three shirts and three ties. What
the hell was I going to wear? I didn't own a suit. I had worn a tie
to my grandfather's funeral when I was fourteen and a lime-green
clip-on bow tie when I worked at a Rite-Way supermarket in
Camperdown as an adolescent. That was my tie-wearing experience. I jumped on a train to Geelong, where my eldest sister
lived, and together we embarked on a shopping expedition whose
outcome can only be described as regrettable. The problem wasn't
that I had champagne taste on a beer budget, but that I had no
taste on a beer budget. At the cheapest menswear store we could
find (in Geelong, a hotly contested title) I saw a mannequin
dressed in a double-breasted beige suit with a black, faux-silk

---

[1]   Albert

shirt and a charcoal tie with a pattern of golden circles. At least, that was how it looked to me, but I am a little bit colour-blind. It reminded me of something Chandler might have worn in *Friends*, so I bought the whole ensemble, plus two more shirts and ties. The suit was far too big, a problem I would kill to have these days. Ever since watching myself on *Sale*, I have understood the expression 'All over him like a cheap suit'—I was more suit than man. The salesman, keen for his commission, told me it looked good. Incredibly, my sister didn't talk me out of buying it. I have questioned her judgement ever since.

To complete the look, I forgot to visit the barber and was left with hair sticking out so far at the sides I looked like the Flying Nun. On a Thursday morning in October 2000, I was a sight to create sore eyes as I caught the train to Burnley Station and made the ten-minute walk to Channel Nine's Bendigo Street studios. I was early, but gradually other contestants arrived. I made hasty judgements: *too old, will be slow on the buzzer; too friendly—no killer instinct; looks focused, could be a threat.* They probably did the same about me: *too young, shocking dress sense—clueless.*

Four hours of formalities later, we were taken to a corner of the studio audience to watch the first of the five episodes to be recorded. Before each episode, a producer announced which contestants would play the next game. The first, the 'Monday' game, came and went. Then Tuesday. Then Wednesday. Then Thursday. Still I sat in the audience. It was 6.15 p.m. when the Friday game was filmed; I had been at Bendigo Street nearly ten hours. The studio audience had started as twenty senior citizens who had been bussed in to enjoy a day out. By early evening they had long since gone home, possibly even to bed, and only four people—my mother, my brother and two strangers—remained when the producers called out: 'Brydon Coverdale'.

I made my television debut in front of a virtually empty studio, introduced on camera by the co-host, Karina Brown, as 'Brydon Coverdale, whose interests include tennis' instead of Brydon Coverdale, who actually enjoyed table-tennis. All of these factors relaxed me.

Meanwhile, something about the buzzers caught my eye. Each one had a bolt in it. A big, metal bolt, right in the middle, just where contestants would have to press down. That wasn't how it was supposed to be. Here I was, about to make my debut on national television, a quarter of a million dollars up for grabs, fixated on this bolt connecting the buzzer to the desk. Some kids dream of wearing a baggy green cap for Australia; for as long as I could remember, I had coveted that red buzzer. It was supposed to be smooth and perfect, like *Sale of the Century* itself. Instead, it was an introduction to the magic of television, where all that matters is how things appear on camera.

I didn't know it but my brain was doing me a favour, distracting itself from what was about to unfold. If my focus was on the buzzer, it meant it wasn't on the cash jackpot or the carry-over champion to my left, who had proven himself a winner. Or on the cameras. I have since learnt the value of distraction in such moments. On *The Chase*, as I sit in my lofty tower while the studio is set up for my final chase, all eyes are watching me and wondering whether I can catch the contestants. I need to find a moment of Zen and empty my brain. My solution is to stare at a strip of cascading lights behind and above the contestants, which has a mesmerising effect. The cash that I'm defending, the score on the board, the contestants, the cameras all disappear while I stare at the rippling lights. And then I'm ready. All extraneous thoughts are gone, and I can focus on each question as it comes, just as, in cricket, a good batter plays each ball on its merits. I didn't understand any of this when I was nineteen, but the bolt in that buzzer drained everything else from my mind.

To my right sat a funeral celebrant named Lynn, to my left a nurse called Ann. And to my far left was David, whose occupation, as far as I was concerned, was 'carry-over champion'. For most of its twenty-one years on air, *Sale*'s format was three contestants per episode. But this was 2000: rebranded as *Sale of the New Century*, it was trying to boost its flagging ratings by expanding to four contestants and eliminating the lowest scorers after rounds two and three. I wasn't worried about that. I was a young man full of trivial facts but equally bursting with hubris. Nobody would have known it to look at me—the quietly spoken, understated teenager, the type little old ladies watching at home would have called 'a nice young man'—but I felt five foot eight and bulletproof. I was destined to win the quarter of a million dollars.

It felt exhilarating when I buzzed in and got off the mark quickly with an easy answer: 'The point at which one is neither gaining nor losing is known as break what?[1]'

Anticipation was the key to success on *Sale*. The time to buzz in was not when you knew the answer, but when you knew that you would know the answer. If you knew your world capitals, for example, the time to buzz was when Glenn Ridge (or Tony Barber in earlier days) was about to give the critical clue. 'What is the capital city of—BUZZ!' The host's momentum meant he would deliver one or two more words after a contestant engaged their buzzer, so when the host finally said '—Denmark', the player who had buzzed early had the answer to themselves[2]. Using this tactic, before long I was in the lead and jumped at the chance to spend some of my points in the gift shop to buy a sewing machine (I gave the machine to my mother; I cared only about the $200 cash Glenn threw in, which paid for my cheap suit).

A whirlwind of questions later, the carry-over champion was knocked out after round three and I was too quick for Ann in the final fast-money round, the 'Mad Minute'. Not only had I won, I had annihilated my competition, finishing on $127—any score over $100 was considered outstanding. After my win I randomly picked a major prize off the board: a suite of bedroom furniture. I wasn't in this for beds and dressing tables; I was here for the jackpot. I was now the carry-over champion, and a break

---

[1] Even

[2] Copenhagen

in the recording schedule meant I had three weeks to prepare for my next day of filming. Three weeks of my housemates telling me all the things they were going to spend my winnings on: a plasma TV for our bachelor pad was the big-ticket item. I was happy to go along with the fun. After my triumph on day one, I felt unbeatable, ready to fulfil my destiny as the next Cary Young.

▼

'Those couches you're sitting on—we've had them redone. The clock, that mirror, this thing. That table. The buffet . . .'

If this is not the house *Sale* bought, it's the house it furnished. Lyn Young scans the living room, racking her brain to recall what else in the house was a *Sale of the Century* prize. It might be easier to point out what wasn't. The trampoline and swing set that are still in the garden, was that from the first episode? The silverware. There was a bed. And the car, of course. Once upon a time Lyn knew the prize list back to front. So did her husband, Cary, but then, he knew everything. Cary appeared on 70 episodes of *Sale* in Australia, plus four in the USA in an international tournament. Armed with a strong memory, the training discipline of a boxer and a deeply competitive nature, Cary was the standard by which all *Sale* champions were judged. After one particularly intense tournament of champions that featured ten episodes filmed back to back, Cary had bruises all the way up his forearm from slamming the buzzer so hard. Did he at least win it? You bet he did.

The dark hair has gone white but the goatee remains. As Cary Young sits down for a chat in his Melbourne home in 2017, at 76 years of age, he thinks back to where his television journey started. Originally from New Zealand, he had married Lyn and moved to her home town, Charters Towers in northern Queensland, where they were living with their two small children and Cary was a meatworker in the abattoir, with a plan to head across the ditch and raise the children in New Zealand. But when *Sale of the Century* debuted in 1980, all plans were put on hold.

'As soon as I started to watch *Sale*, I thought, "Oh, I've got to get on to this,"' Cary recalls.

He was forty years of age, had no official training and no real profession. As a young man in New Zealand, he had worked in customs and mineral exploration. In Charters Towers, some 130 kilometres inland from Townsville, abattoir work was the easiest to pick up. But his real talent was an incredible breadth of knowledge that Cary's fellow meatworkers would never have suspected was hidden behind his quiet exterior.

As a boy, Cary missed a lot of school with bouts of asthma, but convalescence allowed him to read as widely as he wanted. History was his great love, and everything he read he filed in his trap-like memory. When he auditioned for *Sale*, he scored 40 out of 50—enough for the producers to suspect they had a champion on their hands. He had to take several days off work at the abattoir just to travel the 1300 kilometres to Brisbane to try out for the show. It was worth it. Within a few days, Cary was flown to Melbourne to take on a carry-over champion playing his sixth game and going for the car. It was December 1981; *Sale* had been on air for eighteen months and was about to discover that its biggest star was a meatworker from the fringes of the outback.

Sale of the Century might have been new to Cary, but it was not completely unknown to Australian audiences. The same format, more or less, had existed in the early seventies, also hosted by Tony Barber, as *The Great Temptation*, though it was based on an American format that used the *Sale of the Century* name. When the show was revived in 1980, the American title was adopted, and in 2005 it would reappear in yet another guise, this time called *Temptation*, with Ed Phillips as host. There has been talk of another comeback in recent years—*Sale* truly is the John Farnham of quiz shows. The core concept remained the same: three contestants with buzzers, general knowledge questions and prizes that increased in value the longer a player kept winning. On *Sale*, a champion's run culminated with a car, before the cash jackpot was introduced. It was the dominant game show on Australian television for two decades and achieved such gravitas that its first celebrity tournament in 1990 included as contestants Gough Whitlam, Don Chipp and David Lange, who less than a year earlier had still been prime minister of New Zealand. (Lange won the heat and finished runner-up in the final to *60 Minutes* reporter and later *Mastermind* host Jennifer Byrne.)

Sale was such a part of Australia's popular culture that it was frequently parodied on sketch comedy shows—Tony Barber's manic run onto the set at the start of each episode was asking to be mocked. After he was replaced, Tony appeared in a skit

on *The Late Show* in which he was planted in a broadcast van
feeding answers to comedian Jane Kennedy through an earpiece
during a celebrity tournament. It was going well until Tony
ordered some Indian food for dinner, 'forgetting' his mic was
live, and a confused Jane answered 'pappadums' to Glenn Ridge's
next question.

The show's catchphrases entered the national vocabulary, none
more so than 'Who am I?' In each episode there were three 'Who
am I?' questions, which did not automatically add points to a
contestant's score but allowed a pick from the 'Fame Game' board,
consisting of eight famous faces and one home viewer. These
questions could be game-changers. Behind each face was either
a modest prize—a fancy piece of glassware, perhaps, or a small
home appliance—or valuable game points. The $25, equivalent to
five regular correct answers, was added only for the final 'Who
am I?' question and came with its own dramatic sound effects.
Questions began with the host asking, for example, 'Who am I?
I was born in Victoria in 1854 and died in 1880 . . .[1]' and clues
were drip-fed until the correct answer was given. But Cary Young
knew that the dates at the start were the key. If he could master
those, he could master the show.

▼

---

[1]   Ned Kelly. Probably many other people, too, but nobody famous enough to be
the subject of a question.

Back in Cary's living room, sitting on his prize couch, I have in my hands a truly remarkable document. Well, it's remarkable to me anyway. Most people would see it as a random list of names and dates, and it is, but in my eyes it is an Australian quiz-show bible. This is the list that helped Cary Young become an icon of Australian television quizzing. I feel like I'm holding Don Bradman's bat, Rod Laver's racquet or Bert Newton's toupee. There are 85 pages neatly ruled and divided into columns: Name, Born, Died. There are 2803 notable figures listed. The first is Geoffrey Chaucer (1340–1400), a classic place to start. The last is Eartha Kitt (1927–2008), a random finale that presumably reflects the fact that she had just died when Cary last updated his bible. There are names I've never heard before. Michael DeBakey[1]. The Count of Cavour[2]. I'm a professional quizzer, but hit me with those names on *The Chase* and I'd be stumped. Cary started his list in 1980, when *Sale of the Century* began. He realised that encyclopedic knowledge of dates could allow a player to dominate the 'Who am I?' questions, which not only gave you the chance to add big points to your score but also stopped your opponents doing so. Blessed with a good memory and a fascination with dates and human timelines, Cary got to work.

'I started writing down Mozart and Beethoven, and then I thought, "No, it doesn't work like that; Tony doesn't have a list

---

[1] A notable American heart surgeon.

[2] A statesman and key figure in Italian unification.

of all the composers and these other categories—they could be anywhere,'" Cary says.

As a result, his list is in random order. After Mozart comes Michelangelo, then Ernest Hemingway, Enrico Caruso and Abraham Lincoln. Igor Stravinsky is followed by Sidney Nolan, Suzi Quatro and Rolf Boldrewood. The people who are clustered together have nothing in common except that they're people: people whom Cary thought *might* come up in a 'Who am I?' question. Apart from the birth and death dates, and place of birth, there is usually no other information. He didn't need any more. The work involved in preparing the document is breathtaking. This was long before the worldwide web was invented by a computer scientist born in London in 1955[1]. Imagine the reference books Cary must have trawled, the hours he spent writing the names and dates in his clear, neat, block letters. When Cary filmed his first episode, there were 1422 names on his list. He had memorised every single one.

'The first game I ever played on *Sale*, one of the first "Who am I"s was "I was born in Russia in 1828", and I thought, "That's Tolstoy." So I went for it, and it was Tolstoy. But I've got to say, Lyn was tremendous. I realised that thing,' Cary points to his folder of names, 'was invaluable, because if you picked right you got $25. Well, that's five questions. Lyn was invaluable. We'd go to bed at night, get that book out and she'd test me on the dates.'

---

[1]   Tim Berners-Lee

But just like the great billiards player, who Cary could tell you was born in Kalgoorlie in 1898 and died in 1960[1], whose mastery of the game was so complete that authorities changed the rules to level the playing field, Cary's dominance eventually brought about a tweak. In one tournament of champions, the question writers cut him off at the knees by removing the birth and death dates from the questions. He had to quickly adapt and learn a list of birthplaces instead. In his autobiography, the fittingly titled *Who Am I?*, Tony Barber acknowledged that the writers changed the format of these questions to give other players a chance. This, in Tony's opinion, proved that Cary was the best of the best.

There was plenty of opportunity for Cary to measure himself against other champions. After he completed his initial seven-night run, Tony Barber mentioned that maybe, one day, *Sale* would invite its grand champions back for a special tournament. Cary's ears pricked up—he might get to do it all again! The planned move back to New Zealand was put off, the prospect of more *Sale* enough to keep the family in Australia. They also decided that Charters Towers was too far away; they wanted to live in Melbourne, where the show was made, to be on hand for future filming opportunities. Cary, Lyn and their two children arrived in Melbourne in 1984 with no jobs, no family or friends, and no prospects other than *potential* future *Sale* tournaments.

---

[1] Walter Lindrum

The show was so popular that Cary was frequently recognised in Melbourne, and not always for the better.

'He couldn't get work for a long time down here,' Lyn says. 'It's an interesting thing. He didn't have a qualification for anything in particular, and if he went for another job, they'd just look at him and say, "Well, you'd get bored with this." So he found it very hard. Cary and I doorknocked [in sales] for a carpet cleaner when we came here.'

If *Sale* made it hard for Cary to get work, he decided he'd better make *Sale* work for him. The producers did indeed ask their grand champions back for a special tournament, which Cary narrowly lost to Fran Powell, in 1984. But the concept was hugely popular and became a recurring feature, leading to international tournaments with champions from the UK, USA, New Zealand and Canada. Cary soon became the player to beat. During his initial run, a BMW car was the final prize. Over the next decade, he accumulated $332,000 in cash and a literal houseful of prizes. In a 1986 international tournament, he was awarded a Holden Piazza car as the best player; in 2011, having driven the car for 25 years and racked up 200,000 kilometres, he donated it to the National Motor Museum in Adelaide. The car's number plate bore the letters 'CYP'—it was a regular number plate, not a personalised one, but Cary liked to tell people it stood for 'Cary Young's Prize'.

Cary's mental preparation was only half the story. As well as training his mind, he worked his body hard. He had been a boxer as a teenager and getting up for a run at 6 a.m. was second nature.

A wisp of a man ('five foot four and nine stone', Cary says), he has always kept himself in remarkable shape, but he stepped it up whenever a big champions' tournament was approaching. With five episodes filmed per day, he had to be 'up' for hours on end.

'It was most definitely a sporting competition of the mind,' Lyn says, 'but you trained as a sportsman. Five games in a row, and you're there from morning until night, and it's tiring, so you had to be fit. Once you knew you had a competition coming up, you'd step it up and really focus on that. And then you'd taper off and have about three days' rest. And we discovered that on the day it was very important to have carbohydrates running through the system. We used to take natural muesli, and, in between games, Cary would have some muesli. That just kept the metabolism going.'

Personally, I have always baulked at the idea of quizzing being a 'sport', just as I have baulked at concepts such as 'running' and '6 a.m.'. In my view, a sport is a competitive pursuit in which success demands mastery of a physical skill. I consider non-physical contests such as chess, poker and quizzing to be games. But a quiz show such as *Sale of the Century* straddled a hazy middle ground—it was about knowledge, but fundamental to success was speed on the buzzer. Reaction time. And the reaction time of Cary and the show's other greatest champions was scarcely believable. If his physical training gave him the slightest edge, it was worth it.

▼

'There's the Reverend Geoff Clark. Rona Collings, she was the first female champion. Vince Smith. Ian Tweedie—he was one of the first to win the money. Nice guy. There's Fran Powell—she ended up writing the questions.'

I'm standing with Cary in his personal 'Hall of Fame', a little corridor lined with framed publicity photos from his *Sale of the Century* days. There's a shot of his first winning night. Another of him in a tracksuit with a skipping rope, training for the show. I recognise Daphne Fowler, the British quiz champion who became one of the panel of experts on the UK show *Eggheads*. Cary played against Daphne in a *Sale* 'Ashes' tournament. He won, of course, but they kept in touch. There's Matt Parkinson, my fellow Chaser, who won the lot on *Sale* in the early nineties. And David Bock, a chemical engineer from Victoria who was one of Cary's closest rivals for the title of greatest *Sale* champ. One particular photo catches my eye. Four of the show's very best players—Cary, David Bock, David Poltorak and Virginia Noel—going head to head. 'Is that the Mindanao one?' Cary wonders out loud. I can assure him it is.

The 'Mindanao one' was Cary at his peak. It was 1987, and the final in a tournament of champions. The 60-second deciding round is on YouTube, and it is a masterclass in how to succeed on *Sale*. Throughout the minute, Cary consistently buzzes in not when he knows the answer, but when he knows he *will* know it.

'In which large country is the city of —BUZZ—Minsk?[1]'

---

[1] The Soviet Union. Today, the answer would be Belarus.

'What nationality is explorer—*BUZZ*—Sir Edmund—[1]'

But Cary doesn't have it all his own way; these are four proven champions. For most of the minute, he is neck and neck with David Bock, and they are well ahead of Virginia Noel and David Poltorak. David Bock pulls ahead with two brilliant pre-emptive buzzes:

'Who wrote the opera *The—BUZZ—Flying Dutchman*?[2]'

'What kind of animal is a German—*BUZZ* —white-haired—[3]'

With five seconds left, David leads Cary by a question, $100 to $95. Surely the best Cary can do now is a tie? Cary has other ideas, hands firmly on his buzzer, leaning slightly forward like a boxer waiting for a gap through which to punch the winning one-two.

'What, starting with *D*, is another name for—*BUZZ*—an airship?[4]'

Cary nails it. Two seconds on the clock. Scores tied.

'Which Asian country included the island—*BUZZ*—of Min—' (the siren sounds to end the game) '—danao?'

The rules of *Sale* allow that if a player has buzzed he or she has three seconds to answer that question, even if the final siren has sounded. Blessed with the luxury of this time, and knowing he is about to win the tournament, Cary Young puts

---

[1] New Zealander. Even without the surname, it was obvious to Cary that Sir Edmund Hillary was the subject.

[2] Wagner

[3] Dog

[4] Dirigible

both hands up, adjusts his dark blue suit jacket, and coolly states the answer[1], before raising a hand to the audience in appreciation of their applause. His performance could not have been more clutch if it was a pedal in his beloved Piazza. That win granted him a place in a *Sale* world championship, at which he won the $69,000 cash prize.

It is awe-inspiring to witness the best of the best at anything ply their trade, and moments like Cary's 'Mindanao one' can be every bit as enthralling as seeing an athlete overtake a competitor in the final metre of a running race or watching a cricketer hit a six off the last ball to win a game. The same excitement frequently builds on *The Chase* as viewers watch to see whether a quiz expert can get the last few answers in the dying seconds—or whether they will stumble and be beaten.

As quizzers, we are incredibly fortunate that our particular skill set is disproportionately valued. After all, what is it that we really do? We recall stuff, we use our memories. Knowing Leo Tolstoy's date of birth or Frank Sinatra's middle name doesn't mean we're smart. It just means we have excellent memories. And yet, because this ability makes good television, I am frequently recognised on the street and past champions such as Cary are still spotted even now, decades after his successes. Meanwhile, many great Australian scientists, humanitarians or even champions at obscure sports like croquet or squash remain largely unknown. It is not lost on me that, even as I interviewed my childhood

---

[1] Philippines

quizzing idol, the first name I failed to recognise on his list was that of Michael DeBakey, a great American heart surgeon whose innovations saved countless lives. This imbalance often makes me uneasy, and never for a moment do I forget how fortunate I am to have stumbled into the world of television quizzing, where my otherwise useless ability to recall trivial facts is valued so highly.

▼

My own 'Mindanao' moment came in my second episode of *Sale*. Three weeks had passed since I won the first episode, three weeks in which the pressure built inside my own mind. I was no longer just another contestant who could sit quietly in the audience waiting for my chance. I was the carry-over champion. I had a target on my back. And unlike the four-person studio audience who had witnessed my first game, this time there was a full house, including both of my parents, my brother, my girl-friend and two of my housemates. No more flying under the radar. At least this time I'd had a haircut, though, as I struggled to find my mojo in the first episode of the day, I wondered if Angelo the twenty-dollar Victoria Street barber was the Delilah to my Samson.

Despite a very slow start, I found myself in a heated battle with a Tasmanian school teacher named Rodney during the final minute. Contestants could keep track of the scores and time remaining via a television screen to the left of the host. Watching the episode back, all these years later, I can see my eyes flick to the left in the final stages and the panic set in as I

realise Rodney has answered three in a row to level the scores
with two seconds remaining. Fortunately, the last question was
an easy one: 'To pretend not to notice something is to turn
a—*BUZZ*—blind what?'

I answered 'eye', and immediately slumped back in my chair
in relief as the final siren sounded. Rodney buzzed for the last
question as well, but was a split second slower. It came down to
buzzer technique: I had a deliberate method, holding my right
palm firmly on the peak of the buzzer and my left hand on top of
my right, jamming down sharply with both hands for maximum
speed. It was like I was giving the buzzer CPR. Rodney lifted
his hands a centimetre or two before slamming them down on
the buzzer. That fraction of extra distance cost him the game.

This perilously close finish should have served as a warning.
Still, there was no chance of me walking away with the bedroom
furniture and the trekking holiday to Nepal: to me, climbing in
the Himalayas seemed more punishment than reward. I cruised
to victory in my third episode, picked up $5000 from the Cash
Card game, bought a one-megapixel—one!—digital camera in
the gift shop and added a Harley Davidson motorbike to my
major prize swag. Only an hour had passed since Rodney had
almost defeated me, but it seemed like a lifetime. I convinced
myself that if I could see off Rodney, I could beat anyone. I also
reasoned that I had more chance of surviving another five *Sale*
episodes than one ride on the Harley. I felt unstoppable, firmly
believing the sporting cliché that you're only as good as your

last game. Perhaps I should have reflected a little more: by this logic Don Bradman, who made a duck in his final innings, was a complete dud.

My confidence was also buoyed by my dominance of the 'Who am I?' questions. Like Cary Young, I could usually nail these answers from little more than the birth or death dates. Unlike Cary, I didn't have a single master document of thousands of names. But as a curious child, I had pored over encyclopedias and reference books, learning about everyone from Alvar Aalto[1] to Vladimir Zworykin[2]. And while my teenage mates played Nintendo or watched television, I sat at our family PC and typed out pages and pages of names and birthdays of famous people. It is, I admit, very strange behaviour for a teenage boy. I can't imagine what my parents thought of it.

My memory process involves a gigantic mental timeline, century after century of dates, culminating in a cluttered twentieth century subdivided into decades and years with events and names attached. It is invaluable for quizzing. The flip side is that my brain is not set up to remember more useful things. My wife, Zoe, is constantly perplexed that I can instantly recall that, say, Alfred Deakin was born in 1856 and died in 1919, yet I lapse into vagueness trying to remember which freeway exit to

---

[1] Finnish architect and furniture designer, 1898–1976, and the first entry in many dictionaries of biography.

[2] Russian-American inventor and television pioneer, 1888–1982.

take to reach her grandmother's beach house, which we've visited dozens of times. Still, she can take comfort in the fact that I'll never forget her birthday.

On *Sale of the Century*, this mental timeline allowed me to answer 'Who am I?' questions from clues as sparse as:

'Born in Sydney in 1934 and dying in Spain in 1994—[1]'

'Born in 1922 and dying in 1990, I was preparing for life as a secretary when a photograph of me taken by my brother-in-law—[2]'

'Born in Puerto Rico in 1940 and dying in 1994, I was a nightclub performer before arriving in New York in my mid-twenties—[3]'

Occasionally I picked up match points from the Fame Game board, but more often a random selection of goodies: a Wiggles pack for the children I didn't have, some car-care products for the vehicle I didn't own, a queen-size quilt for my single bed and a lingerie package. At least I had a girlfriend to give that to, but then again, I only had a single bed, so ... Like most *Sale* contestants, I made an art form out of the polite smile and nod as these prizes appeared on the board, while thinking, 'What the hell am I going to do with six boxes of car wax?' Then again, there was an Alfa Romeo up for grabs if I lasted seven nights ...

▼

---

[1] Tennis player Lew Hoad, about whom I knew nothing else.

[2] Actress Ava Gardner, whom I had never seen in a single film.

[3] Actor Raul Juliá, whom I at least did know from his role as Gomez in *The Addams Family* movies.

There is a memorable episode of the sitcom *Cheers* in which postman Cliff Clavin appears as a contestant on *Jeopardy!* A running joke is that Cliff claims to know everything about everything, and he constantly bores the bar room with his 'little-known facts', which are indeed little known but not always facts ('The tan became popular in what is known as the Bronze Age.') On *Jeopardy!*, everything falls Cliff's way. The question categories are tailor-made for a postal worker who lives with his mother and hangs out in a bar: 'Civil Servants', 'Stamps from around the World', 'Mothers and Sons', 'Beer', 'Bar Trivia' and 'Celibacy'. Cliff dominates the show until foolishly wagering all of his winnings in the final round. The category is 'Movies' and the clue is: 'Archibald Leach, Bernard Schwartz and Lucille LeSueur'. The correct response is to identify (in the form of a question, as per *Jeopardy!* rules) the movie stars born with those names[1], but all Cliff can come up with is 'Who are three people who've never been in my kitchen?' Cliff's arrogance leads to his humiliation and defeat on national television.

Likewise, my quiz-show dreams were crushed by three people who had never been in my kitchen: Ho Chi Minh, Suzie Wilks from *Changing Rooms* and John from Langwarrin. A feeling of complete and utter dread gripped me as Suzie Wilks' head turned 180 degrees (a sentence that has seldom been written in human history). Simultaneously, I heard the sound effects and saw the flashing $25.

---

[1] Cary Grant, Tony Curtis and Joan Crawford

Half a second later, I heard something else: an audience member's angry 'Aww, fuck!' I later learnt this was my housemate and oldest friend Ben, who was swiftly chastised by my mother.

John from Langwarrin looked as pained as I felt. He didn't want to knock me out (and he was comfortably beaten by Fiona in the final round). It was simply the luck of the draw. The twenty-to-one chance had landed against me. I was in shock, in complete disbelief. I sat there with my elbows on the desk and my chin resting on my hands, not even bothering to feign interest as Glenn Ridge read my *Sale of the Century* epitaph: 'Unfortunately Brydon, we have to say goodbye to you, but you are leaving us with the sewing machine, the leather goods, the sportswear, the car-care package, camera, Wiggles pack, lingerie package, Cash Card $5000, underblanket and quilt, and a total of $13,782. It's been fantastic having you with us, Brydon, thank you very much for playing.'

And just like that, it was over. I was no Cary Young. I was a kid who played *Sale of the Century* pretty well, but I had been overconfident. I would not win the $270,000 or the Alfa Romeo. I had risked the bedroom furniture, Harley Davidson and trip to Nepal—those prizes were now gone. I had nightmares about the experience for years afterwards, and I don't mean figuratively; I often went to sleep and dreamt about losing on *Sale* all over again. On the other hand, the show was like a gateway drug. Suddenly I was looking around the television networks and planning my next move. *The Weakest Link? Wheel of Fortune? Who Wants To Be a Millionaire?* I had plenty of options and, strangely for an introvert, I felt comfortable in front of the cameras. When my episodes began airing, just two days after my defeat in studio, I had a brief glimpse of what it's like to be recognised on the street. For several weeks, people stopped me to say they enjoyed the show.

One memory sticks in my mind: as I hauled my big bag of weekly washing to the laundromat in Errol Street, North Melbourne, an old man stopped to say he and his wife had loved seeing such a young fella do well on *Sale* and when I was introduced as being from West Melbourne they had cheered me on even more. He had lived in the area for most of his life and played footy for North Melbourne in the forties. His name was Stan Radloff; I looked him up later and found that he played sixty games for the Kangaroos and was now in his eighties. Stan could not believe that someone who had been on television would be washing his clothes at a public laundromat. 'Come up to our house,' Stan said, 'we've got a good old Simpson[1] machine; the wife'll do your clothes in that. She'd love to meet ya.' I was too shy to take up the offer and mumbled something about how I wouldn't want to put them out. Oh, well, Stan said, the offer's always there.

I wish I'd gone with him. It would have been so easy to make an old man's day and a connection across the generations. Plus I

---

[1] Little-known fact: the Simpson Desert was named after the washing machine guy. Alfred Allen Simpson, of the Simpson appliance company, financed explorations of the desert in the early twentieth century.

would have got my clothes washed for free. Nearly two decades later, I faced a contestant on *The Chase* and thought his name looked familiar: Ben Radloff. After the game, I asked if he was related to Stan. Turns out Stan, who had died a few years earlier, was his grandfather. I told Ben the story and thought I saw a lump in his throat as he listened.

I still think of Stan when someone recognises me as The Shark and stops for a chat at the supermarket, the playground, cafes and restaurants. I've had young tradies yell from open car windows, 'Hey, Shark!' Sometimes people recognise me but don't know where from. Am I a teacher at their kids' school? Do I work in a shop they go to? They're usually embarrassed when I explain that they don't know me personally but from television. Occasionally I'm embarrassed when, as they rack their brains, I ask them if they watch *The Chase*—and they say no. Without exception, viewers who stop to say hello are friendly, and it is never a hassle. But Stan Radloff remains the only one who has ever offered to help with my laundry.

CHAPTER 3

CHILD'S PLAY

THURSDAY, 23 AUGUST 1990

At the Scout Quiz Night tonight we had our team of six: David, Val, Judi, Chris, Brydon and Lindsay Wilkinson. We won the three sections of the night . . . it was getting a bit embarrassing! We donated back $60 of the $100 prize money. They told us the Coverdale family shouldn't be allowed to sit together as a team! Having a range of ages and interests seems to help in these activities.

I guess that was the first prize I ever won in a trivia competition. Or at least, that I helped win. I was eight years old. I'm sure I would have contributed something to the victory, though not as much as my parents, my teenage sister and brother, and our regular trivia ring-in, my grade three teacher Mr Wilkinson.

Since 1988, my mum has written in her diary each night, religiously. The above is the first reference I can find to me in connection with trivia. Mum was a primary school teacher and places great value on learning, but she prefers not to be the centre of attention. When she wins a game of something—cards, say—she does so apologetically, genuinely pained that everybody else had to lose. Even now, three decades later, I can imagine Mum being embarrassed at us winning every section of the Scout Quiz Night in the small town of Camperdown in south-west Victoria. And while it's not recorded in her diary, I can also picture a possible scene when we won the $100 prize: Mum suggesting we donate it back to the Scouts, us kids insisting we keep it, perhaps Dad proposing the eventual 60/40 compromise. What Mr Wilkinson thought is lost to history[1].

Actually, it's not strictly true that this was my first trivia prize. Two years earlier, when I was six, the Coverdale family trivia team had gone off to another fundraising quiz night and left me at home with my grandmother. My parents said I was too young to go, plus there had to be space on the team for Mr Wilkinson to be rung in. I was furious. Nearly 35 years later, it remains a defining memory, which tells you something. I don't

---

[1] Literally. In an eerie coincidence, I found out a few days after I wrote this paragraph that Mr Wilkinson had died at the age of 80 on the very day I was writing about him. He will be remembered fondly.

recall what I did with my grandmother, Marion, on that fateful night, but chances are we played some sort of game—Go Fish, maybe Monopoly or backgammon. Nana was my dad's mother, and she lived with us throughout my childhood—or, more accurately, we lived with her, in a big old bluestone homestead on the family farm. She was a tough, resilient woman who had been orphaned as a teenager, married a domineering husband and survived breast cancer, Bell's palsy and two serious car accidents in which she wrecked her souped-up Holden Monaro on country roads. She taught me the phrase 'You can't teach your grandmother to suck eggs', when I feebly told her I was just admiring her flowers when in fact I was trampling them searching for a ball I'd lost. She wasn't affectionate but there was a spark to her—and she enjoyed games. Despite the dual crushing blows of missing the trivia team cut and learning that Ricky May, the referee from one of my favourite television shows, *It's a Knockout*, died that evening, I'm sure I had a fun night with Nana.

The next morning, Mum had a surprise for me: a glass beer mug, decorated with a golden picture of a tennis player. She had won it for answering a 'Who am I?' question at the trivia night, identifying which Australian prime minister had been born in Bathurst and worked as an engine driver[1]. She knew this, she said, because I had obsessively learnt the complete list of Australian prime ministers and would reel off information about them day in, day out. And so she gave me the tennis mug,

---

[1] Ben Chifley

ostensibly because I had helped her win it, but perhaps more so to shut me up about being left off the team.

It became a prized childhood possession, up there with my cricket bat, Carlton footy jumper and complete set of *The A-Team* action figurines. Eventually my cricket bat broke, I grew out of my footy jumper and Mr T lost both arms and a leg on a series of suicidal missions. But the tennis mug is intact, all these years later. I used it daily throughout my childhood, and now every time I visit my parents and open the cupboard to get a drink it's still there, staring back at me. It's a reminder of my long journey in trivia, my mother's kindness and the slightly peculiar fact that as a small child I usually drank from a beer glass.

▼

You might wonder how a child of five or six knew the list of Australia's prime ministers. A better question: Why would he want to? I'm not sure I can answer that. All I know is that when I was four, my parents loaded their four kids into our Mitsubishi L300 van and embarked on a family holiday that set me on the path.

As dairy farmers, my parents worked relentlessly. Dad milked the cows twice a day, every day, rain, hail or shine. When I became a journalist and was annoyed at occasionally having to work on Christmas Day, I reminded myself that my father hadn't *occasionally* worked on Christmas Day. He had *always* worked on Christmas Day.

When the cows stopped producing milk for a short period every autumn, we were treated to our annual fortnight-long family holiday. That year, 1986, we went to Canberra. I recall virtually nothing of the trip, but I must have shown an interest in the prime ministerial portraits at Parliament House because my parents bought me a poster listing all the prime ministers from Edmund Barton to Bob Hawke, each with a picture and short biography. I stuck it on my wall next to my bed. And I memorised it. 'Barton, Deakin, Watson, Reid, Deakin, Fisher, Deakin, Fisher . . .' Soon, I could list them all in less than ten seconds flat (I still can, even adding the carnage of 'Rudd, Gillard, Rudd, Abbott, Turnbull, Morrison . . .').

Why? I have no idea. My brain just enjoyed the challenge of committing lists to memory. For the same reason, a few years later I memorised the lyrics of Billy Joel's 'We Didn't Start the Fire', his rapid-fire history of the second half of the twentieth century. Specifically, I was obsessed with names. I literally read the phone book, searching for entries that caught my eye: even now, I remember that the last surname in the Melbourne White Pages of the era was Zzyskov.

I was also fascinated by dates and timelines. Like a lot of kids, I collected things: marbles, footy stickers . . . notable birthdays. Every year, the Australian author and illustrator Roland Harvey published a calendar for kids, often including little notes to show birthdays of famous people. I expanded on his idea, squeezing every date full of birthdays. I look back at a calendar from the mid-1990s and can only shake my head at the variety of names I added. On 12 January, for example, I've written: John Hancock, 1737; Hermann Goering, 1893; Kirstie Alley,

1955[1]; Richie Richardson, 1962; and Vulcan (from the television show *Gladiators*), 1964. (I'd love to watch a time-travel movie with these five celebrating a joint birthday party; John Hancock would give himself top billing.) I collated them from everywhere: books, magazines, newspapers, an 'On This Day' radio segment. If Wikipedia had been invented, I might never have left the house.

I loved television quiz shows, especially *Sale of the Century*, and dreamed of one day being a contestant, but my collecting of information was not done with a specific goal. It wasn't even about quizzing. I simply enjoyed it. I was naturally curious, and I wanted to know things. I wanted to know *everything*. Actually, I tell a lie. I didn't want to know useful stuff. I wasn't interested in what was under the bonnet of a car, but I was curious what 'Edsel is a no go' meant in 'We Didn't Start the Fire'[2]. I had no desire to learn how to milk a cow, but I was fascinated to discover that a current world leader of the era had left school at fifteen to work on his family dairy farm[3]. All the extra information I give on *The Chase* after locking in an answer—that's the product of a lifetime's curiosity. I once interviewed the cricketer and master of the anecdote, Max Walker, who referred to his

---

[1]   It should have been 1951. It was hard to crosscheck sources back then.

[2]   The Ford Edsel, named after Henry Ford's son, was an over-hyped, financially disastrous model released by Ford in 1958. If you've ever seen the early episode of *The Simpsons* in which Homer designs an unconventional car that sends his brother Herb's company broke, that was pretty much based on the Edsel.

[3]   New Zealand prime minister Jim Bolger.

brain as 'a filing cabinet of memories'. It's a neat visual metaphor, but the trick with trivia is opening the right drawer on demand.

Quiz shows weren't my only passion. I also loved the sillier game shows, outlandish as board games made life-sized. On *The Price Is Right*, Larry Emdur watched on as manic contenders guessed the value of a hair-dryer or electric can-opener and then played mini-golf to try to win a car. Rob Brough on *Family Feud* wanted you and your in-laws to 'Name a place teenagers go to kiss?[1]' In *Supermarket Sweep*, Ian Turpie asked contestants to race around a fake Coles store filling their trolleys with the highest value products they could, against a stopwatch. Smart players would always stock up on the maximum number (four) of the most expensive item (nappies). Imagine pitching that to a network executive. But people watched for one simple reason: it was fun. Quiz shows like to think they're different, more highbrow perhaps. But they're all part of the same genre. Not all game shows are quiz shows, but all quiz shows are game shows.

One show I recall fondly was *The Krypton Factor*, which combined observation, logic, intelligence tests and quiz questions while also requiring contestants to complete an army assault course. It was like a mash-up of *Mastermind* and *Ninja Warrior*, which, now that I write those words, sounds like a brilliant format that I will definitely copyright: *Ninja Mastermind*, coming soon. Unusually for a show on Australian television, *The Krypton*

---

[1] The top answer was 'At the movies', if you were wondering.

Factor was produced in New Zealand, though based on a British version. Hosted by Kiwi newsreader Dougal Stevenson from 1987 to 1991, it rewarded the player with the best balance of mental and physical skills. I think, even more than *Sale of the Century*, it was *The Krypton Factor* that first drew me in to television game shows. Often I would create my own obstacle course up the long passageway in our house, replicating as best I could the assault course at the Burnham Military Camp near Christchurch, though I never figured out a way to build my own flying fox. One thing about *The Krypton Factor*: it was great fun to watch. Another thing about *The Krypton Factor*: if Nana needed to get from her lounge room to the toilet at the other end of the passage, she had to jump half a dozen cardboard-box hurdles and crawl under a blanket suspended just above the ground like barbed-wire netting.

Sale of the Century was my other great love. I don't know how many of the questions I could answer when I was six or seven, but that didn't matter. It was about the game, watching a high-stakes competitive endeavour that, unlike cricket or football, would be done and dusted in half an hour, with a clear winner. I don't recall much about my first year in primary school, but I do remember the time the older grades played their version of *Sale of the Century* on stage, with bells for buzzers, and the school sat and watched. And I remember, much like that quiz night in 1988, that I would have given anything to play.

When I reached Grade 6, my teacher was Mr Rob Baker, who had run second in the 1971 Stawell Gift. Mr Baker ran weekly quizzes that pitted students against each other and I thrived on the chance to test myself against my peers. I became so good at these contests that I could sense the other kids rolling their eyes whenever they had to play me. To this day I can recall capital cities ingrained during those battles in Mr Baker's classroom—the capital of Laos[1], say, or the state capital of Alaska[2].

In my first year of high school, I claimed a prize of my own at a school trivia night at which my table of Year 7 students was defeated by a clever bunch of parents. By answering a 'Who am I?' question that asked for the great Australian swimmer born in Balmain in 1937[3], I earned myself a $20 voucher at the local butcher's shop. It wasn't quite the stereotypical meat tray, though it was a precursor to winning $300 worth of chicken meals on a television game show eight years later. But that's a story for another chapter. I used the voucher to try something that I'd never eaten before, buying beef Wellington for the family for dinner. It turned out I didn't much like beef Wellington. But it was a taste of the random potpourri of prizes that lay ahead.

---

[1]   Vientiane

[2]   Juneau

[3]   Dawn Fraser

CHAPTER 4

THAT'S A GOOD QUESTION

THOSE WHO CAN, DO; THOSE WHO CAN'T, TEACH. ISN'T THAT WHAT THEY say? My defeat on *Sale of the Century* showed that I didn't have what it took to win the lot, but I thought maybe I could teach somebody else to go all the way. My brother-in-law Paul, who is married to my eldest sister Lindy, is a repository of obscure information. A librarian-turned–book editor and indexer-turned– university administrator who also once studied engineering, he has a lot of bases covered. And I knew he had dabbled with the idea of appearing on a quiz show; he once told me he had applied for *Sale of the Century* in the 1980s but had forgotten to turn up to the audition. Now that I considered myself an expert, I believed Paul could be a top-shelf contestant—he just needed some confidence and speed training. I had the perfect training tool: my consolation prize, the *Sale of the Century* board game, complete with buzzers.

My main goal was not to improve Paul's knowledge—he easily had enough—but to coach him in the art of anticipation and buzzer speed. They were the keys to success on *Sale*, the skills that would give him a head start. But this would only work if he trained using questions that captured the experience of being on the show. I wasn't convinced that the question booklet that came with the board game would cut it. So I wrote my own questions, which would not only train Paul but also broaden my general knowledge for future quiz-show appearances.

In preparing some 'episodes' for Paul, I copied the *Sale* format and wrote about fifty questions for each game. Finding the time was not a problem; as a journalism student I had only eight or nine contact hours at university each week.

In journalism we were taught to write using the 'inverted pyramid' approach, in which the most important, headline-grabbing information is at the top of the story and the less critical details at the bottom. Questions on *Sale of the Century* were the opposite, which I guess makes them a pyramid. The more obscure details came first, the giveaway information at the end. *Sale* wouldn't ask: 'What collective name for Sweden, Norway and Denmark is sometimes extended to include Finland and Iceland?' because the crux of the question comes too early, and anyone who can't get the answer[1] halfway through isn't going to get there by

---

[1]   Scandinavia

the end. On *Sale*, the question would more likely be: 'Sometimes extended to include Finland and Iceland is what collective name for Sweden, Norway and Denmark?' This version allows a player with good anticipation to buzz in early if they think they know where the clues are leading, but in doing so they take a risk as the question itself has not yet been asked.

To replicate the real-life show, I needed good sources. These days, basically all of human knowledge is available on the internet. Wikipedia, for all the flak it cops from people who think it's unreliable, is the single-most remarkable information source the world has ever seen. Where else could you find entries on subjects as diverse as 'Utegate', 'List of recurring *The Simpsons* characters', 'Australian cricket team in Sri Lanka in 1982–83', and 'Polygamy in Uganda'? But back in 2000, I had no such online source, so I relied on a handful of reference books, plus the Microsoft suite of reference titles from the mid-1990s: Encarta, Cinemania and Bookshelf, all of which I had on CD-ROM (what do those initials stand for?[1]).

Over the next year, I trained Paul on the questions I had written. Prior to the election of George W. Bush, the only father and son to each hold the office of president of the United States were John and John Quincy who?[2] Bounded by Honduras to the north and Costa Rica to the south, the largest republic of

---

[1] Compact disc read-only memory

[2] Adams

Central America is which country beginning with *N*?[1] What term for an important, powerful businessperson can also denote a hard mound or bump on a ski slope?[2] These questions might seem straightforward, but the trick was being the first to buzz in, which meant learning to sense what direction a question was heading. For example, with the question about presidents, contestants with first-rate general knowledge and anticipation should be able to buzz in at 'father and son'. With the question about a businessperson, contestants would be prudent waiting until later.

Any time there was a Coverdale family gathering, I would come armed with printouts of at least four or five episodes' worth of questions and insist on a *Sale* board-game session. Usually, Paul would play against my older brother Chris, who was also very good at trivia. Any combination of family members would take part. At the time, Lindy and Paul had a three-year-old son, Ben, and if he was having a nap we came up with a system to muffle the piercing sound of the board-game buzzers: we stuck a massive wad of Blu Tack over the speaker to act as a silencer. It was crude but effective. In this way, we passed a year of family birthdays and weekend visits.

I was impressed with the way Paul's anticipation and buzzer speed improved. He also passed the *Sale* audition, and I could

---

[1]   Nicaragua
[2]   Mogul

envisage success whenever his call-up arrived. I was self-aware enough to acknowledge that I was behaving rather obsessively. I was like a parent who lives vicariously through their child's sporting exploits—it's just that my 'child' was an in-law eighteen years older than me. But I didn't care that I was obsessive. I felt that Paul needed someone obsessive to push him to make the most of his knowledge. And I knew from experience that it was remarkable how many contestants turned up to film *Sale* having done virtually no preparation—they were simply there for a bit of fun, to see what happened. This seemed unfathomable given the hundreds of thousands of dollars up for grabs. It was absolutely worth training in the skills that would give you an edge. If there's one thing that almost all the quiz show champions I've spoken to have in common, it's that they have taken the opportunity seriously and prepared accordingly.

Then, late in 2001, Paul got the call-up. Sort of. He was asked to be a stand-by contestant, which meant he was unlikely to play just yet. Stand-bys were needed in case a contestant failed to turn up or a carry-over champion chose to walk away with their winnings, meaning an extra position opened up for the next episode. The stand-bys were told that their reward for giving up a day's work was that they would be called up as a regular contestant within weeks. So Paul was in—it was just a question of when. I had done what I could to prepare him. And, looking back now, I had done a hell of a lot: my 'Salequestions' Microsoft Word document from that era, which I still have, contains nearly 4000 questions.

▼

I have stumped David Poltorak. *Nobody* stumps David Poltorak. But I have done it. I have asked him a question that he cannot answer. How many questions has he written for television quiz shows over the thirty-odd years he has been in the business? He has no idea. He has never stopped to think about it. But what happens next tells you the secret to David Poltorak's success.

'My interest in quizzing comes from a lifelong feverish curiosity about anything that I don't know,' David says. 'I've just got to know it.'

And so it is with the question of questions. A few days after I asked David how many questions he thought he had written, we spoke again. His curiosity had got the better of him, so he did some tallying.

'Of the ones that I can count,' he says, 'it comes to 108,295.'

Of the ones he can count. The real number is certainly higher, because he hasn't kept all the questions from all the quiz shows he has worked on. He can't even *remember* all the quiz shows he has worked on.

'I look back at this folder of the shows I've worked on and some of them—I have no memory of them,' David says. 'I just don't know what they are. I've got abbreviations for the names of shows that mean nothing to me now.'

David's first question-writing experience came in the late 1980s, when he was asked to contribute to the short-lived ABC quiz shows *University Challenge* and *The Oz Game*. By then, he was an established quizzing name, having scooped the $244,000 cash jackpot on *Sale of the Century* in 1986 and set an all-time record score of $200 in his final episode. His long list of credits as writer or adjudicator also includes *Who Wants To Be a Millionaire?*, *Hot Seat*, *Temptation*, *The Einstein Factor*, *Are You Smarter than a Fifth Grader?*, *Think Tank*, *Pointless*, *Mastermind* and many more. But his bread and butter was *Sale of the Century*: four years after he became a champion contestant, he was asked to become the show's question writer and adjudicator when another former champ, Fran Powell, stepped down. In eleven years in the job, David wrote almost 80,000 questions for *Sale*.

'What I had to do for the entire run of that show was write 180 questions a week, even though they only ever used 120 tops,' David says. 'I remember they just had cardboard boxes full of question cards. It meant that you were working like a demon. It was exhausting.'

You may be reading this and thinking that 180 questions don't seem like a lot. What's the capital of Italy? What sport did Rod Laver play? How many centimetres in a metre?[1] Bang, I've just written three in under a minute. Sure, but are they interesting questions? Not really. And anyway, how long before I'd run out of steam coming up with quick questions off the top of my head? How long before I would start repeating myself? Not very long at all. Imagine writing 180 questions per week that were unique, interesting, challenging, meticulously worded, well referenced

---

[1] Rome, tennis and 100.

and covered a balanced mix of subjects and difficulty levels—and doing it every week for a decade. It's true that anyone can write a trivia question, but not everyone can do it well—certainly not 80,000 times.

These days, quiz shows will typically require at least two reliable online sources for any question, after which a verifier will try to 'break' the question: search for reasons that the answer may be incorrect or the wording problematic. Perhaps the information is outdated or the question is ambiguous. A hypothetical example of the latter: 'In which Australian state is Kangaroo Island?' Most people would answer South Australia, and they would be correct. But there is also a Kangaroo Island in Tasmania. And in Western Australia. And in Queensland. A contestant who gave any of those answers could not therefore be marked incorrect. To avoid problems, the question would need to be rewritten in such a way as to lead *only* to South Australia, for example: 'Australia's third-largest island, Kangaroo Island, is in which state?'

But in the *Sale* days, sources were limited and verification basic. David was responsible for writing what could be described as the 'regular' questions, while another writer produced the shorter, snappier 'fast money' ones as well as the 'Who am I?' questions. And the verification process consisted, more or less, of David and the other writer reading each other's questions and ticking them off before they were physically typed onto question cards by a clatter of typists[1]. One source for each question was

---

[1]   I've heard of a pool of typists, but I prefer my made-up collective noun.

the norm, and a limited number of hard-copy sources made up the show's reference library: *Encyclopaedia Britannica*, *World Book Encyclopedia*, several dictionaries, *The Guinness Book of Records*, *Brewer's Dictionary of Phrase and Fable*, *Rock and Pop Day By Day* and several others. Current affairs questions came from *Time* magazine or a reputable newspaper such as the *Sydney Morning Herald*. Watching old episodes now, I am struck by the nature of the questions: I wouldn't exactly call them highbrow, but the word that comes to mind is 'classical'. The reason for that is simple: they reflect the sources used.

'It meant that the questions all tended to be a little bit on the daggy side,' David says, 'so when you could put something in that was current, it always felt jazzy.'

As the in-studio adjudicator, David also faced the challenge of arbitrating issues that came up during recording. This meant determining whether an answer given by a contestant, but not listed as the correct answer on the host's question card, could be considered acceptable. Filming would be halted while David looked into the issue, and, pre-internet, hard-copy sources could only help so much.

'If we did have issues with questions on the day, we would have to call someone,' David says. 'I would be calling libraries, I'd be calling sports bodies, and I'd be hoping that the issue arose before 5 p.m. so that there's someone there.'

Given the volume of questions needed for *Sale*, it is surprising how seldom mistakes arose. The same is true of most quiz shows, when you stop and think about it. But being a question writer or adjudicator is like being a cricket umpire: the public rarely appreciates how often it is done well, but everyone notices when a mistake is made. I recall a 2001 episode of *The Weakest Link*— not a show David worked on—in which a contestant was asked the name of Australia's new governor-general and said 'Peter Hollingworth'. He was sternly told by host Cornelia Frances that he was incorrect, and the answer was 'Hollingsworth'. The network received phone calls, letters to the editor flooded the newspapers: there was no 's' in the governor-general's surname, and the contestant should have been marked correct. It was the show's sourcing that was wrong. Fortunately, that contestant went on to win the $32,000 episode prize anyway, so a major controversy was avoided.

On *Sale*, David says, mistakes were acknowledged and contestants brought back for another episode if it was found they had been dudded by a question error. But sometimes, the show had to stand firm despite public uproar, as when David wrote a question asking what was the major export product of Nauru. The answer was phosphate, but a contestant said 'guano', the fossilised bird droppings from which the country's phosphate was extracted.

'There was an almighty outcry from the audience: lots and lots of letters,' David says. 'It got to the point where we had a letter from the Nauru High Commissioner, who, pre-empting ScoMo by several years, said, "I'm holding a rock of phosphate in my office. It sits on my desk as a paperweight; I can assure you that phosphate is the correct answer."'

By the time David started working on *Who Wants To Be a Millionaire?* new worlds of data had been opened up by the internet. But that didn't mean it was a free-for-all. The web might have been known as the information superhighway, but quiz shows still wanted writers to stay in their lane.

'There was huge nervousness about using the internet as a reference source,' David says, 'and the only things at that point that would be considered allowable as references from the net were reputable mastheads or the BBC. The gold standard was *Britannica*, because it was a book that was on paper, and they were written by a different species, apparently.'

While that sounds like a safety-first approach, it could lead to unexpected problems. On *Millionaire* in 2002, Victorian teacher Michael Mawson was asked, for $125,000, what the Rosetta Stone was made of, with the options being alabaster, basalt, granite and obsidian. Michael was leaning towards granite until he used his 50-50 lifeline, which left basalt and obsidian. He took a stab at obsidian, but basalt was deemed correct. And you would think the sourcing, from several trusted encyclopedias including *Britannica*, was rock solid. Unfortunately, those printed tomes were out of date. It had always been believed that the Rosetta Stone was basalt but testing in 1998–99 by the British Museum, at which the artefact is held, had shown it was made of granodiorite, which is similar to granite but with a slightly different composition. The museum had updated its records, but the change hadn't yet made it into the encyclopedias. Michael Mawson was later invited back to have a shot at the $250,000 level, the producers conceding that his comments on the show indicated that he was leaning towards the 'most correct' answer, granite, before the 50-50 lifeline took that option away. For $250,000, Michael was asked who was the first US astronaut to walk in space[1]; unsure of the answer, he walked away with $125,000.

I share David Poltorak's scepticism about the printed word being intrinsically superior to the internet. Even the world's great encyclopedias make mistakes, and as for relying on books that market themselves as 'quiz books'—forget it. *The Penguin Ultimate Trivia Quiz Game Book* from the 1980s is one of many examples from my reference shelf. The very first question in the book asks, 'What have Dr Benjamin Spock, Errol Flynn and the Emperor Nero got in common?' The answer is that the unlikely trio all competed at the Olympics, at rowing, boxing and chariot racing respectively. Except that it's wrong. Spock was indeed an Olympic gold medallist in rowing before he became a world-renowned paediatrician and Nero bribed his way into the Ancient Olympics, but Flynn was as much an Olympic boxer as I am a rhythmic gymnast. It was a fiction created by Hollywood executives to promote a film of his in the 1930s, and fifty years later it was still occasionally being spouted as fact. And once a 'fact' is in a book, it can't be corrected. The odd false piece of information may turn up on Wikipedia, but a worldwide army of editors is constantly checking articles and making corrections, flagging problems and discussing points of debate. In my view,

---

[1] Ed White

the occasional error is a small price to pay for having virtually every piece of information you could ever want right there at your fingertips.

'To me Wikipedia is just so far ahead of virtually anything else and where there are issues, it'll flag them,' David says. 'And it's foot-noted to buggery.'

Accurate sourcing is just one of many factors a question writer must consider when coming up with ideas. On shows where players answer against a clock, the writers often have guidelines relating to the length of questions, so that no player is disadvantaged by having long and cumbersome questions compared to another contestant. There is also the issue of difficulty. There is scope for easy, medium and hard questions on almost any quiz show, but skew the balance too far and you'll end up with boring television. David learnt that the hard way in his first job as a writer for a quiz show, on *University Challenge* in the late 1980s.

'We had no guidelines and we just wrote questions far too hard for the students who we ended up getting as contestants,' David says. 'There were just so many awkward silences on screen. They all sat there and looked at each other bemused and just thought, "I don't know, do you?" It was ugly television. It was just horrible.'

It can be surprisingly tricky to determine whether a question is easy, medium or hard. Some questions that might seem straightforward to the question writer can prove impossible for a contestant. This can often prove the case with 'complete the common saying'–type questions, because what you view as 'common' depends to a large extent on your upbringing. 'Six of one, half a dozen of the other' might make total sense to me, while mystifying someone else. It can also be generational. David says that his children, for example, 'live in an idiom-less world'.

Judging the difficulty became more important for David when he started working on *Who Wants To Be a Millionaire?*, a format that involved a clear hierarchy in which the questions started as very easy and became harder. Writers would be asked to supply questions for specific difficulty levels and the so-called 'level one' questions (the easiest ones) were often the hardest to write.

I recall a contestant on *Hot Seat*, the afternoon successor to the prime-time *Millionaire*, being asked at the $1000 level for the name of the world's largest gold nugget, found at Bendigo in 1869. Was it the Welcome . . . Digger, Battler, Stranger or Back Kotter. Under the pressure of a ticking clock, he locked in 'Welcome Back Kotter'. Host Eddie McGuire was incredulous that the contestant had chosen the joke answer, but in a strange way I could under-stand the thinking of a young man who had never heard of either the Welcome Stranger nugget or the television show *Welcome Back, Kotter*. 'Back Kotter' was such a weird option, what was it doing there? Why would they make up something like that? Maybe it's right? Lock it in. Eddie couldn't fathom someone not having heard of *Welcome Back, Kotter*, the 1970s sitcom that starred a young John Travolta. But the contestant was the same age as me; *Welcome Back, Kotter* had finished before we were born. I've never seen an episode. Eddie McGuire was a teenager when the series was in its prime; he reeled off the names of all the main characters, clearly knowing the show well. Different generation, different set of knowledge. Mind you, I'm guilty of the same: I assume everyone knows *The Simpsons* and *Seinfeld* as well as I do, because they were the shows I loved when I was a teenager. But Jerry Seinfeld, thirty-something when his sitcom was at its peak, is now pushing seventy. There's a good chance anyone under thirty may be totally unfamiliar with *Seinfeld*—not that there's anything wrong with that.

'Those "level ones" were the toughest by far,' David says. 'Really hard. And as you moved up the scale to the harder levels, you felt this weight lifting because then it was open slather.'

Only a few times on Australian *Millionaire* has the million-dollar question been seen, and one of those was a question David recalls having written himself. It asked how many people had walked on the moon, with the options being 10, 12, 14 and 16. Contestant William Laing decided to walk away with the $500,000 instead of taking the risk of playing for the million, though when asked which answer he would have locked in he chose the correct one[1].

'I really liked that question as an example of the sort of question which is hard but knowable,' David says. 'If you sit there

---

[1]   Twelve. And who was the last man to walk on the moon? That's a classic example of a trick question. On the final Apollo mission in 1972, Eugene Cernan became the eleventh man on the moon and Harrison Schmitt the twelfth. So, Schmitt is the answer, right? Wrong. Because Schmitt re-entered the lunar module first, Cernan is the last person to have walked on the moon. As I said, a trick question, and one that should therefore be avoided by trivia writers.

and you don't know, you think, "Oh, why don't I know the number of manned moon missions?"'

He's right: it is a good million-dollar question, one that rewards knowledge rather than guesswork, and a fact that would have viewers at home wondering why it wasn't better known. Sometimes it's the questions that go unanswered that make the best television.

That was certainly the case back in David's days as a contestant on *Sale of the Century*. Just like me, David had a heart-stopping finish to his second episode, but whereas I answered an easy question correctly in the last second to win, David survived because he and his rival both held fire on a difficult final question that neither of them knew: Which American wrote the novel *Go Tell It on the Mountain*?[1] Luckily for David, he was already $4 ahead; had his opponent answered correctly, David Poltorak would have been a one-night *Sale* champion, a quarter of a million dollars poorer, and would almost certainly have had a completely different career path. At the time, he drove taxis in between gigs as a comedy writer and screenwriter; maybe that would still be his life. Both he and the other contestant had bought prizes in the gift shop during the episode; David says he later heard that the losing player had stomped around at the back of the set after the episode, muttering to himself, 'I shouldn't have bought the dining suite.' Every meal the contestant ate off that table in the years that followed probably tasted bitter. I was

---

[1] James Baldwin

fascinated to learn that David's second-night experience was so similar to mine, and it turns out we're not alone.

'Tony Barber would warn contestants of the second-night syndrome and it was a much-observed phenomenon where people who had done well to win their first night would then just collapse on the second,' David says. 'And there was much theorising as to what was going on. My own view was that partly it was a bit like an act doing an opening night show and then the second night just isn't as good because you're reliving the first night, instead of being in that moment.'

I think it's also a question of perspective. In your first game, as the challenger, you are risking nothing; as the carry-over champion, your second episode is your first experience of having something to lose, of being the hunted instead of the hunter. David started his *Sale* journey with the cash jackpot as his only goal, but he took an interesting approach by frequently buying prizes in the gift shop, not only to bolster his winnings but because he believed contestants who took risks and spent money made for better television. No doubt that was his script-writing background reminding him of what makes the best 'story' for viewers. But on his final episode, playing for the cash jackpot, he bought nothing—only because he wanted to see how high a score he could achieve. The answer? The all-time record, never broken, of $200.

'And I felt, "Well, I've kind of earned it. I've earned this bloody jackpot because I've got a really good score as well,"' David says.

David's success meant that he was invited back for some tournaments of champions, but he never managed to beat Cary Young.

David was good enough to reach a final question tie-break against Cary on one occasion, but tie-breaks were always a 'Who Am I?' question—Cary's greatest strength. From as little as 'Born in the Darling Downs in 1868' Cary was able to nail the answer[1]—and ice the game. Within a couple of years, David was on the other side of the camera, as the show's writer and adjudicator, and the longer he worked on quiz shows the more he assumed that his days as a television contestant were over. And, apart from a brief and unsuccessful appearance on a show called *QuizMaster* in 2002, that seemed to be the case.

Then, in 2020, Channel Seven aired a spin-off from *The Chase* that was called *Beat the Chasers*. It flipped the regular show on its head: instead of contestants working as a team against one chaser, the chasers played as a team against one contestant. The contestants could choose how many chasers to take on, with the highest jackpots available for those who tried to take down all four of us. It was such a formidable task that a number of past quiz-show champions turned up to try their hand at the unique challenge. And when at one point we heard host Andrew O'Keefe call out the name of the next contestant—'David Poltorak!'—we knew our biggest test was at hand. All of us knew David by reputation as a *Sale* champ and question writer, but he was almost unrecognisable after three decades of virtually no television appearances. He had won the lot on *Sale* with a full head of

---

[1] Steele Rudd (the pen name of Arthur Hoey Davis), the author who created the characters 'Dad and Dave'.

hair at age 31; here he stood before us at 65, wearing glasses, his remaining hair cropped almost to invisibility. He had the knowledge to defeat us, but did he still have the speed?

The answer was a resounding yes. David was the show's biggest winner, earning $150,000 for beating the four Australian chasers: Issa Schultz, Matt Parkinson, Cheryl Toh and me. For most of the two-minute speed battle—the game would be lost by whichever side's time expired first—correct answers bounced back and forth between David and the chasers. In the dying seconds, we were asked: 'In music notation, how many demisemi-quavers are in one crotchet?[1]' Issa, who has played music since his childhood, audibly said, 'Oh, goodness me!' Cheryl buzzed in and incorrectly guessed sixteen, but someone had to take a punt: Matt and I were sitting like stunned mullets, still trying to work out what language the question was in. I was on more comfortable ground when I quickly answered the next question: 'Which hit '80s sitcom features the Keaton family?[2]' But David won the game by answering his next question correctly: 'The UK's nuclear arms program is named for what pronged spear?[3]' Our time expired, and David Poltorak had done it again. He had once again proved that he could answer the questions, after thirty years of asking them.

---

[1]   Eight. I call this sort of question a 'stopper', one that completely halts your momentum. It requires a different type of thinking to answer: first knowledge of musical theory, and then quick mathematical conversions.

[2]   *Family Ties*

[3]   Trident

'When I did get the job on *Sale*, I thought, "This'll be interesting for a year,"' David says. 'And I was just sucked into the maw of television. It was so much fun so much of the time. There was a lot of pressure to do it well, and I know I had a lot of sleepless nights and I had shocking headaches on the day after records, because you're just intensely staring at the screen for hours and your mind's racing. But that's part of the fun as well. It was great having that experience.'

▼

One hundred and eight thousand questions. At least. I thought I had done pretty well to write 4000 questions while training Paul. To be fair, it wasn't my job. When Paul went to the studio as a stand-by contestant, I came along to sit in the audience and watch the filming unfold, confident that he was well prepared. I recall chatting to Paul, who was wearing a suit and tie, ready to play if required. Another of the stand-bys did get the chance to play but Paul was not needed. His disappointment was tempered by the knowledge that he would be called up in the coming weeks and the dry run could only help his preparation. There were only a couple of weeks of filming left in 2001, but Paul would surely be one of the first cabs off the rank in the new year.

Unfortunately, Paul had put himself in the right place at the wrong time. In early December, shortly after his stand-by experience, Channel Nine announced that *Sale of the Century* would be rested in the new year:

TV GAME SHOW SHAFTED

The 21-year-old TV game show *Sale of the Century* is to be taken off the air for the first half of next year and replaced by a new quiz show called *Shafted*. The Nine Network said a revamped *Sale of the Century*, minus host Glenn Ridge, who has fronted the program for 11 years, and his sidekicks, Karina Brown and Peter Smith, will return to the network mid-next year.

Sydney Morning Herald, 8 December 2001

No *Sale of the Century*? The show had been on air for my entire life. It wasn't just part of the furniture, it was where you *won* the furniture. Cancelling *Sale of the Century* was as unthinkable as axing the news. But ratings were struggling. The new backstabbing reality shows such as *Big Brother*, *Survivor* and *The Mole* were all the rage, not to mention Channel Seven's *The Weakest Link*, which had debuted in 2001 and brought a new edginess to the genre. *Sale of the Century* had survived for two decades by being a nice, classy, friendly game where the men wore suits and ties, the women were asked to wear 'after five' attire and everyone shook hands politely. Apparently, that was now uncool.

Sale of the Century's replacement, *Shafted*, was another entry in the trend towards nasty formats. It was hosted by Red Symons, who had made his name first as the lead guitarist in the band Skyhooks in the 1970s, and then as the grumpy, sarcastic judge on the 'Red Faces' talent segment on the long-running variety show *Hey, Hey It's Saturday*. Red also had brains: on a celebrity episode of *Who Wants To Be a Millionaire?* in 2000, he reached the level at which he could play for $500,000. By an interesting quirk of fate, the phone-a-friend lifeline Red used to correctly answer the $250,000 question (Who, in 1960, was the first Australian of the Year?[1]) was the Channel Nine news reporter Brett McLeod, who had been one of my brother-in-law Paul's best friends growing up. On the $500,000 question, Red crashed back down to $32,000 by overconfidently locking in 'architecture' when asked in which field sixteenth-century Italian Benvenuto Cellini achieved fame[2]. Red's television persona was as something of an arrogant killjoy, which made him a natural fit for *Shafted*, a show in which he could pull a lever to drop contestants through a trapdoor, and which ended with two contestants deciding whether to share the prize money or trick their opponent and take it for themselves. At its core, *Shafted* was still a general knowledge quiz show but, as a viewer, I reacted strongly against the nastiness. It seems I wasn't alone. After only eight weeks on air, network executives pulled their own lever and *Shafted* disappeared through the studio floor, never to be seen again.

Now that *Shafted* had failed, surely *Sale* would be back. But perhaps the talk of being rested was simply the network's way of phasing the show out with a minimum of fuss. *Shafted* was replaced

---

[1] Macfarlane Burnet, the virologist who won a Nobel Prize in Physiology or Medicine in 1960 for his theory of acquired immune tolerance.

[2] The answer was sculpture.

with reruns of the sitcom *Frasier*, which proved a surprisingly popular—and cheap—replacement. For a loyal *Sale* fan, this was the ultimate insult, because it felt like Nine preferred to produce nothing rather than produce *Sale of the Century*. Still, I was convinced the show would come back. I liked *Frasier*, but surely his *bon mots* couldn't carry such an important timeslot forever.

And so I kept writing my practice questions throughout 2002, as much for my own improvement as for anything. By the time I gave up, I had written enough questions for roughly 70 episodes.

As yet, Paul still hasn't made it on to a quiz show as a contestant, which is a shame, because I believe he could have great success. His voice has appeared on television, though: in 2003, he was my phone-a-friend on *Who Wants To Be a Millionaire?* But that's a story for another chapter. Meanwhile, in my efforts to train Paul, I had stumbled upon what I believe is the best quiz training of all: writing your own questions. By researching, carefully phrasing and physically typing out these 4000 questions, I had carved them so deeply into my brain that I could answer nearly all of them even twenty years later. I use the same training method while preparing for *The Chase* and have written many thousands of practice questions specifically for that purpose. These days, I also write 125 quiz questions per week for newspapers around Australia, so that's another 6500 questions a year. I'm only twenty-odd years off matching David Poltorak.

CHAPTER 5

NOT THE WEAKEST LINK

Dear Ruthless Determined & Confident one!
Thank you for your interest in auditioning for Dog Eat Dog,
the new prime time game show set to air nationally on the
Seven Network. As you can imagine, with a huge cash prize
guaranteed to go off each week we've had an incredible response
to the show. We will not be doing any more contestant auditions
for Series One. We will however keep your details on file for
Series Two . . .

I can't remember the first thing about *Dog Eat Dog*. Couldn't tell you who hosted it, how the game worked, nothing. All I know is that it didn't last long. But, flicking through my folder of old game-show memorabilia, I found this letter, dated 28 November 2001. Apparently, I had applied to go on the show about the same time Paul was called up as a *Sale of the Century* stand-by. Some brief online research reveals that *Dog Eat Dog* aired on Channel Seven in 2002 and featured a mixture of maths, language and logic challenges, as well as a rock-climbing segment and a final general knowledge round. It bore some similarities to my childhood favourite *The Krypton Factor*, but with an unhealthy dose of the mean-spiritedness that marked game shows of the early 2000s: for example, it had a designated 'Losers Bench'. It was hosted by actress Simone Kessell, who also in 2002 was one of the *Undercover Angels*, along with Jackie O and Katie Underwood, on a bizarre *Charlie's Angels*–inspired reality series hosted by then nineteen-year-old Ian Thorpe. A *Sydney Morning Herald* reviewer labelled *Undercover Angels* 'the worst show in the history of the world', which was pretty outlandish considering *The Jerry Springer Show* existed. *Dog Eat Dog* was pulled after two episodes, although it briefly reappeared in Channel Seven's summer schedule later that year before it was taken off life support.

In hindsight, I'm surprised I applied for *Dog Eat Dog* before seeing the show, because that was not my usual modus operandi. I preferred to know what I was getting into, especially during that backstabbing era. A brief flurry of these shows involved varying degrees of treachery, which I suspect was a direct response to the enormous success of *Survivor*, the granddaddy of all reality competition shows. *Survivor* was based around competitors making and breaking alliances, lying and in-fighting. The first American *Survivor* series in 2000 had been won by Richard

Hatch, a corporate trainer who made Machiavelli look like a good bloke misunderstood.

Survivor was a phenomenon—I lived in a share-house at the time and watched on, stunned, as Richard was voted the winner by his fellow contestants despite his arrogant, conniving behaviour. The turkeys had not so much voted for Christmas as voted for the turkey farmer who fattened them up and sold them for profit. The show was hugely popular in Australia, the finale drawing more than 600,000 viewers in Melbourne alone and beating an AFL preliminary final in the ratings. That bears repeating. It beat an AFL preliminary final. In Melbourne. That's like out-rating the pope's mass in the Vatican City. No wonder Eddie McGuire's *Who Wants To Be a Millionaire?* invited Richard Hatch to appear on a celebrity special the following month. What nobody expected was for Richard to bomb out on the fourth question: 'What is 11 multiplied by 12?[1]' Too quickly he locked in 123. I'm not sure I've ever seen Eddie McGuire speechless apart from that moment, when his show lost its drawcard after four questions. Suddenly, Eddie needed a lifeline of his own.

After the ratings triumph of *Survivor*, it was no surprise that networks looked for shows with an edge. *Dog Eat Dog* was one of several. In early 2001, Kerri-Anne Kennerley became the first woman to be the solo host of a quiz show in Australia when she fronted Channel Ten's *Greed*, based on a US format developed by Dick Clark. It was a team-based game that featured a theoretical

---

[1] Come on, you didn't really expect me to answer this one for you.

million-dollar top prize that could be shared among the contestants, but there were a couple of catches. The team captain had
the sole discretion as to whether the team played on to risk more
and more money, which could lead to tension if some players
wanted to walk away with their winnings. More cruel was the
'Terminator' segment, where a randomly chosen contestant could
challenge one of their teammates to a one-question shoot-out,
with the losing player eliminated and the winning player taking
the loser's share of prize money. The show wasn't called *Greed*
for nothing. It also explained why the king of television confron-
tations, Jerry Springer, was hosting the British version. But this
was not what Australians expected of game shows. The meanest
that *Sale of the Century* ever got was introducing a 'Take Five' to
the Cash Card gamble, which involved taking $5 off the score of
an opponent. *Sale* was so civilised that this was jarring to watch,
and contestants were always apologetic when taking $5 off a
competitor, like a tennis player whose shot accidentally catches
the net cord.

Shafted was even grubbier in the way it tempted contestants
to behave horribly. Based on a British program, *Shafted* began by
dumping one of its six contestants before the first question had
even been asked. It proceeded into quiz rounds that involved each
contestant choosing how many points they were willing to risk
per question, based on the category. That was okay. There were
also occasional 'half questions', whose first few words came up on
the screen before contestants had to wager money on whether they
thought they could answer it correctly, though the questions often

went in an unexpected direction. An example: 'Manhattan is one of . . .', before diverting to '. . . the films by which director?[1]' That was tricksy, but as a sparingly used gimmick it was interesting.

Where *Shafted* lost me was in its elimination of contestants, and in its final head-to-head game. The leading player after each round chose a contestant to 'shaft', and that contestant then pleaded their case, hoping the 'shafter' would change their mind and pick on someone else. I found an episode on YouTube and it made for depressing, even offensive, viewing. In one round, the leader, Laurie, nominated a player named Peter to be shafted because 'He's got the same name as my brother-in-law, and I don't like him very much'. In a later round, Laurie was set to be shafted by another contestant, Craig. Here is the discussion that followed.

Laurie: 'I think you're making a mistake because you're leaving yourself with two women, and we know how unreliable they can be.'

Craig: 'I'm with you, Laurie. See you later, Lisa.'

Red: 'Geez, it's got ugly in here. Lisa, you've been shafted— royally. And when we come back from the break we'll have more ugliness and sexism.'

There's not much to say about that, except . . . wow. There was, at least, some poetic justice. The endgame was a version of the 'prisoner's dilemma', an experiment in game theory first conceived by mathematicians in 1950. The way it worked on

---

[1] Woody Allen

Shafted was that the final two contestants decided whether to share the prize money or attempt to take it all themselves. Each player secretly chose one of two options: 'share' or 'shaft'. If both chose 'share', the prize money was split evenly between them. If one picked 'shaft' and the other chose 'share', the one who shafted won the lot. But if they both picked 'shaft', nobody won anything. You'll be pleased to know that Laurie and Craig, who reached the final two, walked away empty-handed after trying to shaft each other. Their uppance had well and truly come. The 'double shaft' was the most common result. Few players walked away with cash during the 40-episode run of *Shafted*, and even fewer did so by sharing. Stephen Hall, a comedian and writer who became a *Temptation* grand champion in 2005, worked on *Shafted* as a question writer. He now writes a blog titled 'How To Win Game Shows' (I heartily recommended Stephen's work), and wrote of the feeling behind the scenes on *Shafted*:

> Often, when working on *Shafted*, I'd feel quite dispirited at the end of the day. Time and time again, it became clear that we were empowering our contestants to lie to each other, betray each other, cheat each other and just generally behave poorly. We weren't exactly celebrating humanity at its best here. As per the UK version of the show, every time both finalists shafted each other (resulting in them both going home empty-handed), it was feel-bad television at its most depressing. And I'm sorry to say that this was—by far—the endgame's most common outcome. Both finalists would earnestly promise each other

they'd share, before immediately going back on their word and shafting each other. It always resulted in two sad, ashamed, regretful people kicking themselves for being so nasty.

I completely understand Stephen's sentiment. After watching the Laurie and Craig episode on YouTube, I felt dirty. I didn't just want to clear my internet history, I wanted to disinfect it. There were no winners from such a show, not even the network. The ratings for *Shafted* steadily declined until it was axed after less than three months on air. The episode I watched was the last one. As the credits rolled, announcer Pete Smith advised that at 7 p.m. next week, Nine would air 'the award-winning fun of *Frasier*'. That it was Pete Smith making this announcement was another reminder of how the timeslot had fallen. He had been the classy, erudite voice of 'Saaaaale of the Century'; now he was a voice from quiz-show heaven reading the obituary of the replacement that was heading for game-show hell.

At the core of these shows (and others like 2002's *Fear Factor*, which wanted contestants to eat bulls' testicles and lie in a box filled with snakes for a chance to win money) was the idea that viewers wanted nothing more than to watch ordinary people in uncomfortable situations. It was a flawed assumption—though *I'm a Celebrity, Get Me Out of Here* later proved it was great fun to watch *celebrities* eat disgusting food and confront their phobias. But in my opinion, the mash-up of genteel game show and nasty reality television was never likely to work. *Survivor* was a whole new genre, and viewers could accept and even love the backstabbing because they came in without preconceived ideas. But for shows like *Shafted*, Stephen Hall's description is apt: it was feel-bad television. None of these programs lasted long.

The Weakest Link was the most successful; it aired for more than a hundred episodes over fifteen months from early 2001 to 2002. It was the only one of these 'edgier' quiz shows that entered the cultural zeitgeist. Two decades later, despite the show's short run, you occasionally still hear someone imitate Cornelia Frances: 'You are the weakest link. Goodbye.' It was also the only one of these 'nasty' shows for which I auditioned. Part of that was because of my reluctance to apply for a show until I had seen it. Having watched *Greed*, I could see that, while there was some malice in the Terminator segment, at its core the show was mostly trivia, with big money up for grabs. I would have auditioned had it stayed on air long enough. But I wasn't masochistic enough to go on *Shafted*, where the potential to win money was so small. As for *Dog Eat Dog*, it didn't last long enough for me to show them what a 'ruthless, determined and confident one' I was. But, early in 2001, I decided *The Weakest Link* was worth a shot. Paul's *Sale* experience had shown me that time was of the essence.

The original version of *The Weakest Link* had been a great success in the UK, where it was hosted by Anne Robinson, who had made her name writing caustic tabloid newspaper columns before moving to radio and television. Whereas the quiz show host was traditionally a more benevolent figure, if sometimes a bit stuffy, Robinson's approach was to deliver withering put-downs to the contestants and, frankly, scare them. She was so good at it that when NBC bought the rights to produce an American version, they flew in Robinson to host it. In Australia, the job went to Cornelia Frances, known for playing nasty characters in soap operas, and who, with her red hair and glasses, bore a striking resemblance to Anne Robinson.

The show began with nine contestants, each standing at a podium, in a semicircle around the host. Across eight rounds of questions, the group would build up a sizeable bank of prize money, which would ultimately be won by just one person. After each round, players would vote the 'weakest link' off the team, and this contestant had to leave their podium and navigate the 'Walk of Shame' out of the studio. The final two contestants played head-to-head for the cash jackpot in a best-of-five-questions final round. Weaker players were usually voted off earliest because their incorrect answers cost the team money, but stronger contestants were sometimes targeted towards the end, when they posed a threat. Because contestants could see the names being written by the players nearest to them, voting blocs frequently formed, because there was safety in numbers. Cornelia would also ask contestants why they voted for a player, which often led to narky comments.

I wasn't concerned about insults from the host, or even from other contestants—that was part of the fun. And while I didn't love the idea of voting players off, I could handle it for the chance at a big cash prize. And, because *The Weakest Link* aired in prime time, Channel Seven put up decent cash. The winning player often pocketed $30,000, $40,000 or more. The audition made it clear that personality would be far more important than on *Sale of the Century*. One of the profiling questions was something like: 'If you were an animal, what sort of animal would you be?' I wasn't yet The Shark, but I knew I needed to give the producers a reason to cast me. I wrote that I would be a crocodile: still and silent for long periods, watching everything unfold around me, but ready to strike at the right moment. I felt this would appeal to the casting team, but there was also some truth to it. I could picture myself blending into the background, quietly biding my time while the little fish flapped and floundered. And when the opportunity arose, I would show that I had been a threat all along. Would that win me the money? Would I even make it on to the show? Only time would tell.

▼

When Deb Stewart started working on *The Weakest Link* in 2001, she had opened the door to a whole new world. In the '90s, Deb had worked behind the scenes on *Tonight Live with Steve Vizard*, a late-night comedy interview show that went in unexpected directions at the whim of the host and the guests. She also had experience in news and current affairs, which was unpredictable and required fast reactions as stories developed. On a quiz show, none of those principles applied.

'Quiz was a completely different ball game because it has a real discipline compared to those sort of shows, which thrive on being spontaneous,' Deb says. 'On a quiz show, you need to button everything up. You can't have anything ambiguous, because you're dealing with someone's potential to win possibly a life-changing amount of money.'

Twenty years later, Deb is still working on quiz shows, as executive producer of *The Chase Australia*. Along the way, her game-show producing credits have included *Who Wants To Be a Millionaire?*, *Deal or No Deal*, *1 vs 100*, *The Million Dollar Drop* and *Think Tank*. She has seen formats rise and fall, some that have struggled and some that have thrived. But it all started with *The Weakest Link*, which is widely remembered by Australians and was rebooted in 2021, yet was only moderately successful in its original run.

'I know towards the end of *The Weakest Link*, I started to get a bit uncomfortable, because my boys were in primary school and "You are the weakest link. Goodbye" was becoming a bit of a bullying catchphrase,' Deb says. 'And I remember feeling uncomfortable about that. I thought Cornelia did it really well; I thought she was great. She hit the right tone. But I did start to notice that.'

When the show was cancelled in 2002, the world had changed vastly since its premiere in February 2001. The September 11 terrorist attacks in the USA had effects from which the world has, in some ways, not recovered. I wonder if it also had less significant effects, such as altering what people wanted to watch on television. If television is a way to escape the real world, then, in the wake of a terrible tragedy, feel-good television will likely thrive more than shows with an unfriendly streak.

'You want escapism. That's what it's always been about,' Deb says. 'It's easy to be nasty. It's very easy to say hateful, hurtful things to people. But it's not clever. And I think that's where those shows went wrong, because they were so constructed. It wasn't even necessarily contestants reacting to what was happening— they had already decided what they were going to say. I think people found it uncomfortable.'

At least *The Weakest Link* did offer one guaranteed feel-good moment, because *somebody* would always win a hefty jackpot. *Shafted* couldn't even give viewers that. And watching people win is generally more satisfying than watching them lose.

'My experience is, from being in the control room and down on the studio floor when there's an exciting game, everyone's holding their breath waiting to see, can they do it?' Deb says. 'And they're just euphoric if the person does it, they're so happy for them. It's a really lovely thing. If you've got contestants who people relate to . . . then they want to be a part of what's happening. It's like a sport—they're cheering them on, encouraging them from the stands. I've also worked on a lot of sport, and I see a good quiz show as a sport, because you have to bring your best game, which is your mindset.'

There it is again, the comparison between game shows and sport. The parallels are unmistakable. Tennis, golf, cricket, football—they're all games. *The Chase, Millionaire, Sale of the Century, Mastermind*—they're all games too. The two groups might come from different branches of the family tree, but they're not-too-distant cousins. They are all played competitively to a set of rules. The rules might be complicated—I challenge any soccer lover to explain the offside rule succinctly—but that doesn't always matter if the spectacle is entertaining enough.

'*Deal or No Deal* went for about eleven years,' Deb says, 'and let me tell you, there were a lot of people who still didn't know how that show worked. But they watched it every night, and they loved it. I think it was a bit like going along to the casino and standing next to people at the pokies.'

Sometimes a format simply cannot overcome a complicated rule. *Jeopardy!* is the pinnacle of quiz shows in the United States, where it was broadcast on and off from 1964 to 1979 before being revived in 1984 and running ever since. When long-serving host Alex Trebek died in 2020 at the age of 80, there was such an outpouring of grief that it was like America had lost its favourite uncle. I love *Jeopardy!* In my opinion, it brilliantly marries highbrow and lowbrow trivia, and, by sorting its questions into twelve categories that change every day, it ensures a wonderful variety. Except—and here's the problem—they're not really questions. They are answers. *Jeopardy!*'s quirk is that it requires contestants to respond in the form of a question. To take a real example, in the category 'Tough Geography', players were given this clue: 'The Gulf of Aden guards the southern entrance to this sea.' To be marked correct, a contestant needed to say: 'What is the Red Sea?' If they simply said 'The Red Sea', they would be incorrect. Of course, in real life, if you asked someone 'What is the Red Sea?' and they answered 'The Gulf of Aden guards the southern entrance to this sea,' you'd tell them to stop talking in riddles.

When Channel Ten aired a local version of the show in 1993, with Tony Barber as host, Australians struggled to adjust. In his autobiography, Barber wrote that while viewers who liked the show *really* liked the show, a focus group had revealed that the majority of people found it too confusing that answers had to be in the form of a question. It was like trying to introduce cricket to Americans: they might enjoy it if they gave it a chance, but most couldn't be bothered.

A similar format hesitancy struck another Channel Ten adaptation in 2018. One of the UK's most successful modern quiz shows has been *Pointless*, in which two-player teams are given questions or language puzzles that have multiple correct answers. Much like in *Family Feud*, these questions have previously been put to a survey group of 100 people. But, whereas the aim in *Family Feud* was to name the most popular answer, *Pointless* reversed this by challenging contestants to guess the correct answers that the fewest surveyed people had included in their responses. For example, if the category was 'US presidents', answers like Ronald Reagan or Barack Obama might have been said by 70 or 80 of the hundred, whereas only one or two may have thought of a more obscure president such as Calvin Coolidge. As in golf, the lower the score the better. The ultimate goal is to name a 'pointless' response—a correct answer that none of the hundred surveyed people had said. This greatly appealed to my love of useless, obscure information; I liked that it rewarded all correct answers but gave greater reward to contestants with the deepest knowledge.

The Australian *Pointless* was hosted by comedian Mark Humphries, who I believe did an excellent job with Andrew Rochford as his co-host. And fitting *Pointless* into a half-hour commercial timeslot compared to the UK version's 45-minute run-time also eliminated much of the tedious waffle that afflicts many British game shows. But Australian viewers didn't warm to *Pointless*. Perhaps its 6 p.m. timeslot—up against the major news bulletins on Seven and Nine—didn't help. *Pointless* lasted two seasons before Ten decided that it was, indeed, pointless.

That was a great disappointment to Mark Humphries, who had cheekily put his hand up via Twitter to host the Australian production, having become an avid fan of the British version. Mark had been a game-show viewer as a child, but *Pointless* was unlike anything he had seen before. He particularly liked the fact that *Pointless* did not reward contestants and viewers who thought like everyone else.

'*Pointless* was the first quiz show where I almost had a physical reaction of, wow, this is really clever, this is really different,' Mark says. 'There's something about getting a pointless answer—in that theoretical group of 100 people, you would be the only one that would have come up with that, and that makes you feel unique.'

I agreed. What quizzer doesn't like displaying their knowledge of obscure facts? It also gave me great satisfaction to watch some of the jackpot-winning answers: a young man who worked in sports media named nineteenth-century cricketer Jack Blackham in the category Australian Test wicketkeepers; a contestant pair came up with the capital cities of Suriname and Guyana[1] in the category of South American capitals. The prize money wasn't big—the jackpot started at $2000 and another $2000 was added each episode until it was won—but the entertainment level was high, or so I thought.

The ratings never hit the level required. Why did such a successful British format (the show has been on air for more than a decade) not work here? Mark Humphries believes there were several factors. He wonders if his own transition from a comedian producing short satirical videos for SBS to mainstream game-show host happened too quickly; in my opinion, he was great. More importantly, slashing the run-time to half what it was in Britain cut out the waffle but also left little room for witty banter, and plenty of the best material ended up on the cutting-room floor. But I think the fundamental issue was that many viewers simply didn't understand or appreciate the cleverness of the core concept: that certain correct answers were better than others.

'I was genuinely shocked that that was a recurring issue,' Mark says. 'People would tell me in the street that they didn't get it. And I didn't get that they didn't get it. I was really confused by that. That was disappointing. It also seemed to be simultaneously too highbrow for people who loved *Family Feud* and not highbrow enough for people who loved the British *Pointless*. It was in a sort of no-man's land.'

---

[1] Paramaribo and Georgetown respectively

Australian television history is littered with game shows that struggled to make it past one or two seasons. In my lifetime alone I can recall *1 v 100*, *All-Star Squares*, *Cash Bonanza*, *The Con Test*, *Dog Eat Dog*, *Greed*, *Hot Streak*, *Jeopardy!*, *Keynotes*, *Million Dollar Chance of a Lifetime*, *The Million Dollar Drop*, *The Oz Game*, *Pass the Buck*, *Press Your Luck*, *Shafted*, *Strike It Lucky* and *Think Tank*. If *Pointless* had ever had a category called 'Australian game shows', most of the above would have been pointless answers. One show was dragged after a single episode: *The Master*, a 2006 quiz show that pitted contestants against *Who Wants To Be a Millionaire?* champion Martin Flood.

Sometimes it's not the format's fault. All sorts of factors can affect a game show's success. The timeslot is critical, although in the current era of streaming and catch-up it's less important. There is also the question of general viewing trends. One show that Deb Stewart worked on that she believed had great potential was *The Million Dollar Drop*, which Eddie McGuire hosted in 2011. The concept was that two people with a pre-existing relationship—spouses, siblings, friends—were given $1 million in cash, made up of bundled $20 notes. Across eight multiple-choice questions, they piled the cash onto trapdoors that corresponded with answer options. They could hedge their bets by splitting the money between different answers, but any cash that fell through the trapdoor of an incorrect answer was lost forever. Whatever they retained after eight questions, they won. I recall Zoe, my wife, who had also enjoyed watching *The Million Pound Drop* in the UK, really enjoyed the dynamic of the show. But here, it lasted only six episodes.

'I thought that was a really interesting concept,' Deb says. 'I liked the psychology of two people having to trust each other when answering seemingly accessible questions, then agreeing on how to divide the money between answer options. It was an insight into people's relationships under the pressure of competing, and that has always interested me. There was a lot that I liked about that, but I think it was just at the wrong time. I think prime-time quiz shows in Australia were just starting to wane. Reality just came in and gave it all a hip-and-shoulder.'

Deb believes simplicity is the key to what makes a successful quiz show format. There is a reason *Sale of the Century* lasted for twenty years—the questions and answers were the stars. The same is true of *Who Wants To Be a Millionaire?* and its afternoon spin-off *Millionaire Hot Seat*. The same is true of *The Chase*. These shows lend themselves to what is sometimes called 'play-along-ability', encouraging viewers at home to answer the questions as they watch. *How did he not know that!? Ooh, that was a good guess! I knew that one!*

There is more opportunity to play along on *The Chase* than on almost any other quiz show, because such a large number of questions are used. My rough, back-of-the-envelope estimate is that across four cash-builder rounds, four head-to-head rounds and two final chases, at least 120 questions will be asked in a typical episode. And when you consider that we have filmed more than a thousand episodes, you can do the maths—unless you're

Richard Hatch. In fact, the number of questions produced by the show's writers is much higher again, because for any given episode at least 200 questions will be prepared and ready to go.

Since *The Chase Australia* premiered in September 2015, the show has dominated its timeslot of 5 p.m. to 6 p.m., so much that at times our ratings numbers have been more in line with prime-time figures.

The final chase, leading into the 6 p.m. news bulletin, may be the most jam-packed endgame that television quiz shows have ever seen. The contestants first have two minutes to answer as many questions correctly as possible before the chaser is given two minutes to catch that target. If chasers and the players answer at a reasonable speed, it's quite common for roughly 25 questions to be asked in a two-minute chase, so 50 questions can comfortably be asked in the last five minutes of the show. On *Sale of the Century*, with champion players answering at maximum speed, the final 'mad minute' would top out at about 18 questions. The hour-long *Millionaire Hot Seat* has capacity for only 30 questions across the entire show.

Due to the volume of questions on *The Chase*, there are inevitably answers that the chasers miss, while people at home think 'How did they not know that one!?' That can be especially empowering for the vast numbers of children who watch the show. I can recall any number of answers I've missed that my kids have nailed instantly. For example, under time pressure in a final chase, I mistakenly answered 'rabbits' to the question: 'A children's book by Beatrix Potter is *The Tale of Two Bad* . . .

what?' We have the full set of Beatrix Potter books at home, and my children instantly knew the correct answer[1] when they heard the question.

Our host, Larry Emdur, took on the job in 2021, completing a career grand slam of game-show roles. Most famously, he was the smiling face of *The Price Is Right* during the 1990s, often literally holding the hands of nervous contestants as they guessed how much a tin of pineapple cost or rolled oversized novelty dice to estimate the price of a car. Larry's other hosting duties have included *Wheel of Fortune* and *The Main Event*, as well as some bizarre curios of Australian television history. There was *Cash Bonanza*, filmed at Movie World on the Gold Coast, which was connected to lottery scratchies and featured contestants in cowboy hats. There were the short-lived *Celebrity Splash* and *Celebrity Dog School*, in which famous people tried to master high diving and dog training tasks respectively. And there was Larry's first very brief foray into game show hosting, on *Family Double Dare* in the late 1980s when he was in his mid-twenties. Larry certainly didn't expect, at 56, to be suddenly hosting a 'proper' quiz show for the first time, but he has slotted in seamlessly.

'None of it's in my wheelhouse,' Larry says of *The Chase*. 'And my wheelhouse is a funky place, because I've done so much crap television. But each and every one of those crap shows has been an invaluable lesson for me. I did a show called *Celebrity Splash*, which was in front of an audience of 2000 people. And same with

---

[1]   Mice

Cash Bonanza actually—this massive, massive audience. And the reason I wanted to do those shows was to experience that, and that made me a better host. My wheelhouse is like this sort of garage with old busted bits of game shows, but what it all equates to is that I feel comfortable hosting stuff. *The Chase* represents a huge challenge to me because of the volume of questions, the speed at which the questions are asked. I truly am intimidated by you guys, and the contestants. I am, by far, the dumbest guy in the room. But it's not my role to be the smart guy, it's my role to be the circus master.'

Circus master was an apt description for *The Price Is Right*, so silly were most of the games. But, as much as I might tell myself *The Chase* is more highbrow, I know deep down it's just as outlandish for me to dress up in a blue suit, call myself The Shark and answer questions about ancient history or rap music or Olympic medallists. And I'm fine with that. The point of any game show is to entertain, to have fun. And quiz shows *are* game shows. It didn't take Larry Emdur long to work out that *The Chase* was not that far removed from *The Price Is Right*.

In fact, the stakes were sometimes higher on *The Price Is Right*, where contestants could win cars, luxury holidays and a final showcase that by the mid-2000s was sometimes worth more than half a million dollars. At other times, even the smallest of prizes could make a huge difference to a contestant. Larry has seen the full gamut of contestants, all of whom have different motivations for appearing on a game show.

'For some people it's "I need $50,000 because my husband half-renovated the bathroom ten years ago and I'm washing my face with a hose,"' Larry says. 'Then for other people, it's like "I'm on TV, I'm answering questions against Sharkie!" For a lot of people, that's enough; it's such a special thing. Here's my favourite story. There was a woman on *The Price Is Right*—single mother with four kids. And she wanted a microwave oven, just to help her at dinner time. And she couldn't afford a microwave oven—it's a couple of hundred bucks. And she was playing for a microwave oven. I'll always remember it, because it was so special to her, so exciting, so nerve-racking, and she was just playing a stupid game where she had to get three numbers in a row, but it could have gone either way. And we were so involved in this story. And I'd already resigned myself—a couple of times on *The Price Is Right*, I thought, "I'm going to give the prize to them anyway and if the boss makes me pay the boss makes me pay." And she won it and you could see it was special. That stuff sticks with me. That moment for her, dinner time and breakfast time with her four kids, for an unemployed single mum—that made a huge difference to her.'

The joy of seeing people win, and of playing along at home and wondering if you could have won too—that's key to a game show's success. It's also why Larry Emdur has kept coming back to the genre. He wasn't a game show viewer growing up, he didn't get into the media to become a game show host, and, after *Family Double Dare* tanked, he assumed he was done with game shows entirely. More than thirty years later, he's a game show icon—and he loves the genre.

'It's about playing along at home and empowering people to think they could have done it,' Larry says. 'That's the engagement. That's different to the news, it's different to *The Morning Show*, it's different to *Home and Away*. It's a very special piece of the puzzle. I love that. I love the reaction I get from people in the street.'

Ultimately, it's feel-good television. Which is why, in my opinion, shows like *The Price Is Right* and *Sale of the Century* have such high nostalgia value, while mean-spirited shows such as *Shafted* and *The Weakest Link* didn't pass the test of time. There's enough nastiness in the world without manufacturing it on a game show as well.

▼

Until researching this chapter, I would have sworn that I first met Deb Stewart when *The Chase Australia* started in 2015. I would have been wrong. The evidence is staring me in the face, on an old VHS tape my parents recently found at their house. Gathering together all the footage of my various game show appearances while writing this book, I was pretty sure I would find everything except *The Weakest Link*. I was a contestant on the show in 2001 and I knew my parents had recorded it, but I hadn't seen the video in at least fifteen years. I assumed it had been mislabelled, taped over or otherwise lost. But here it is, after all this time. And there is my youthful, beardless face, pontificating about the result of the episode as the credits roll. And there is the familiar name in the credits. Line producer: Deb Stewart. I sent her a screenshot of my head next to her name. She replied: 'Wow! I did work on your ep! I would have done your exit interview.'

There is a reason my exit interview ran as the credits rolled: I was not voted off during the episode. I did not do the Walk of Shame. I was not the weakest link. Six months after my *Sale of the Century* heartache, still nineteen, I played against one other contestant, head-to-head, for more money than I had earned in my life: $30,700. And the final, winner-take-all round began with these words from Cornelia Frances: 'Brydon, as the strongest link you have the choice of who will go first . . .'

▼

I should clarify something. I didn't do *the* Walk of Shame, but I did *a* Walk of Shame before the show was recorded. Contestants were required to bring three changes of clothing, to ensure they had something deemed suitable by Channel Seven. I can't remember what shirts I took, but as the wardrobe supervisor ran her sceptical eye over them, I suffered an early blow to my confidence. Sheepishly, and ashamed at my lack of style, I was guided to a corner, where she chose for me a plain yellow shirt from her stock collection. I felt like the unsophisticated slob who turns up to a fancy dining venue without a jacket and has to wear one from the restaurant's lost and found.

Still, that didn't matter. I was here for the quizzing. And the money. There were nine contestants in the green room that day, and as we nervously awaited our opportunity, we sized each other up. There was Sue, Noel, Fred, Marc, Lara, Alexandra, Simon, Peter and me. Who were the threats? Who looked like weak links? There were some half-hearted attempts at forming alliances, but I knew this was futile. What mattered was where you would be positioned in the semicircle and who was next to you. I didn't want to get stuck on one of the ends. From there, you could see only one other contestant writing on their vote card, an immediate disadvantage. If there was safety in numbers, there was danger in isolation.

In the studio, we were each shown to our podium. And there was mine, on the end, to the far left of the host. I stood behind my podium, cursing my luck. We introduced ourselves on camera: 'I'm Brydon, 19, arts student from West Melbourne.' To my left was Sue, 38, a distribution supervisor from Fernvale. She seemed nice enough. To her left was Fred, 46, a teacher from Kingsgrove. I had been sitting next to Fred in the green room; I wasn't sure I trusted him. Time would tell. In the meantime, I had little choice but to hitch my wagon to Sue's, and I wondered if she would hitch hers to Fred's.

The game involved the host reading one question to each player around the semicircle in turn. The first round lasted two and a half minutes, but, as players were eliminated, the rounds became shorter. The cash jackpot built as chains of correct answers were completed, and any player could, on their turn, 'bank' the money on behalf of the team before Cornelia asked the next question. An incorrect answer lost the team whatever amount was unbanked. So there were tactics in judging when to bank, but it was mostly about answering correctly. In the first round, only two questions came my way. The first, I answered correctly: 'In what language is *caramba* an exclamation of surprise or dismay?[1]' But my brain froze on my second question: 'What sweet name is given to alternate stripes of white and a colour?[2]' Fortunately for me, Noel missed both of his questions—'Of which continent is the Iberian Peninsula a part?[3] and 'In TV transmission, the acronym PAL stands for phase alternating what?[4]' He was the logical candidate to go, and six of us voted for him. But, interestingly, there were a couple of dissenters. Alexandra voted for Fred, and Fred voted for . . . Brydon. So there were two wins for me: I hadn't been voted off and I'd proven myself a good judge of character. Cornelia asked a few of us why we'd voted for Noel. I said he seemed to be struggling under the pressure, to which Cornelia shot back that I had only managed one correct answer myself. In a quick retort that was a little narky and a little Sharky, I pointed out that I had only missed one.

---

[1] Spanish. Thank you Bart Simpson and his 'Ay caramba!' catchphrase; the amount of trivia questions I've worked out over the years from *The Simpsons* references is unbelievable.

[2] Candy stripes

[3] Europe—that's where you'll find Spain and Portugal.

[4] Line

As the rounds progressed, players were picked off one by one. Often, it was the player who had been the weakest link in the round. The first-round elimination of Noel put a physical gap between the trio of Fred, Sue and me, and the rest of the group. So we ended up voting in a bloc. Lara left in round two, then Peter in round three. In round four, Fred was voted off, protesting that it was only because he was a threat. When asked by Cornelia why he had voted for Fred, Simon, who was positioned exactly opposite me, said: 'Kill a snake by chopping off its head.' That was pretty clearly a reference to the Fred–Sue–Brydon triumvirate—and it didn't bode well for Sue and me.

Indeed, Sue was the next to go. Suddenly I was isolated. Four players remained: me on one end, Simon on the other, with Alexandra and Marc next to each other near the middle. Surely I was dead and buried. My only hope was if Simon and I happened to vote the same way and force a tied vote count, in which case the casting vote went to whoever was the strongest link in that round. It was in Simon's interests to vote with me, because otherwise Marc and Alexandra, who could see each other's vote cards, would unquestionably turn on him after me. But how would I know whom Simon was voting for? As we picked up our Sharpies to write on the vote card, I scanned the faces of the three remaining contestants and found my answer. As I glanced at Simon, he looked me straight in the eyes and mouthed a single word at me: 'Marc.' Thank you, Simon, 30, engineer from Carlton! Alexandra and Marc voted for me; Simon and I voted for Marc. And the casting vote rested with the strongest link: me.

I had answered all three of my questions correctly in that round, including a total guess at 'What part of a house may be mansard in shape?[1]' And with that, Marc was gone. I stuck with Simon in the next round; we voted off Alexandra, and the two underdogs on each end of the semicircle had made it to the $30,700 play-off.

Twenty years after the episode, I couldn't recall how I had performed during the general rounds. But, as I watched it unfold on this old videotape, I was surprised at how well I did. I missed only three of 26 questions over the eight rounds, and when I entered the head-to-head with Simon I had strung together 17 correct answers in a row. My questions had ranged from the simple—'In Australia what animal do we associate with a pedestrian crossing?[2]'—to the kind of questions a nineteen-year-old had no business knowing—'*Born Free* is the story of a lioness with what name beginning with E?[3]' *Born Free*, a 1960 nonfiction book by naturalist Joy Adamson that was adapted into a 1966 film, was classic cultural fodder for Baby Boomers but certainly not for my generation. All I knew about it was the name of the lioness. Why? Because that had been a question in the original Trivial Pursuit board game that I played as a child—one of the questions that had, for some reason, stuck in my head.

As the strongest link, I chose to answer first in the head-to-head round, reasoning that if I kept getting my answers correct,

---

[1]   Roof
[2]   Zebra
[3]   Elsa

the pressure on Simon would grow. My first question was one that most nineteen-year-olds would have struggled with but which I knew from a well-worn *Who's Who in the 20th Century* reference book that I devoured as a teenager: 'What is the profession of Princess Margaret's former husband, Lord Snowdon?[1]' Simon had no trouble with his first question either: 'Which US broadcasting millionaire has donated millions to reduce United Nations debt?[2]' But then I hit a rocky patch: 'Originally an Aboriginal word, what is a dangerous stretch of water where waves break over rocks?[3]' This was completely unfamiliar to me. Time ticked by as I racked my brain for anything. All I could do was feebly answer 'Billabong', knowing it was incorrect, but any guess was better than a pass.

Simon took a 2–1 lead by correctly answering: 'What is the old pre-decimal coin that was worth one quarter of a penny?[4]' I needed something in my zone; I couldn't afford another miss. So when Cornelia asked me, 'Which Australian author has written a novel called *The True History of the Kelly Gang*?[5]' my heart sank. I had never heard of it. I tossed around a few names in my head, but nothing sounded likely. In the end, I answered 'Henry Reynolds', the historian whose work I had often cited in my Year 12 Australian history class. By the time I answered, I must

---

[1] Photographer
[2] Ted Turner
[3] Bombora
[4] Farthing
[5] Peter Carey

have forgotten about the word 'novel' in the question and focused too much on 'history'. You may wonder how I had never heard of *The True History of the Kelly Gang*, a well-known work by one of Australia's most acclaimed authors. The answer is that when the episode was filmed, the book had been out for barely a year. Six months later, it won the Booker Prize and everyone was talking about it. But in March 2001 it was not yet within my sphere of knowledge.

Missing that question was a disastrous blow, compounded when Simon was served up an easy one for his third: 'Which president served the longest total term of years in US history?[1]' So Simon led 3–1. My hopes of a $30,700 cash prize—an outrageous amount for a second-year university student—were hanging by a thread. I needed to answer my fourth question correctly to stay in the game. 'In which German city in 1938 did a British prime minister sign an agreement with Hitler?[2]' I took my time, ran through the logic in my head. I was sure this had been covered

---

[1] Franklin D. Roosevelt, who was elected to four terms in office, dying early in his fourth term. Although convention dictated that US presidents should only serve two terms, that was based solely on the precedent set by George Washington, who chose not to run for a third term. During World War II, FDR reasoned that America needed continuity of leadership. He threw convention out the window and the public backed him at the ballot box. But concerns about the precedent he had set led to the Twenty-Second Amendment, which was ratified in 1951 and limited presidential tenure to two elected terms.

[2] Munich. The Munich Agreement is remembered these days for the optimistic 'Peace for our time' speech that British PM Neville Chamberlain delivered upon returning home to the UK. Less than a year later, World War II began.

in high school history classes. I came up with the correct answer, but was still playing catch-up. Simon could win with his next question: 'Which Australian author wrote a novel about the papacy called *The Shoes of the Fisherman?[1]*'

Oh no! I knew this one. Why didn't I choose to play second! 'Colleen McCullough,' Simon answered. *Colleen McCullough! He's missed it! I'm still in the hunt!* If I could answer my fifth question correctly and Simon missed his fifth, we would go to sudden death.

Cornelia asked my final question: 'What is the name of the isthmus that connects North and South America?'[2] And with that, I said goodbye to $30,700. I had no idea. I'm not even sure I knew what 'isthmus' meant. All I could think of was 'Central America', and I was doubtful the answer would be that generic. I fumbled around in the filing cabinet of my brain, but the drawers were empty. Eventually, dejectedly, I answered Central America. 'That answer is . . . incorrect,' Cornelia confirmed. I was done. Simon walked away with the cash, thinking all his isthmuses had come at once. I walked off, reeling from another devastating television experience, to be interviewed by Deb Stewart. Plus, of course, because it wasn't mine, I even had to give Channel Seven the shirt off my back.

---

[1]   Morris West. He's what I call an 'op-shop' author—hugely popular in his day, but almost forgotten now. My nana worked in an op shop in Camperdown and often brought home books from the shop—there were certainly a few Morris Wests among them.

[2]   Isthmus of Panama

At uni the day after the episode aired, everyone was an expert. 'The Isthmus of Panama, I did that in high school geography!' someone told me. 'How could you not know "bombora"?' another classmate wondered. But everything is easy if you know it. Easier still if you don't have 30 grand on the line. I had not been voted off. I had not done the Walk of Shame. I was not the weakest link. But I had also not won the money. Of course, I relived the experience and wondered what if. What would have happened had I chosen to go second in the final round? I might have performed better with Simon's questions, but perhaps he would have whizzed through mine. It was all academic. Simon was invited back for a 'Strongest Links' champions' episode, which he won. He added another $46,600 to his prize money. On the one hand, this made me feel slightly better: it had taken the best of the best to defeat me. On the other hand, I was once again left wondering, 'What if?'

Reliving the experience twenty years later, I wondered what the win had done for Simon. In 2002, I saw him pop up on *QuizMaster*, a show that invited winners from quiz shows to compete against each other, but after that he seemed to disappear from the quizzing scene. I remembered his surname was Hoffman, seared into my brain as the man who vanquished me. It didn't take much to track him down: there he was, on LinkedIn, based in Perth. On a whim, I sent Simon an email and mentioned that I was writing a book. 'Always happy to re-live my brush with fame,' he replied. A couple of hours later, we were on the phone, reminiscing. Indeed, Simon had not appeared on any shows since *QuizMaster*; he felt he had hit his peak and walked away on a high. His total winnings from *The Weakest Link* — nearly $80,000 — went most of the way to buying a one-bedroom apartment in Perth, which he sold a few years later and parlayed into a deposit on a house in Melbourne.

'It was great fun,' Simon says of *The Weakest Link*. 'I loved the psycho-drama of it. In the end, trivia was a relatively small component. And if I remember it correctly, *Survivor* was still pretty fresh then, and it really did feel a lot more like *Survivor* than *Sale of the Century*. And the social engineering was what I thought was the most interesting part of the game . . . For me, the difficulty was trying to balance who to gang up with. I think what I was thinking at the time was that we were both in danger, for being too good. And, as you got to the end of the game, it was a real disadvantage to be good. So it was a good bet for both of us to knock off the weakest players so they didn't knock us off.'

When he won the champions' episode, Simon took another strong player, Jacob, through to the final with him. In the best of five head-to-head round for $46,600, they finished at 4–4 after five questions each and entered sudden death.

'We ended up going through fifteen questions,' Simon says. 'There were a couple of times where we both missed, and then we both kept hitting it. It was quite good fun by the end of it. It kind of freaked everyone out, because they literally did run out of questions.'

There was one question I couldn't resist asking Simon. In recent years, had he made the connection that he had once beaten The Shark from *The Chase*?

'I didn't,' he says. 'I'm going to have to remind everyone of that! It makes the win that much sweeter!'

I was pleased to hear the win had set Simon up financially at a relatively young age. I took my defeat on *The Weakest Link* better than I had my *Sale* loss, partially because I had no regrets about the final round. The answers that I had missed I simply didn't know. Winning on *Sale* had been my dream; *The Weakest Link* was a bit of fun but not a show that I loved. Within a year, *The Weakest Link* was dead and buried, and so too was the trend of nastiness in quiz shows. That was fine by me. My contestant career was only just beginning. It wasn't long before I found a game show format where the bucks stopped with me.

CHAPTER 6

THE BUCK STOPS HERE

DO YOU REMEMBER A GAME SHOW CALLED *PASS THE BUCK*? COME ON, be honest. *Nobody* remembers *Pass the Buck*. John Burgess hosted *Pass the Buck* and I'm not convinced even *he* would remember *Pass the Buck*. I'm sure I have mentioned *Pass the Buck* in this paragraph more times than anybody has thought about the show in twenty years. Anybody, that is, except me. I have reason to remember *Pass the Buck* every single morning, when I get up and make myself an espresso with the Quaha Napoletana Series II coffee machine that I won on the show. It's a terrific, proper espresso machine—none of this over-packaged coffee-pod stuff—and it's the oldest game-show prize that I still use. I won it on *Pass the Buck* in 2002, along with some other stuff—but we'll get to that. I don't want to ruin the suspense by telling you about my pineapple clock just yet.

On the same day that Channel Nine premiered *Shafted* as a replacement for *Sale of the Century*, *Pass the Buck* debuted in the afternoon, at Burgo o'clock. The show was hosted by John Burgess and replaced *Burgo's Catch Phrase*, which had been hosted by John Burgess, and found itself up against Channel Seven's *Wheel of Fortune*, which had previously been hosted by John Burgess. Each episode of *Pass the Buck* started with ten contestants and one John Burgess. The contestants stood in a line at the top of a wide set of steps, with the immaculately coiffed Burgo at the bottom.

The basic premise was that Burgo asked a question that had multiple correct answers—'Name a city that has hosted the Summer Olympics', for example—and each player in turn had to give a correct answer to stay in the game. This continued until a contestant either answered incorrectly or repeated an answer that had already been given. That player was eliminated, and the remaining contestants took one step down and did it all again. When two players were left, they went head-to-head. The grand prize was a new car, which a carry-over champion would earn for winning five nights in a row. But that was almost impossible, because if you made a single mistake in five episodes, you were dead. Oh, and did I mention, you had only three seconds to provide each correct answer? To win the car, a contestant would have to outlast 45 challengers, walking a tightrope of trivia, memory and wordplay with no safety net. In terms of difficulty,

Pass the Buck packed a heavyweight's punch in the guise of a lightweight afternoon format.

For those reasons, when I arrived on a Saturday in March 2002 at the Channel Nine studio in Bendigo Street, Richmond—the scene of my *Sale of the Century* trauma from a year and a half prior—I had no expectations. There were so many uncontrollable factors in *Pass the Buck*; I was simply hoping to enjoy myself. Winning one episode would be a bonus. Still, I wasn't going unprepared. I had noticed that eliminated contestants generally fell into one of three categories: those who hadn't listened and repeated someone else's answer; those who had the rug pulled from under them when their answer was taken by the previous player; and those who simply couldn't think of a valid answer. So my first task was to listen closely—to the question and the answers given by other contestants. Secondly, I had to make certain that, where possible, I had two or more answers ready. If one of those answers was taken by another contestant, I needed to keep thinking so that I always had options. There wasn't much to be done about the third category. If I simply couldn't think of a correct answer, all I could do was have a stab.

Another tactic was to give the most obvious answer and keep obscure ones for emergency back-up. This, I hoped, would rob other players of the easy answer they had in mind. And if I made it to the final four, a further strategic consideration came into play. Until that point, contestants answered in the order they stood, from left to right. But at the final-four stage, contestants who gave a correct answer then nominated which player must answer next. My tactic here was simple: I would always 'pass the buck' straight back to whoever had just passed it to me. This would give that opponent very limited thinking time to come up with a new answer, and it might also discourage contestants from passing the buck to me. It seemed such an obvious tactic that I was amazed how few contestants appeared to employ it.

As with *Sale of the Century*, five episodes were filmed in a day. Backstage, the nine challengers in my group were told ours would be the second episode. I shared a dressing-room with a friendly prison officer named Peter, who was in his late twenties. We chatted about the show and our shared love of cricket, and agreed that if we made it to the final four we would not pass the buck to each other. It was a gentlemen's agreement that we hoped might slightly increase our chances of reaching the head-to-head and the prize round that followed. That was fine by me, because it fitted the tactic I had already decided upon.

It wasn't long before we were ushered into the studio and shown to our positions at the top of the staircase. There I stood, seventh from the left, in a pale green short-sleeved shirt and baggy cream-coloured corduroy pants. I might have learnt about tactics, but I hadn't learnt a thing about fashion. There was my new backstage buddy Peter, second from the right. And there, second from the left, was the carry-over champion, a tall, bald man in a dark polo shirt.

Oh shit. It's Neven.

Neven. The name alone was enough to send a shiver up my spine. It was a name that carried with it certain connotations.

Notoriety, even. It would be hard enough to win *Pass the Buck* without one of the most skilled and feared quiz players in the country standing in my way.

I wasn't alone in recognising Neven. As we each introduced ourselves on camera—'I'm Brydon, I'm twenty and I'm a journalism student'—the final player in line, a pub trivia operator named Leon Fent, summed it up perfectly: 'G'day, I'm Leon, and my ambition in life is to beat Neven at something'.

Easier said than done.

▼

Neven.

The trivia world knew him by one name, like Madonna or Prince. And oh boy, did the trivia world know him. While writing this chapter, I got in touch with Leon Fent to ask if Neven was a regular at Leon's pub trivia nights, and if that was how he knew him. The short answer was yes. The long answer was long. Leon's summary of Neven: 'No doubt one of the smartest blokes I've known, but a flawed genius.'

At least Neven hadn't been banned from any of Leon's trivia nights. But his presence at pub trivia was, shall we say, a little fraught. Why? Because Neven would always win. On his own. Often while reading a book, or doing a crossword, trying very hard to look like he wasn't trying very hard. *A Current Affair* once featured a story about how 26 Melbourne venues had barred him from their trivia nights. The grabs from other patrons were revealing. 'He's a smart-arse. I think he just likes to show off,' said one man. 'A pain in the arse,' was one woman's description. Pub trivia operator Ritchie Hewett told *A Current Affair*: 'People feel that he's not only smart, but he's rubbing their noses in it as well.' When the reporter commented to Neven that he didn't seem very well liked in the pubs, Neven answered: 'I've faced it all my life, actually, I haven't really fit in. And it hasn't helped that I don't drink. But if you sit on a drink, like a lemon squash, all night and answer all the questions right, why would they like me? In fact it's bad for business, actually.'

An article in *The Age* in 1996 explored what Neven admitted was an addiction to radio quizzes, which he would call up, play and usually win. 'People love me and hate me,' Neven told the paper, 'but they mainly used to hate me so that's an improvement.'

I knew Neven's name mostly from Tony Delroy's midnight quiz on ABC Radio. There, he was known as 'Neven from St Kilda'. Or 'Carl from Heidelberg'. Or any number of other names that he made up to avoid the month-long ban that callers incurred after they won the quiz. His other trick was to deliberately fluff the final question, so he wouldn't win, and therefore was free to call back the next night. For Neven, the ABC quiz was never about the prizes.

If you think that Neven Solian—yes, he has a surname, like Madonna and Prince[1]—sounds like a fascinating character study worthy of his own story, you're right. And that story was

---

[1] Madonna Ciccone and Prince Nelson

told wonderfully well in a 2016 documentary, *The Trivialist*, by Melbourne filmmaker Ronen Becker. *The Trivialist* is an incredible tale that explores what makes Neven tick, and I cannot recommend it highly enough. It won the Best Foreign Documentary Feature award at the Atlanta Docufest film festival, and it's a mystery to me why it hasn't gained much attention in Australia. Explaining to Becker why he used fake names and voices on the ABC quiz, Neven admits that on one occasion he even used helium to sound like a woman and would use an 'ethnic' name and try to 'sound ethnic'.

'When you were banned for a month for winning a CD or winning a show, you'd want to come back,' Neven says in the documentary. 'So that's when I got a bit naughty. I started impersonating people and throwing voices.'

As 'Carl from Heidelberg', he even ran the table by answering correctly all 25 questions, and then cheekily sent a shout-out to Neven from St Kilda. It was like a Batman villain leaving a calling card to show off. Sometimes it seemed the questions were the easiest part of the quiz for Neven: the biggest challenge was fooling Tony Delroy and his producers into thinking he was someone else. Sometimes they cut him off midway through a run, when they suspected it was really Neven on the line instead of Peter or Michael or Beryl. Neven was working as a taxi driver on the lonely overnight shift and was by his own admission 'down and out'. Calling the midnight quiz added excitement to his life, and it gave him a buzz to be heard nationally. But, much like in pub trivia, Neven's domination could also kill the buzz for anyone else who hoped to win, or even play.

And yet my overriding feeling after watching *The Trivialist* was pity. Neven obviously had brains. He had struggled through life and had trouble interacting with people. In his own words: 'Money was always very easy, but relationships were hard.' That statement, though, needs clarification. Money was only easy once he started using his prodigious memory to plunder trivia competitions. Before that, Neven was $25,000 in debt, occasionally even going without meals. As a young man, he had missed out on qualifying to study medicine by the barest of margins, then spent eleven years at university switching from subject to subject without earning a degree. He worked as a taxi driver but, out of pride, told people he was a 'road traffic consultant'. Then, in his mid-thirties, Neven studied for eighteen months for *Sale of the Century*, only to turn up to the studio drunk on the morning of filming because he had struggled to sleep the previous night and knocked himself out with half a bottle of Grand Marnier from his mother's cupboard at 3.30 a.m. The ultimate irony was that Neven, the almost teetotal taxi driver, had to get a cab to Channel Nine on the morning of his episode because he couldn't drive himself.

Somehow, after a few early jitters, Neven won his *Sale* episode. And then another. Then another. His year and a half of study was paying off. When he eventually picked the Audi Cabriolet off the prize board, he chose to walk away with the car and a total prize pool worth more than $120,000 instead of playing on for a few more nights and going for the cash jackpot. Like me, Neven saw *Sale* as just the beginning. But if I thought I was obsessive, writing several thousand practice questions for my brother-in-law and applying for game shows, I was an amateur compared to Neven. He says that at one point he was clearing $1000 a week from trivia competitions on commercial radio, and in total he picked up close to $60,000 worth of cash and prizes from radio quizzes. As with the ABC's midnight quiz, Neven started using fake names and even gave friends and acquaintances a cut in return for permission to use their names and addresses for delivery of the winnings. His life became the obsessive pursuit of trivia.

In 2000, he appeared on *Who Wants To Be a Millionaire?* with the goal of impressing a waitress, in what Neven admitted was an 'unrequited love'. He deliberately dragged out his answers, talking in circles and riddles before locking in his responses, trying to spread his appearance across two episodes. This, he hoped, would increase the chances of the woman seeing him on television. He won $32,000 and succeeded in coming back for a second week, but then was knocked out by this question: 'The desire of long-term hostages to cooperate with their captors is called the what syndrome?[1]' The options were Berlin, Amsterdam, Warsaw and Stockholm. I felt this was an easy question, perhaps because it featured in one of my favourite films, a 1988 action flick

---

[1] Stockholm syndrome

set at Nakatomi Plaza[1]. Neven, apparently, had never heard of the syndrome. Still, it felt like an appropriate question: more than a few viewers probably experienced something like Stockholm Syndrome watching Neven excruciatingly discuss every answer option the previous week.

Another win came on the television show *QuizMaster* in 2002. That's the show that pitted trivia legends against each other, and from which David Poltorak walked away with nothing. The *QuizMaster* format required four players to battle it out over an episode, with the winner then choosing one opponent as a back-up in the final big-money round. With proven champion William Laing as his second, Neven earned $150,000 on *QuizMaster* and then crash-tackled William to the ground in celebration. William had won $500,000 on *Millionaire* by walking away from the question of how many people had set foot on the moon; Neven had won only $32,000 and admitted, in *The Trivialist* documentary, that he was bugged by William being 'sixteen times the quiz player or the man I was' due to that ratio of winnings. He wanted, he said, to 'hurt' William, but they soon made up and became friendly.

---

[1] *Die Hard*. Here's my favourite piece of *Die Hard* trivia. *Die Hard* was based on a novel by Roderick Thorp, the sequel to an earlier book by Thorp that had been adapted into a 1968 film called *The Detective*. The film studio was contractually obligated to offer the role of John McClane to the actor who had starred in the 1968 film. Fortunately, seventy-something Frank Sinatra politely declined, and it was Bruce Willis instead of Old Blue Eyes who slaughtered terrorists and yelled 'yippee-ki-yay, motherfucker'.

The following year, a *Herald Sun* article explored Neven and his many bans from pub trivia. One host compared Neven turning up at a pub to 'an A-grade tennis player going back to play beginners'. The writer of that article, Craig Sherborne, tracked Neven down to the small flat in which he was living and saw his bookcase filled with encyclopedias and piles of paper on which quiz questions were written. Five years later, Sherborne wrote about Neven for *The Monthly* magazine in a strange piece that read like an open letter to Neven—but a contemptuous, insulting one. *The Monthly*'s slogan is 'nothing without context', yet the context of this article was a mystery to me. Neven was not in the news at the time, as far as I can tell. I wondered if the earlier meeting had simply given Sherborne such an enmity for Neven that even five years later he had to get it off his chest. But I found *The Monthly* piece distasteful and unnecessary. It referred to Neven's calling as 'the petty pursuit of quizzes and trivia, an inane branch of esotericism'. Perhaps that sentence cut a little close to the bone. Sure, some trivia is inane. So is some literature, some music, some film. There are plenty of things I can't stand, from pretentious poetry to Adam Sandler's comedy, but I wouldn't insult people who devote themselves to such things. Who are we to judge what someone else deems a worthy pursuit?

Perhaps while reading the article thirteen years after it was written, and having just watched *The Trivialist*, I also had the benefit of understanding some of the reasons for Neven's behaviour. Nothing without context. Neven's father was absent for much of his childhood, and then he felt weighed down by the burden of failing to pass the entrance exam to study medicine. He admitted to being a show-off, having a superiority complex and wanting to become the greatest trivia player in an effort to reach his father, hoping that he may be watching.

'What I had was a store of knowledge,' Neven says in the documentary. 'I wouldn't even say I was intelligent. I was like a one-trick pony. I tried everything to get recognition, because my father rejected me. I was just so hurt . . . I found that hurting other people, and being noticed for hurt, would be a way of being recognised.'

The documentary gives the impression that Neven is remarkably self-aware of his shortcomings. That may be explained by a piece of context missing from what I have so far told you: Neven's outlook changed after he found religion. In an interview on a Christian radio program called *Real Faith*, Neven said he had previously had a 'rapacious appetite' to make up for the times he 'couldn't get a degree or failed scholastically'.

'I was a show-off,' Neven told interviewer Eric Skattebo. 'Probably this is in response to people putting me down for not having qualified. Even relatives would say I was a loser . . . so I wanted to prove myself constantly. So I'd get into near punch-ups in hotels, and even on television I'd be showing off, [on] radio. It was just all about me. I was my own god.'

Neven wanted to prove he had made it, but proving it wasn't enough—he wanted to shove it down everybody's throats. He came to love being hated, and fed off that negative emotion.

'Even though I was pretty hopeless socially, I got a high out of being rejected,' he says. 'I found that was fascinating. There was a wrong sort of energy about it.'

Then, one day, he realised the foolishness of it all. He came to accept what deep down he had always known: that his relentless acquisition of knowledge did not amount to wisdom.

'I always knew this somehow,' Neven says. 'I always realised that knowledge was beneath intelligence, which was beneath wisdom.'

Neven became involved in the controversial and now defunct Rise Up Australia Party, which aimed to curb multiculturalism and was led by an evangelical pastor. Yet Neven also believes in generosity.

'We have a very strong evangelism at the Pentecostal church I go to,' he says in the *Real Faith* interview. 'I just give money away as God tells me to. I also do the thing in the supermarket queue, I give money away or I pay for their goods. Although the last time a person said, "I don't trust your god, why are you giving me money?" It was quite funny.'

Neven can afford to do this partly because he lives an ascetic lifestyle and partly because, in his own words, he has been overly blessed with finance. There is one particularly lucrative aspect of Neven's trivia life that I have not even touched on yet: he says he has won close to $600,000 from trivia machines in pubs. It speaks volumes that such a figure is no more than a footnote in his story.

After finding religion, he also located and reconciled with his elderly father, and says he has found the peace that he never previously had.

'My father has also taught me how to cook, and my mother is the second-best cook in the world,' he says in the radio interview. 'And I make a meal for, if not strangers, acquaintances, every two weeks . . . now I actually serve others at every opportunity, and there's a great reward in that.'

It is difficult to comprehend that the old Neven and the new Neven are the same person.

'I've been through the darkest suicidal times,' Neven says in the *Real Faith* interview. 'And now I realise every breath is a gift.'

▼

Now you know why, when I discovered that Neven was the *Pass the Buck* carry-over champion on my episode, my internal response was: 'Oh shit.' Of course, I didn't know his life story then, but I knew enough to consider him an awesome trivia machine. I'm sure I would have been even more intimidated had I known that Leon Fent was also a former *Sale of the Century* champion who had won the car and all the prizes in the mid-1990s, but walked away instead of risking it all to play for the $68,000 cash jackpot. In hindsight, it was a pretty stacked field.

Each episode began with a randomly selected player being asked the first question. Neven, chosen first, was asked: 'The lat is one basic unit of European currency. Including those being replaced by the Euro, can you name another?' A question like that was Trivia 101. I had little doubt that Neven could name them all. He sensibly took one of the easiest answers, franc, and the next couple of players went for lira and pound, before the fourth contestant was unable to come up with a valid response. I had survived one question without saying a word (although I had several answers in mind: deutschmark, escudo, peseta[1]).

The second question was directed at Helen, the player next to me: 'According to the *Macquarie Dictionary*, can you name a place of worship?' Helen answered 'church', and then it was my first turn. Watching the episode all these years later, I notice my eyes flick to my right, confirming that I am definitely next. As tactically prepared as I was, one thing surprised me: there was no cue for contestants to know it was their turn to answer. You had to keep track of the order yourself, quite a challenge when you were supposed to be looking straight at the cameras. I have no doubt that plenty of players fell because they didn't realise it was their turn.

I answered 'synagogue' and breathed a sigh of relief as I heard the audio effect that confirmed a correct answer. Mosque, cathedral and chapel were also answered, but when the 'buck' moved back to the far left-hand end of the line, contestant Luke said nothing. I wonder if he even realised it was his turn; the challenge of keeping track was infinitely harder for the player at the far left, because there were eight contestants physically separating you from your predecessor, the player at the far right. An audio

---

[1]   The currencies of Germany, Portugal and Spain respectively.

or lighting cue was needed to tell players it was their turn, and perhaps such little wrinkles would have been ironed out had *Pass the Buck* lasted more than a few months. As it was, we were all guinea pigs in a format that must have been only in its ninth or tenth day of filming.

Next, Neven was asked to 'Give the name of any winner of the Australian Golf Open since 1980'. He confidently and correctly answered 'Greg Norman', but the next player bombed out by saying Tiger Woods. I was pleased the question hadn't reached me: I knew the list would be dominated by Australian players but didn't know which ones, and it was 50-50 whether I would have plucked a correct answer like Robert Allenby or Peter Senior, or an incorrect one such as Ian Baker-Finch or Wayne Grady.

I had made it to the first ad break. Three questions down, and all I'd had to say was 'synagogue'. *Pass the Buck* was fast moving and unforgiving, but with just a few correct answers you could advance rapidly. After the first break came a wordplay game; in this case, the name 'KEATING' was shown on screen and players were asked to give any English word of three letters that could be made from those letters. This was a different skill, but it suited me. When I was a teenager, living on a farm after all my siblings had moved out of home, I spent hours playing PC games. One of my regulars was a basic Windows game called Wordstalk, more or less a rip-off of Boggle, requiring you to make words from a four-by-four grid of letters. Anagrams always amused me. (You may think *this* is an inane branch of esotericism, but a couple of my favourites are very appropriate anagrams of 'Old West action' and 'Nerd amid late TV'[1].)

I answered 'tea' for a three-letter word from 'Keating', while others ticked off 'tin', 'tan', 'gin', 'ate' and 'eat'. After Leon at far right said 'ate', the camera showed Neven at far left peering across, trying to keep track of his turn. He quickly turned back to look at the word on screen, his eyes wide as he scrambled for an answer, and he said something like 'teak' or 'tik'. Either way, he was incorrect. Burgo ran through some other possible answers, after which Neven said out of the corner of his mouth, 'git', clearly referring to his own mistake. It was quite a funny line: Neven could be amusing and quick-witted, and here he was also self-deprecating. But I wasn't sorry to see him leave with his $6000-odd worth of prizes. I was thrilled. It felt like the number one seed in a tennis tournament falling in the second round. Suddenly, the game was wide open. And Leon Fent, one of six contestants still standing, had achieved his life's ambition: he had beaten Neven at something.

Again, the next question didn't reach me, and again I was pleased. It asked for any of the top ten countries with the highest life expectancy for women. Only ten countries out of roughly two hundred on the planet were valid answers, and aside from Japan, which usually tops longevity lists, it was potluck. Sure, you could narrow the pool down to wealthy countries, but where to

---

[1] Clint Eastwood and David Letterman. These are known as 'aptagrams', anagrams whose meaning is relevant to the original words.

from there? Would Norway be on the list? Germany? Canada? Iceland? It would have been guesswork, with little thinking time. We did well with ranks of British nobility, ticking off earl, duke, duchess, viscount, king, queen, prince, princess, baron and marquis, before Helen answered 'lord', only to be told that it was a courtesy title only.

Incredibly, I had reached the final four having given only three answers: 'synagogue', 'tea' and 'prince'. You could be Steven Bradbury and win this show—just hold your feet and wait for everyone to fall over. Also in the final four was Leon, a nurse named Roie and my backstage mate Peter. So there was one person who wouldn't pass the buck to me, at least. The final four had the chance for a brief on-camera chat with Burgo. I told him I wanted to become a sports journalist, specialising in cricket; I'm quite proud that a few years later I achieved it.

The next question was word-related: Give a number less than twenty that, when spelled, has only one syllable. I was first and answered 'ten'; honouring my pact with Peter, I then had to pass the buck to Roie or Leon. I picked Roie, probably because she was next to me and I could see her nametag; one of the toughest challenges was remembering the other contestants' names. Roie said 'six' and threw it back to me; I answered 'four' and gave it straight back to Roie. And then she moved to Leon. My tactic of a quick return of serve had paid off. Roie and Leon went back and forth, back and forth, exhausting virtually the entire list: 'two', 'one', 'eight', 'three', 'five', 'nine' and 'twelve'. Stumped, Leon couldn't think of another and was eliminated. I couldn't think of one, either. I was sure we had named them all. When Burgo informed Leon that the only answer left on the list was 'nought', Leon looked unimpressed. I would have been, too. Firstly, while '0' is technically a number, it felt like a trick answer. Secondly, I would generally refer to that digit as 'zero' rather than 'nought'. The adjudicators were not wrong, but I still think Leon was stiffed.

The final question before the head-to-head round was the 'Memory Moment'. This was a strange and daunting round that featured eighteen random words flashing up on the screen in quick succession for players to memorise. The challenge was simple: say a word from the list, pass the buck to someone else and keep going for as long as possible. And it truly was a meaningless group of words. In this episode, the full list was 'evaporation', 'fate', 'box', 'helium', 'sword', 'breakfast', 'punk', 'departure', 'shovel', 'weather', 'tertiary', 'freeway', 'complex', 'sunshine', 'whatever', 'delirious', 'tomorrow' and 'chimpanzee'.

I cannot stress how challenging this task was. Having studied psychology at high school and university, I knew research had shown that humans could generally only hold seven to nine items in their short-term memory. To recall any more, you needed techniques such as 'memory chunking' to group individual pieces of information together to form one larger piece. That's why ten-digit phone numbers are generally 'chunked' together in a 'four, three, three' format. For example, to register as a contestant on *Who Wants To Be a Millionaire?*, you had to call 1902554649. Ten digits crammed together are hard to recall, but by chunking the numbers together in manageable groups—1902, then 554, then 649—it was much easier. Now go back to the list of eighteen random words and see if you can find a way to remember more than seven. Perhaps you can put some together in a 'story': It is my fate to have breakfast with a chimpanzee tomorrow. Study the list long enough, and you might come up with chunks for them all.

Unfortunately, on *Pass the Buck*, the time you had to make these connections was basically zero. Sorry, nought. It took less than 40 seconds for the eighteen words to flash up, one at a time, with the audio reinforcement of Burgo saying each word as it appeared. Each word was on screen for less than two seconds. Chunking was impossible, because it happened too fast and the words were so unrelated. All I could do was choose some words to repeat in my head, repeat, repeat, repeat until I had to give an answer. If I was first in line, my first response would always be the last word in the list, which was freshest in mind and therefore likely to be recalled by my opponents. I also tried to remember a couple of 'dull' words that did not stand out by conjuring up vivid imagery. I reasoned that because words like 'whatever' or 'tertiary' were less memorable than 'breakfast' or 'punk', I should keep a couple of these boring words in my back pocket as a safety net.

I was first, so I used 'chimpanzee' and passed the buck to Roie. She went for 'breakfast' and passed it back to me. I said 'punk' and went straight back to Roie. Again, she'd had enough and, after answering 'freeway', moved to Peter. They battled it out, I didn't have to answer again and Roie was eliminated when she repeated my answer of 'punk'. Peter and I were through to the final round; our pre-game alliance had actually worked. And so had my tactic of passing the buck straight to whoever passed it to me: twice I had thus put the pressure on Roie and twice she had decided to avoid me. In this way, I advanced while minimising the number of answers I had to give.

My final challenge was to defeat Peter in a 90-second head-to-head round. This was the only portion of the game that allowed any leeway for incorrect answers, although they could still be costly. It was, essentially, a minute and a half of questions in the same style as the rest of the game: multiple answers, back and forth, until someone gave an incorrect response. Burgo then asked a new question, and on it went until the buzzer. The winner was the contestant with the most correct answers. The questions were wideranging. We were asked for any method of post used by Australia Post (for example, Express Post or Registered Post); any noun from the nursery rhyme 'Simple Simon'; a number from one to ten in French; patron saints of the UK; any Jack Nicholson film released since 1975; the ten most common elements in the Earth's crust; and any four-letter word rhyming with 'file'. I scored eight ('pieman', 'wares'; *As Good As It Gets*, *Wolf*; 'hydrogen'[1]; 'pile', 'wile' and 'mile'). Peter managed five ('fair'; *Batman*; 'dial', 'tile' and 'bile').

---

[1] I was lucky to get away with this one: hydrogen is tenth on the list, and only marginally ahead of phosphorus at No. 11. Peter answered carbon, which seemed a good guess, but it surprisingly sits in 17th place. The top ten are oxygen, silicon, aluminium, iron, calcium, sodium, magnesium, potassium, titanium and hydrogen.

I had done it. I was the *Pass the Buck* champion. I had seen off nine opponents, including two proven quiz-show high-performers. The game was tough, and I was constantly paddling to stay afloat, but I had come in with strategies that had worked. I'd had some luck—I was pleased the questions on longevity and golf hadn't reached me—but I had also worked hard. Now I could relax and play the prize round, knowing that, whatever happened, I would be back as carry-over champ.

The prize round was about as straightforward an endgame as any in television game shows. There was no downside and almost no skill involved. It was similar to the 'Memory Moment' round, except here ten prizes flashed up on the screen, after which I had twenty seconds to name as many of the prizes as I could. Whatever I named, I won. Simple as that. There was always a cash prize, but the dollar figure varied and you had to name the correct amount. My plan was to say the cash first then prioritise any other prizes I really wanted. Anything beyond that was a bonus. As it happened, I failed to recall only one prize—a digital camera (but I still had my state-of-the-art 1 megapixel digital camera from *Sale*, so that was all right). What did I win? Five hundred dollars cash, the coffee machine, a food processor, a leather handbag, women's sportswear, a cutlery set, a lawn trimmer, meal vouchers and a 'dice clock'. When naming this last one, I said 'Clock?' in a questioning tone, unsure that my eyes had really seen the kitschy red clock in the shape of the dice. I was pretty sure I didn't want it, but hey, a prize is a prize. When the goodies were eventually delivered, the company that produced the dice clock must have run out, and they substituted an equally kitschy clock in the shape of a pineapple. I suspect I ended up donating it to an op shop. The meal vouchers turned out to be $200 from the Hard Rock Café; I took my family out for a celebratory dinner later in the year. Remarkably, the food processor still works two decades later, now handed down to a family member.

Don't worry; I won't bore you with blow-by-blow descriptions of every moment on *Pass the Buck*. Suffice to say, I won my second episode. And my third. And my fourth. Watching the shows back, I am struck by how calm I appear. And how frustrated and resigned my opponents look when I keep spitting out answers. I've been a competitive table-tennis player since childhood and I play a defensive game: I just keep getting the ball back, and back, and back, and hope to eventually force my opponent into a mistake. I saw a similarity in my *Pass the Buck* performance: I kept getting answers back, and back, and back, and eventually my opponents had faltered. In a few hours of filming, I had already outlasted 36 contestants: nine more and the Hyundai Elantra was mine. Yes, I was about to play for a new car.

Except that I wasn't really 'about to' do it. The filming day was done. I had a near two-week wait before the next day in studio. Two weeks to stew on the opportunity in front of me. But this was different from the break after my first *Sale of the Century* win. Here, I had nothing to lose—the prizes I had won could not be taken away, no matter how willing I was to risk the dice/pineapple clock. I spent these two weeks trying to keep my brain in *Pass the Buck* mode. As I travelled to and from university, I re-created the 'Memory Moment' round. I would think of eighteen random words, whatever popped into my head—fence, porthole, lemur, apology, biscuit—and then see how many I could recall a minute later. It was a flawed training method—I wrote nothing down, so could not tell how I had performed—but my aim was simply to keep my mind in the zone.

A fortnight later, on a Friday evening, I returned to Channel Nine to film what would be, win or lose, my final *Pass the Buck* episode. And when I walked into the studio, I was surprised to see a red Hyundai Elantra right there by the stage: Channel Nine was going all out to make this episode a big event for a show that had not yet captured the imagination of the viewing public. I don't recall being particularly nervous. Nobody had survived five nights on *Pass the Buck*, and even now I had no real expectation of being the first. I intended to concentrate on each question as it came, looking no further ahead. I was ready, but I'm not sure Burgo was. As the contestants stood at the top of the staircase after our introductions, Burgo made special mention of the young man playing for the car: 'Brydon Cloverdale'. I contorted my mouth into a questioning face and looked over to one of the producers; Burgo re-recorded the line, correctly pronouncing my name, but they didn't bother editing out my puzzled 'What the hell?' look, which seemed completely out of place when the show aired.

Again, contestants fell quickly. I answered a couple of easy wordplay questions, named Billy McMahon as a post-war

Australian prime minister and Cairns as one of Queensland's top ten most populous cities. And with that, I was through to the final four. Two more questions and I would be almost there. On 'member nations of the OECD', I answered the United Kingdom and Japan, again hammering the contestant who kept passing it to me until she started targeting someone else. Australia, the USA, Germany, France and the Netherlands were all named by the time I had another turn; I tried for New Zealand, and that got me through to the Memory Moment. Watching the recording now, as one of the words—finger—flashed up on the screen, you can just make out that I stuck out the index finger on my right hand, a surreptitious physical reminder. It helped me get through to the head-to-head.

Now there were 90 seconds between me and a new car. Ninety seconds and an opponent named Leanne. I simply had to focus on each question as it came. One of Australia's top five most respected sportspersons, according to Sweeney Research? In 2002, I'd have been amazed if Cathy Freeman wasn't number one, so I gave her name. Correct. Leanne tried Allan Border, but he was too long retired: 1–0 to me. Any word from the chorus of The Rolling Stones hit *Satisfaction*? I took the obvious answer, 'satisfaction', and Leanne accidentally answered multiple words: 2–0 to me. A character from *The Partridge Family*? Trouble. I had never watched it. 'Joey?' I tried. Incorrect. Leanne outdid me on counties of Ireland, getting Dublin and Cork to my Limerick: 3–2 to me. The next question—Hugh Jackman films—went to Leanne, who couldn't name one[1]. Any Best Picture Oscar winner from the 1990s? Beautiful, beautiful! A classic trivia list. I answered *The Silence of the Lambs* and could have named a few more, but Leanne passed. It was 4–2 to me, and time was running out. I was watching the countdown clock and could see the car was almost mine. A chemical element beginning with C? I knew then that I had it won. I could name at least four or five of them—copper, carbon, cobalt, calcium, chlorine—and there was no way Leanne would have time to make up the deficit.

The time expired, celebratory sirens sounded and I had bloody won it! I had won a car! I should have been laughing, pumping my fists, whooping like a maniac, and yet . . . I wasn't. I was barely even smiling. I was a twenty-year-old introvert who had enjoyed playing the game—in a previous episode Burgo had called me 'a very quiet young man'. Internally I *was* excited, but externally, you could barely tell I was alive. Not surprisingly, the producers re-shot the winning moment, and asked if I could perhaps, possibly, please, look excited. So the version that went to air had me plastering on a big fake smile and taking some deep breaths, my attempt to act out relief that it was all over. On a scale of nought to ten for excitement, I had at best lifted from a zero to a two.

Burgo opened the Elantra door and showed me in; I sat in the passenger seat, looking around, still deadpan. The producers must

---

[1]   This was a much harder question in 2002 than it would be today, as Hugh Jackman had appeared in only six films. I had one up my sleeve—*Swordfish*—but didn't need it.

have been perplexed, and disappointed, when they couldn't get a reaction out of me. They had given away the car for the first time! They could promo the hell out of this! But I gave them zip, zilch, nil, all words Leon might have answered to stay in the game. I like to think I'm more expressive these days, though I'm still not naturally effusive. Zoe tells me I often don't react to situations in the typical, expected way. Some people find this off-putting—obviously. But it's the way I've always been. Often it's because I'm focused on an internal dialogue, concentrating on my own thoughts. So when Burgo was showing me the car, I was probably thinking something like, 'Damn, I don't get to play *Pass the Buck* any more' or 'I'd better ring Mum and Dad and tell them I've won'. The same internal focus that helped me block out distractions and concentrate while playing the game also prevented me from spontaneously celebrating my win.

My episodes started airing less than a week later. And then, the prizes began rolling in. At the time I lived with my girlfriend, Kirsty, in a one-bedroom villa unit in the Melbourne bayside suburb of Brighton East, and it turned into a mini logistics centre. Every prize supplier organised their own delivery and I had won nearly thirty individual prizes, so I took calls day in, day out, from couriers who had some random package for me. Some prizes I had to collect in person. I had won $1000 of women's clothing and trekked out to the Black Pepper factory outlet to choose what I wanted. The factory workers probably wondered what I wanted with $1000 of women's clothes.

Another prize was a $300 voucher from Lenard's Chicken; over the next year, I became a regular at their store at Southland shopping centre, ticking off a few dollars' worth of enchiladas or kievs every few weeks. We took a free five-night holiday to the Murray Downs golf resort at Swan Hill, a bit lost on us since neither Kirsty nor I played golf. We spent three nights at the Grand Hotel on Melbourne's Spencer Street in the lead-up to Christmas, a fun time to enjoy the hustle and bustle of the CBD. Some prizes I gave to family members, while others I sold in the *Trading Post*, seeking out a Darryl Kerrigan who wanted not jousting sticks but a leaf blower or a lawn edger. A set of collectible teddy bears and a home gym set-up ended up at my parents' house, and remain there to this day.

A $380 three-piece set of Venetian glassware became a one-piece set within about a minute of my opening the box, when I set off to carry the items into a different room, tripped over another prize and a vase and bowl fell to the floor and shattered into pieces. Oh well. Less to clutter up the tiny unit. A 'ring watch' was exactly as described: a tiny watch that fitted around one finger. There was as much chance of me using it as the pineapple clock. I didn't set out in life to become a tacky version of Paul Keating, but like the ex–prime minister I was apparently now a collector of rare timepieces. I had no idea what to do with a rangehood; I doubt I knew what a rangehood was. I didn't think it would sell in the *Trading Post*, so I just left it in its box and shoved it in a closet. When I moved house, it came with me. And again. And again. Always in the too-hard basket, it travelled with me to seven different homes and was about to be loaded up for another move in 2021 when Zoe tapped me on the shoulder and said, 'It's time.' We listed it on Facebook Marketplace and within a few days had found a buyer for a rangehood that was simultaneously brand new and nineteen years old. I'd owned it for nearly half my life. Farewell, old friend, I thought, as I reluctantly put it outside the front door for the buyer to collect. Go and extract those fumes like you were always meant to.

Back to 2002. I had spent eighteen months offloading car-care products from *Sale of the Century* to friends and family members; now I had won even more. When they turned up, I was perplexed to receive an entire box of something called 'wet tyre shine'. As the name suggested, it apparently made your tyres look wet. And shiny. Why this was desirable was a mystery. I thought water would have had the same effect. I was not the type to wash a car, let alone shine it, let alone shine the *tyres*. I think I gave some of it to my parents, because they also bought the Hyundai Elantra off me. I didn't need a car. My parents saved me the hassle of trying to sell it. Between that injection of funds and the $2850 in cash I had won, *Pass the Buck* set me up nicely for life after university. Unfortunately, the show hadn't set itself up for life beyond a few more weeks. *Pass the Buck* was quietly axed and Nine passed the buck back to *Burgo's Catch Phrase*, the show that *Pass the Buck* had replaced. Twenty years later, few people remember it. But pop around to my place and I'll make you an espresso. Burgo's shout.

CHAPTER 7

MILLION DOLLAR QUESTIONS

'FROM 1969 TO 1985,' I SAY TO MY BROTHER-IN-LAW, PAUL, 'SPAIN CLOSED its border with which neighbour? France, Gibraltar, Andorra, Portugal. Twenty seconds.'

'Not really sure, but possibly Gibraltar.'

'How sure?'

'Fifty per cent, 60 per cent.'

I wonder about my sister. 'Does Lindy know?'

'Don't think so.'

And time is up. I have $32,000 on the line—almost a year's wages. Not only that, but a free, no-risk shot at $64,000 if I get this right. The problem is, I have no idea. Literally no idea. Why would Spain have closed one of its borders for sixteen years? I can't work it out. I don't know enough about modern European history. I have abandoned any thought of answering the question myself. Now I am asking myself a different question: How much do I trust my brother-in-law's 'Fifty per cent, 60 per cent'? Eddie McGuire asks me: 'Have you ever had a $15,000 bet before?' At twenty-one years of age, I've barely had a fifteen-dollar bet before. But I'm not here to walk away from this opportunity. It's time to take the plunge.

▼

Good trivia players should know a fair bit about Mark Twain. His real name?[1] The unusual connection between his years of birth and death, 1835 and 1910?[2] His response to incorrect reports that he had died?[3] Of course, his best-known writings are literary icons: *The Adventures of Tom Sawyer* and *The Adventures of Huckleberry Finn*. But the work of Twain's with which I most identify is an obscure short story titled *How I Edited an Agricultural Paper*. In it, Twain writes from the point of view of an unqualified man who stands in when the regular editor goes on holiday. 'Turnips should never be pulled, it injures them,' he writes. 'It is much better to send a boy up and let him shake the tree.' Talk about feeling seen. I have never felt as ill equipped for anything as when I started my first journalism job out of university, reporting for the agricultural newspaper *Stock & Land*.

---

[1] Samuel Langhorne Clemens

[2] They were both years in which Halley's Comet appeared. In 1909, Twain wrote, presciently: 'I came in with Halley's Comet in 1835. It is coming again next year, and I expect to go out with it.'

[3] 'The report of my death was an exaggeration.'

I was so ignorant that had a farmer told me with a straight face that his turnip trees were struggling, I might have believed him.

After my *Pass the Buck* triumph, I finished my journalism studies at RMIT University and graduated with honours. I could write a catchy intro that would draw the readers in. I could come up with a quirky, unique feature story. But I knew I wasn't suited to so-called 'hard' journalism. I dreaded the prospect of covering the police beat for a daily newspaper or having to cultivate secret sources. I enjoyed the writing part of journalism but not the talking-to-people part, which is fairly fundamental to the profession. I narrowly missed out on a cadetship with *The Age*; in hindsight I suspect the interview panel could tell I was unsure I even wanted the job.

When I applied for a junior reporting position with *Stock & Land*, I was just as half-hearted. I had grown up on a dairy farm but never milked a cow, and I couldn't wait to leave my small country town when I finished school. But during the interview, the editor either didn't notice my apathy or else his own apathy trumped mine. I was reminded of the Ben Folds Five song 'The Battle of Who Could Care Less'. I guess it was him, because I got the job. My title was 'property and markets reporter', which meant that every Thursday or Friday I would drive to a country town in Victoria—Euroa, Warrnambool, Bairnsdale, Wodonga, Wycheproof, anywhere and everywhere—to report on sales of farms and livestock. I was so far out of my depth it wasn't funny. Interviewing a Gippsland dairy farmer whose property was on the market, I followed his directions and drove the newspaper's

Ford Falcon through a muddy paddock to find a good spot for a photo. As the vehicle started to spin its wheels and get bogged, I asked the farmer, who was sitting in my passenger seat, if he thought it could handle the terrain. 'Dunno, mate,' he said, washing his hands of the situation. 'It's your car.'

Saleyards were an intimidating, blokey environment where the auctioneers moved quickly along the railings, jabbering out numbers and words that meant so little to me they might have been speaking in tongues. Sometimes I couldn't even spot the bids, often no more than sly winks at the auctioneer as buyers chatted away to each other. I was truly in another world. All I could do was find an agent after the sale, stick my recorder in front of him and ask: 'So, happy with the prices?'

Stock & Land's senior markets analyst, Mike 'Nicko' Nixon, was a hard-drinking former stock and station agent who wrote his reports by hand and faxed them to our Melbourne office. He was a legend, the Keith Richards of the livestock industry. And his number two was little old me, who couldn't even read the music. Every week, farmers and agents around Victoria devoured Nicko's 'What's in Store' column, which showcased his incredible understanding of the trends in 'store' markets[1]. A few months after I started at the paper, Nicko died suddenly in a Wodonga motel room while on the road to cover a sale. For a couple of

[1] At store markets, cattle or sheep are often sold to other farmers to restock their farms; prime markets are the sales that feature 'finished' animals ready for purchase by meat processors.

weeks, until he was replaced, I had to write the 'What's in Store' column, despite having admitted in my job interview six months earlier that I didn't know the difference between a 'store sale' and a 'prime sale'. Turnips, anyone?

This was the world in which I unexpectedly found myself in 2003, when my parallel career as a game show contestant culminated in an appearance on *Who Wants To Be a Millionaire?* I knew this show had the potential to change my life. I might not win a million dollars. But then again, maybe I would. Half a million would be pretty damn fine as well. Or a quarter. Hell, I'd take $32,000. My starting salary at *Stock & Land* was just a tick over $30,000 a year (nobody goes into journalism for the money), so that too was a life-changing amount. Based on the original British version, the show had arrived on Channel Nine in 1999, when I was in Year 12, and instantly I was hooked. At the same time, Channel Seven launched its own short-lived, big-money, prime-time quiz show, *Million Dollar Chance of a Lifetime*, hosted by Brisbane newsreader Frank Warrick. On that show, contestants were not given multiple-choice options or shown the next question before deciding whether to play on or take their winnings. This made it nearly impossible to imagine anyone earning the million, but then again, winning a million dollars *should* be hard. On *Millionaire*, contestants were always shown the next question, could walk away at any time and had three 'lifelines' to help them get through the fifteen questions to a million dollars: they could ask the audience, phone a friend or use '50-50' to eliminate two of the four answer options. I was convinced the top prize would go off semi-regularly and so were the producers. How wrong we were.

When it started, *Who Wants To Be a Millionaire?* was 'event television', the kind of prime-time spectacle that left you feeling on the outer if you hadn't watched it. Plenty of contestants had won hundreds of thousands of dollars on *Sale of the Century*, but there was something mesmerising about a million dollars. Where else but in a lottery could you become an instant millionaire? The American version of the show, hosted by Regis Philbin, was highly successful and its million-dollar prize went off six times in the first year alone. But some of their million-dollar questions seemed too easy. One contestant won the million by answering which of Lesotho, Burkina Faso, Mongolia and Luxembourg was entirely surrounded by one other country[1]. Another had to nominate whether Paddington Bear was from India, Peru, Canada or Iceland[2]. I'm not saying these are *easy* questions, but most decent trivia players would know the answers. The first millionaire winner in the USA, John Carpenter, cruised through without using a lifeline, and only phoned a friend (his father) on the final question to brag that he was about to win a million dollars[3]. To

---

[1] Lesotho, a small kingdom that is entirely surrounded by South Africa.

[2] Paddington is from 'Darkest Peru'.

[3] His question: Which of these presidents appeared on the television series *Laugh-In*—Lyndon Johnson, Richard Nixon, Jimmy Carter, Gerald Ford. The answer was Nixon. During the 1968 election campaign, *Laugh-In* invited both Nixon and his Democratic opponent Hubert Humphrey to appear on the show. Humphrey declined and later conceded that it probably cost him the election.

me, that suggested the questions should have been harder. On the original British version, it took more than two years to find a million-pound winner: Judith Keppel (later one of the panel of *Eggheads*), who correctly identified which king—Henry I, Henry II, Richard I or Henry V—was married to Eleanor of Aquitaine[1].

In Australia, it took six years before a contestant took the plunge and played for, and won, the million dollars. In the early years, the show's first big winner was Paddy Spooner, a 32-year-old British backpacker who walked away with $250,000 after nailing the year in which the last convicts transported from Britain arrived at Fremantle[2]. I had been educated in Australian schools but had no idea of this answer. Paddy said the correct year out loud before the options even appeared. How did an Englishman know so much about Australian history? Turns out he'd studied it. Hard. In 2021, Paddy Spooner and his friend Keith Burgess released a book titled *Quiz: The Consortium The Truth*, which details the way they helped contestants reach the hot seat on the British version of the show in exchange for a cut of the winnings. Paddy discovered all the tricks of the trade, scooping £250,000 on the British *Who Wants To Be a Millionaire?* and also appearing on the Irish version. But all of that came after his appearance on the Australian version. In the late 1980s, Paddy cleaned up by playing pub trivia machines in the United Kingdom; in his best week he won £890. He was also successful

---

[1] Henry II

[2] 1868

on the British version of *Sale of the Century*[1] and had come to Australia in the late nineties in the hope of appearing on our show, hosted by Glenn Ridge. To that end, he spent every day for a month in the La Trobe Reading Room, the magnificent octagonal space at the State Library of Victoria, absorbing information. He focused on the *Chronicle of Australia* book, in which each double page was dedicated to a different year in Australian history, with entries written in the style of newspaper clippings. It was the perfect way for an Englishman to complete a crash course in Australian history. It wasn't a highbrow encyclopedia, but it didn't need to be. Similarly, I find that children's reference books are the perfect study tools for quiz shows, because the most relevant information is presented clearly and in bite-sized pieces, rather than being hidden away in long, scholarly text.

While Paddy was here, ads began for *Who Wants To Be a Millionaire?*, which he knew from back home. Part of the genius of the original British version was that, to register as a contestant, you had to call a premium phone number and the massive income from the flood of calls helped make the production profitable. And here's the thing: you could call as many times as you wanted. Paddy Spooner knew that calling over and over and over would give him the best chance of receiving a callback, so, while sleeping

---

[1] *Sale of the Century* had been reasonably successful in the UK in the 1970s, less so when it was revived in 1989. That revival is best remembered these days for one notable contestant: Simon Cowell, who, before he was famous, was introduced as 'a record company director from London'. He won his episode, and took home some kitchen utensils as a prize.

on a friend's floor and with just a few weeks left on his Australian visa, he hammered the phone number 215 times at a cost of 50 cents per call. That $107.50, and his intense study at the State Library, paid off in the most magnificent fashion.

After Paddy's quarter-million dollar triumph, the winnings stagnated for more than a year. The show gave away $32,000 here, $16,000 there. It wasn't until July 2000—fifteen months after Paddy Spooner—that another contestant walked away with $250,000. That player was Brett McDonald, a 34-year-old Perth labourer whose two main goals were to buy a bowling machine for his cricket club and a car for himself. He won the cash by remembering the artist who had been awarded the previous year's Archibald Prize (using his 50-50 lifeline, he was left deciding between Euan Macleod and Henry Mulholland[1]) and opted not to play for half a million dollars when asked whether Colombia, Ecuador, Peru or Venezuela was the largest South American country by area that was wholly above the equator[2]. Tragically, Brett McDonald was killed just a few months later in a crash while driving the sporty Honda Prelude that he had purchased with his winnings. It was a heartbreaking reminder that one never knew how a life-changing win might manifest itself.

---

[1]   The answer was Euan Macleod, who won the 1999 Archibald Prize for the evocatively titled *Self-portrait/head like a hole*.

[2]   Venezuela. Brett said that, had he played, he would have answered Colombia. He would have fallen back to $32,000 had he done so, because, while Colombia is larger than Venezuela, it straddles the Equator.

Brett McDonald had called the registration phone number just three times, to Paddy Spooner's 215. I'm not sure what my tally was over the four years until I reached the hot seat, but probably somewhere in the middle. In 2002, I was selected to be one of the ten contestants who would play the 'Fastest Finger First' segment during an episode. At that time, these questions required two answers; the player with the fastest correct response joined host Eddie McGuire for a chance at a million dollars. But I bungled my two opportunities. When asked which two US states out of Oregon, Arizona, Kentucky and Georgia did not have coastlines[1], I incorrectly picked Georgia and Kentucky, knowing that Oregon was on the Pacific Ocean, but wrongly guessing in the heat of the moment that Arizona might have a small southern coastline. Later, when asked which two of these people—Boy George, George Michael, Andrew Ridgeley and Angry Anderson—were in the pop duo Wham!, I made a stupid error: I leapt before I looked. I knew the answers were George Michael and Andrew Ridgeley, but in the pursuit of speed I pressed the first George I saw—Boy George—and realised my mistake too late.

The following year, while I was sitting at my *Stock & Land* desk wondering how to fill the next week's eight-page property section, my mobile phone rang. It was *Who Wants To Be a Millionaire?* again. I quickly ducked into the fax room for privacy. While the machine hammered away, telling me the prices from

---

[1] Arizona and Kentucky

the morning's cattle sale at Pakenham, a television producer asked me a series of general knowledge questions. And with that, I had another opportunity on the show. This time, I knew I had to read the Fastest Finger answer options more carefully, but I also knew I couldn't compromise too much on speed. There was no use being correct if I wasn't first. Even great quizzers found the challenge elusive: *Sale of the Century* legend Cary Young reached the Fastest Finger segment but never the hot seat.

After the ten contestants—all men—waved and were introduced, the fastest-finger question popped up: 'Which two animals are types of horses? Donkey, mustang, pony, zebra?' It would have been easy, in the rush for speed, to think the question was asking about the horse family and press either donkey or zebra. But having once placed Boy George in Wham!, I took an extra fraction of a second, realised pony and mustang were the answers and locked them in. Only three of us answered correctly; in just 1.65 seconds, I was the quickest. I shoved the swinging Fastest Finger monitor out of my way and bounded up to shake Eddie McGuire's hand, adrenaline coursing through my body. I was about to sit in the seat where Paddy Spooner and Brett McDonald had won $250,000, and where a few contestants such as Trevor Sauer, William Laing and Maria McCabe had each taken home half a million dollars. I doubted I would be the first to win a million; I just hoped the experience was about to change my life—for the better.

▼

Martin Flood still remembers the look on the face of his thirteen-year-old son, James. One million dollars should have brought tears of joy, but these tears were not of joy. They showed only a teenage boy's dismay. The newspaper had hinted at it, a television report had raised it. But it couldn't be true. Could it?

'He was standing at the door of his bedroom,' Martin says, 'and he had tears in his eyes. He said, "Dad, you didn't cheat, did you?"'

Martin's other son, nine-year-old Liam, was similarly distressed.

'I found Liam,' Martin recalls, 'with the big cheque under the table, crying, saying, "They're never going to give you the million dollars!"'

Channel Nine did give Martin the million dollars, of course, and he hadn't cheated. He had simply taken *Who Wants To Be a Millionaire?* more seriously than any other player in the history of the Australian show. On a scale of one to ten for *Millionaire* preparedness, I was at best a five. Martin was off the charts; like Spinal Tap's amps, he went to eleven. When he sat in the hot seat opposite Eddie McGuire, he was absolutely convinced that he would win the million dollars. In his mind, it wasn't 'all or nothing'. It was 'all'.

'I would have been devastated if I had to walk off there with 500 grand,' Martin says. 'That sounds weird, and I often look back now and think, how did I do that? Because I am so out of it now, I get things wrong watching on TV, and I'm not fast. But at the time I knew I was going to win, I had no question about it.'

I'm sitting in Martin's living room in Sydney, chatting to him about his triumph on *Who Wants To Be a Millionaire?* in 2005, when he became just the second person, after Rob 'Coach' Fulton, to win the million on the Australian show. Remarkably, after nobody won the top prize for the first six years, Rob and Martin both did so within a month. Rob's final question asked which television show debuted first out of *Bewitched*, *Get Smart*, *Hogan's Heroes* and *I Dream of Jeannie*. I thought this was a monstrously hard question. Unlike the million-dollar questions from the USA and Britain that I quoted earlier in this chapter, this required a contestant to know *four* pieces of information. On top of that, I couldn't envisage how a player could know the answer short of having studied the Internet Movie Database or a similar source and having the page headlines (*Get Smart* 1965–1970; *Hogan's Heroes* 1965–1971 etc.) embedded in a photographic memory.

But Rob wanted to go for the million and revealed his thinking. He convinced himself that *Get Smart* seemed like it was from the late sixties and ruled that out. Rob recalled that, as a young child in hospital, he had once been held by John Banner, who played Sergeant Schultz in *Hogan's Heroes* and was on a promotional tour of Australia. This had occurred in 1969 and, in Rob's mind, that narrowed the options down to *Bewitched* and *I Dream of Jeannie*. He visualised the opening credits of *I Dream of Jeannie*, in which a one-man space capsule crash-lands on the beach; Rob mentally pinpointed that to 1963, the year the single-astronaut Mercury space program ended. And he felt that the décor and style of *Bewitched* fitted the late fifties and early sixties. He locked in *Bewitched* on that logic. It was flawed logic. As it happened, the four shows had premiered within a year of each other: *Bewitched* in September 1964 (certainly not the fifties, and in fact it spilled further into the seventies than any of the others), and the remaining three in September 1965. But what separated Rob from all the players who had previously seen the million-dollar question was that he was prepared to risk $468,000.

A month later, 41-year-old Martin Flood was not just prepared to take the plunge, he wasn't prepared to *not* take the plunge. After all, he had studied for five years for this opportunity. That doesn't mean he went to the odd quiz night and played a bit of Trivial Pursuit. Oh no. Martin *studied*, with the explicit aim of winning a million dollars on *Who Wants To Be a Millionaire?* He studied not just trivia, but the show itself. Sitting in the hot seat, he probably knew *Who Wants To Be a Millionaire?* better than anyone who worked on the show. Better than Eddie McGuire. He knew which topics had been question subjects before, and therefore weren't worth studying, because they tended not to come up again. He got to understand the wording of questions, the little clues to look out for. He deduced that at the higher levels, the obvious answers were almost never the right ones. He knew the precise details of how and in what circumstances he would use his lifelines. His phone-a-friend was in fact a group of about a dozen people in a room, a phone-a-friend *community* who had trained together, perfecting the technique to best use that invaluable lifeline. He wrote himself a JavaScript computer program to simulate the Fastest Finger First questions, training and training and training to ensure he would make it into the hot seat when the opportunity arose. He was, nominally, an IT worker at Westpac Bank, but he considered it a soul-destroying job. For five years his real occupation was something else entirely: apprentice millionaire.

'I was *obsessed*,' Martin says. 'Absolutely. It was beyond a dedication. I couldn't talk about anything else for five years. People would talk to me about something, and I would bring up last Monday night's episode. And then when they'd change the conversation, I'd think, "What are you doing, we're talking about *Who Wants To Be a Millionaire?*" And I would really start to think, "This is wrong, how can they change the topic, it's like they're not interested."'

There are many remarkable aspects of Martin Flood's story, but perhaps the most surprising is that when his obsession began, he wasn't even what you would call a 'trivia person'. He started his preparation from scratch.

'What I learnt was that you *can* start from somewhere, you don't have to be born with it or have done it most of your life,' Martin says. 'Some of these things you can look at and think, "I might give that a go, you never know." The first couple of times I watched *Millionaire*, I thought it was silly. This phoning a friend, what's that all about? That's just weird. I didn't know who Eddie was.'

But Martin watched it. And after eighteen months, he realised that a lot of people were winning hefty sums of money. He set his mind to the task of training to appear on the show, joining an acquaintance named Dave, the brother of one of Martin's friends, on his regular pub trivia team. Frequently, Martin sat at the Hornsby RSL trivia night with Dave and the team, and by his own admission contributed little of value in the early days. But the journey to a million dollars begins with a single question, and one question from the Hornsby RSL—it concerned Adolf Hitler being named *Time* magazine's Man of the Year for 1938—later helped Martin earn his seven-figure payday.

For all of Martin's training, there were variables he couldn't control. By 2005, each person was allowed to call the registration line only once per episode—no more stacking the deck like Paddy Spooner. Unlike in Britain, the Australian show made enough profit from advertising that it didn't need the phone line as its major income source. Still, Martin managed to reach the circle of ten contestants on four occasions from early 2004 until late 2005, but, despite his training for Fastest Finger First, he couldn't control the speed of other contestants or the type of question. Fastest Finger had evolved and by now required contestants to place four options in their correct order. While Eddie McGuire read the question aloud, contestants had a few seconds to mentally speculate what the possible answers might be before they appeared on screen. Sometimes it was easy to predict, sometimes impossible. Martin wanted the former, because then all he had to do was spot the answers and press them, instead of wasting precious milliseconds parsing the answers once they appeared.

On Martin's first appearance, in early 2004, an outstanding quizzer named David Morgan won $250,000, having reached the hot seat by answering this Fastest Finger First question: 'Put these Roman numerals in order, starting with the highest: (A) D, (B) C, (C) M, (D) L[1].' You could know your Roman numerals perfectly and still mess that up, with both C and D appearing twice. Most people did mess it up, Martin included. Only two contestants answered correctly—David Morgan and another player who took more than ten seconds to work it out. And so it went for Martin's first three trips to Melbourne, where the show was filmed. By late 2005, he was mentally exhausted, almost ready to take a break. But on his fourth trip, Martin was thrilled when the Fastest Finger question appeared on the screen: 'Place the following in order to form a famous scientific equation'. It had to be $e = mc^2$. There was no other scientific equation famous enough. Primed, and ready to stab the buttons in order, Martin punched in e, $=$, m, c^2, and did it in 1.78 seconds, winning comfortably. Another contender, a casino dealer named Brian Cripps, was on his eighth attempt in the circle of contestants; he answered correctly and quickly but was unlucky to come up against Martin Flood, the nearest thing *Millionaire* ever had to a card counter.

Remarkably, for all his five years of study, Martin pocketed $125,000 (by answering the first twelve questions) without having to rely on lists he had specifically studied. These questions he answered from picking up information in day-to-day life. That's

---

[1]   M (1000), D (500), C (100), L (50)

the very definition of *general knowledge* and the platform on which all trivia players build their mental database. Not that he was certain of all the answers immediately. Alan Bond's first occupation—greenkeeper, boilermaker, pastry cook or sign-writer[1]—was little more than a vague recollection that earned him $16,000. To confirm his own instinct about which country was home to the volcano Mount Pinatubo (Bangladesh, Japan, Indonesia or Philippines[2]), he used his ask-the-audience lifeline to reach the safe level of $32,000.

But the most remarkable answer, and the one that raised suspicions of cheating, was for $125,000: 'Which brand of champagne is sprayed from the podium at Formula 1 Grand Prix races?' The options were Bollinger, Moët & Chandon, Mumm and Veuve Clicquot. I thought this was a very hard question, arguably the trickiest in his entire set: Formula One racing is only moderately popular in Australia, and even within the sport this was a niche fact. Out of curiosity, I watched some race highlights from the era while researching Martin's story, and I saw no advertising hoardings for the company in question around the racetrack, which meant unless you watched the podium presentation, and unless the commentators mentioned the brand (which they didn't always), there was hardly any way to know the answer. Adding to the difficulty, the brand in question had only taken over the sponsorship rights five years earlier, from one of the other brands

---

[1] Signwriter

[2] Philippines

mentioned in the question. So this was not only a hard, niche piece of minutiae, but one that had recently changed. I wouldn't have had a clue. To watch Martin Flood in the hot seat, it seemed that neither did he.

For six and a half minutes, he talked through the options. It took him nearly a minute even to say out loud that his first thought was Bollinger. Later, he made the valid observation that Bollinger might have stuck out at him simply because it was answer A, and appeared on screen first. Often, I have the same experience on *The Chase*; the three answer options appear simultaneously for viewers at home, but on the monitors in studio, the answers come up one at a time. If I see answer A and think, 'Yes, that sounds right', it can be mighty hard to change my mind. On *Millionaire*, Martin spent the first four minutes leaning towards Bollinger, having ruled out Moët & Chandon and Veuve Clicquot. Unconvinced that any of his phone-a-friends would know the answer, he ploughed on alone. And then he closed his eyes, and said to himself 'Mumm . . . Mumm . . .' as if chanting a mantra. Five and a half minutes in, he was now leaning towards Mumm. After another minute of thinking, he locked in Mumm, the correct answer. To watch his process without the full backstory, I could see why the producers were mystified. Most contestants in Martin's situation would have used a lifeline, and he had both phone-a-friend and 50-50 still available. Contestants with no lifelines left would typically either stick with their first instinct or walk away with $64,000. That's what I would have done. But walking away wasn't an option for Martin.

'When the question came up I thought, "I'll recognise the answer", because I often studied stuff with the view that I don't have to commit it to memory, I don't have to buzz in and say it, I just have to recognise it,' Martin tells me. 'And I was able to do that with a lot of questions with plenty of time, sitting there working it out. And the four [champagne] options came up—and I couldn't see it.'

However, something did stir in his filing cabinet of memories. But in which drawer? And did he have the key? He realised that he *had* heard this before. He hadn't actively studied it, but a specific visual and auditory memory edged to the surface. He could see himself, three or four years earlier, in the lounge at his old house, holding the remote control and flipping through channels, when he hovered on a Formula One podium presentation. The information was in his memory, he was sure of it. Sitting in the *Millionaire* hot seat, Martin could hear two Formula One commentators in the back of his mind, and he thought they had said the name of the champagne brand. 'They're spraying the Bollinger' or 'They're spraying the Mumm'. So he had heard it. He ruled out Moët & Chandon and Veuve Clicquot because he didn't know those brand names—and now he was confident the answer was something of which he *had* heard. He was lucky that his memory was not more than five years old, because before that Moet & Chandon *had* supplied the champagne for podium presentations. Eventually, the memory told him something else: it was a short name. And then he heard it.

'My head even tilted a bit, which then becomes more of an auditory memory,' Martin says. 'And I suddenly heard him say, "They're spraying the Mumm." I thought, that's it! It's Mumm! It took me a while to get that. I was really excited about that question when I finished. That proved to me that I've got this, I've nailed this. Because that was really hard for me to recall what the answer was. It was one of those ones that I'd never thought about.'

Martin is fascinated by the mechanics of memory, and since his *Millionaire* appearance he has learnt that the best way to access memories like the Mumm one is to close your eyes and visualise yourself back in the moment. What can you see? What can you hear? It's not a particularly useful method for me on *The Chase*, because it takes time. Nor is it much good on the modern *Millionaire Hot Seat*, in which players answer against a ticking clock. But on the old prime-time version of *Millionaire*, there was no time limit—perfect for Martin's approach. Of course, memory isn't perfect. Long-term studies have shown that even for major events, such as 9/11, the average person is surprisingly bad at recalling where they were and whom they were with when they found out about the terrorist attacks. Of course, everyone *thinks* they remember those details vividly, but researchers have proven that often we are wrong.

'I've got a real thing about memory,' Martin says. 'It's who we are. Without memory, what have you got? A lot of people remember stuff that didn't actually happen. I've come across a lot of situations like that. I don't tend to have that, I don't think. But then again, how would I know?'

Martin reached $250,000 by identifying which of Cecil Day-Lewis, Cecil Rhodes, C.S. Forester and C.S. Lewis had the given names Cecil Scott. There were a couple of strands to his thinking. Because Martin relentlessly analysed every question asked on *Millionaire*, he knew that Lewis and Rhodes had both been the subject of questions in the recent past and he had observed that the show didn't repeat topics that were so specific. Mostly, though, he remembered a phone call with a trivia friend named Chris, in which they looked up various real names and middle names of famous people. Martin knew that during that call he had looked up both C.S. Lewis and C.S. Forester on Wikipedia, and in his mind's eye he could see the names 'Cecil Scott' on his computer screen. He just had to recall which person he was looking up at the time. He felt reasonably sure that the name he had seen for Lewis was a little unusual, not something plain like 'Cecil Scott', although he couldn't remember exactly what it was[1]. He trusted that the information was somewhere in his mind, and Cecil Scott Forester earned him a quarter of a million dollars.

But Martin's mannerisms and unusual way of working out the answers flummoxed the producers and Eddie McGuire. The $250,000 question was the final question of the episode and, as Martin walked off the set, he was patted down by security to

---

[1] Clive Staples Lewis

ensure he wasn't wearing a wire or didn't have a phone strapped to his body to receive vibrating signals from an outside source. In a 2021 radio interview with Kyle and Jackie O on KIIS FM, McGuire admitted that by the end of that episode he thought there was something amiss with Martin Flood, that '. . . absolutely something was wrong, that he was hot'.

An infamous cheating scandal had plagued the British version a few years earlier, when Army Major Charles Ingram won the million pounds but was later convicted in court of 'procuring the execution of a valuable security by deception'. Ingram had been a contestant in 2001 and had seemed to be struggling early on, using two of his lifelines within the first seven questions, which netted him just £4000. He baffled the host, Chris Tarrant, by talking in circles, changing his mind and sometimes going for answers that he admitted he had never heard of. This was the case with the million-pound question when he correctly identified the number that was one followed by one hundred zeroes[1]. Ingram, his wife Diana, who was in the studio audience, and another contestant named Tecwen Whittock, who was in the Fastest Finger circle, were all prosecuted over what investigators believed was a conspiracy to fraudulently win the money. The accusation was that Charles talked through the answers to allow Tecwen to cough when the correct answer was mentioned. In 2003, the trio was convicted, and Charles Ingram was never paid the prize money.

---

[1]   A googol

The case re-entered the cultural zeitgeist in 2020, when it was the subject of a three-part television drama series titled *Quiz*, directed by Stephen Frears. (Can you name the two films for which Frears has been nominated for the Best Director Oscar?[1]) The dramatisation seemed quite sympathetic to the Ingrams and Whittock; my feeling having watched the show was that perhaps they didn't cheat, but then again, it was a scripted drama, not a documentary[2]. Either way I could see how producers of a quiz show giving away enormous sums of money might be edgy, rightly or wrongly, about anyone who behaved unusually. This was the backdrop against which Martin Flood was searched and investigated two years later, although he assumed it was all standard procedure.

'They went through the whole searching stuff,' Martin says, 'and the whole time, I just did not see any of the red flags that they thought I was cheating. Because it was so left of field.'

---

[1] *The Grifters* (1990) and *The Queen* (2006)

[2] A fascinating subplot in *Quiz* involves the aforementioned Paddy Spooner and a so-called 'consortium' that helped contestants get on the show. Spooner and Keith Burgess detailed their system in 2021 in the book *Quiz: The Consortium The Truth*. It was an operation of military precision in which they helped potential contestants hammer the phone lines and answer the audition questions upon being called back and coordinated a 'phone-a-friend' team from a special 'data room'. The system was so successful that during the five years it operated, they helped 55 quizzers into the 'hot seat' in the UK, players who collectively won 26 per cent of the total payouts by *Millionaire* during that time. Of course, Spooner and Burgess took a healthy cut of the winnings as payment for their service. I recommend their book if you'd like to find out more about their system.

Martin's first episode was filmed in late September 2005 and scheduled to air on 7 November. In October there was a month-long break in production, during which Martin took time off work to study intensively for his final two questions. His second episode was filmed on 7 November, a few hours before his first episode hit the airwaves. So, he was rather confused when Eddie McGuire introduced him during that second episode with statements such as 'last week, in one of our most controversial and talked-about shows . . .' and 'it's been the talk of the town'. You can see the bewilderment on Martin's face; he knows the episode hasn't even aired yet. So how could it be controversial? How could it be the talk of the town when nobody has seen it?

'I was sitting there thinking, this hasn't gone to air yet. What does that mean?' Martin says. 'But the second thought was, none of this stuff matters, I have to sit here and blank my mind out.'

That was the focus of a champion. Clear your mind. Take it one question at a time. Avoid all distractions. Martin had spent five years preparing for this; he couldn't let anything steer him off course now. His sons, James and Liam, were in the studio audience with Martin's brother John; Martin's wife, Robyn, had not travelled to Melbourne, having recently started a new job as CEO of the Arrow Bone Marrow Transplant Foundation. The following morning, after his million-dollar episode had been filmed and his first episode had aired, the Floods received a phone call from Robyn's sister, telling them to check the newspaper.

QUIZ CHAMP QUERY

Channel 9 has investigated whether a *Who Wants to Be a Millionaire* contestant—who goes on to win the million dollar jackpot in an episode next week—cheated, *Confidential* understands. The network studied footage and brought in psychologists to help them determine whether a repeat of the British *Who Wants to Be a Millionaire* coughing scam in 2001 has been repeated by the Sydney-based contestant. IT analyst Martin Flood's behaviour raised the suspicion of the live audience and technicians in the control room . . .

The Daily Telegraph, 8 November 2005

The story was also featured on Channel Nine's *A Current Affair* program; both it and the newspaper article clarified that Martin had been cleared of any wrongdoing and that the network was comfortable with him playing on for the million dollars. But to have such a suggestion aired in public was shocking. Not only that, but this was the first Martin had heard of any investigation. His sons weren't the only ones who were distressed.

'I was really upset,' Martin says. 'And I was never given my right of reply in the media. Hardly anyone rang me. I think I got one person ringing me for an interview on the phone.'

Back at work on Tuesday morning, Martin walked into a regular 10 a.m. meeting and was met with deathly silence from the large group present. The million-dollar episode was yet to air, but that morning's newspaper had already reported both his million-dollar win and the investigation. One workmate smiled at him but nobody else made eye contact. Clearly, everyone had seen the paper and had probably watched him reach $250,000 the previous night.

'Of course we felt complete heels,' Eddie McGuire said in the KIIS-FM interview in 2021. 'We almost put the rubber glove on to check this bloke, to see what was going on. Anyway, bottom line was that he won the million dollars and was fantastic and was a worthy winner. But it is interesting that the people who really set themselves to do it, they go to extremes to do so and they do stand out [from] the rank and file people who come on and have a punt and have a day out on the telly.'

Having spent several hours with Martin at his home in Sydney, I can see what Eddie means about going to extremes. By his own admission, Martin has an obsessive personality. He is also curious and constantly analysing everything: it is the only interview for this book in which I felt that I was being interviewed myself, as Martin asked about my experiences and we each took in information about the other. You can almost see him mentally filing things away, always the analyst. Robyn, who stayed out of Martin's quiz obsession, made an interesting observation.

'Can I just say, when you went on there, I said you'd either come home with nothing or you'd win the million,' Robyn says, 'because that's your personality.'

She was right, of course. For $500,000, Martin was asked how many independent countries border the Caspian Sea—four, five, six or seven. He smiled after the options were revealed;

Martin was obsessed with the Caspian Sea. He knew it back to front. He had a globe at his house, and every time he walked past the globe, he would look at the Caspian Sea. Why? Because, as with C.S. Forester, in five years of obsessive viewing and analysing, Martin had never seen a question about the Caspian Sea on *Millionaire*. Or, indeed, anywhere. But he knew it would come up someday, somewhere. Still, he didn't rush into his answer. He trusted his process and considered the options in turn. He was pretty sure the answer was five. As he deliberated, he explained his mental picture: Russia and Kazakhstan were to the north, Iran to the south and Azerbaijan to the west, with its capital city, Baku, on a peninsula jutting into the sea. Martin was sure there was another country to the east, one of the '-stans', though he couldn't remember which. Reluctantly, he used his phone-a-friend lifeline to call his Hornsby RSL trivia buddy Dave Brissett, who had been on *Millionaire* a few years earlier.

During his own run, Dave struck a tricky question at the $300 level—is the person who adjusts the focus on a film camera a focus mover, focus pusher, focus minder or focus puller?[1]—and had to call Martin for help. Except it wasn't just Martin, it was their phone-a-friend team, made up of eight people that day.

---

[1] Focus puller. I would have known the answer from seeing the job title in film credits, but this struck me as a very hard question for the 'gimme' level of $300. I wondered if it was a case of writers and producers working in the television industry assuming that because they knew the term so did everyone.

Only one of the eight knew the answer—a film buff, who often stayed to watch the credits.

'That was the scariest moment, being his phone-a-friend,' Martin says. 'Eddie gets on the speakerphone and it's like god on the phone. It was such an intense moment getting this call from Mr TV.'

By the time Martin was in the hot seat, the group was made up of about a dozen people crammed into a room, set up with books and lists and all manner of sources. But all he needed was his globe, which Dave had at hand. In the 30 seconds allocated for Martin to ask the question and Dave to answer, Dave spun the globe, found the Caspian Sea, tallied up the countries—Russia, Kazakhstan, Turkmenistan, Iran and Azerbaijan—and said he was pretty sure it was five. His memory confirmed, Martin locked the answer in. Half a million dollars in his kitty, he was now ready for the moment for which he had been waiting five years: the million-dollar question.

Who was never *Time* magazine's 'Man of the Year'? Adolf Hitler, Ayatollah Khomeini, Joseph Stalin or Mao Zedong?

Martin's first reaction on camera: 'This is one of those "not" questions.' As was the case for Rob Fulton, knowing one piece of information was insufficient. He wasn't being asked which king was married to Eleanor of Aquitaine, or what you called one followed by a hundred zeroes, or where Paddington Bear was from—all questions for which a single piece of knowledge was enough. To win the million, Martin effectively needed to know the entire list of *Time*'s Man of the Year, later renamed Person of the Year. Remarkably, after five years of it being one of those things that he meant to study but never got around to, Martin had looked over it just three days before his million-dollar episode.

Still, he couldn't pinpoint the answer immediately; it was too long a list to memorise. He could rule out Hitler, thanks to that Hornsby RSL trivia night five years earlier. And he was pretty sure the Ayatollah Khomeini was on the list—Martin could picture the cover from 1979. Stalin and Mao were the mysteries. Martin didn't say any of this on camera, because he had the 50-50 lifeline up his sleeve; he didn't know if the producers might change the 50-50 options based on his comments, and he was hoping Hitler, the one he was most certain had been Man of the Year, would be one of the two remaining answers. But his 50-50 left Khomeini and Mao; at least Stalin was off the table. Still, this was the million-dollar question, and Martin would not be rushed. A further eight minutes of deliberation followed as he made certain he could lock in Mao.

During his fifteen-question run, Martin had been the picture of a poker face, talking through answers but rarely giving away his full thought process. That wasn't a deliberate strategy, it simply reflected the way he had trained. For five years, he would record *Millionaire* and watch it late at night when everyone else was asleep, pacing the house quietly and working his way to the answers. When he got his chance in the hot seat, he enjoyed every moment; to him, it was the most comfortable place on earth. After he had settled on Mao as his final answer, Martin quoted Shakespeare, mentioned some charities he wanted to donate money to and dragged it out. He didn't want to lock the final answer in, not because of nerves but because he didn't want the experience to end.

For five years he had visualised this moment and virtually every part of the process. The only thing he hadn't visualised, because the possibility never occurred to him, was accepting a cheque for anything less than a million. Before flying to Melbourne, before he even reached the hot seat, Martin had gone so far as to fill in a deposit slip from the bank for one million dollars—another psychological trick to build his self-belief. Carrying that deposit slip in his pocket made him feel like the million was already his. He finally locked in Mao, and Eddie McGuire said the magical words: 'You've won a million dollars!' And then, the confetti, the flowers, the champagne—with no sense of occasion, Channel Nine gave Martin a bottle of Bollinger instead of Mumm. Martin was joined by his brother and sons on set, as well as Rob Fulton, whom Channel Nine had invited. Martin's five-year journey ended as he always believed it would: with Eddie McGuire handing him a cheque for one million dollars[1].

Three years later, the Academy Award for Best Picture was won by *Slumdog Millionaire*, which told the fictional story of Jamal Malik winning the top prize on the Indian version of *Who Wants To Be a Millionaire?* The movie opens with a question,

---

[1] The cheque handed over by Eddie in the studio was only a prop—as for all contestants, the real bankable cheque arrived in the mail a couple of weeks after the episode aired.

asking how Jamal did it—A: He cheated, B: He's lucky, C: He's a genius, D: It is written. Having spoken at length to Martin Flood about his experience, and having watched his episodes a number of times, it is tempting to say that, like Jamal, it was written for Martin to win the million. To some degree, he seems to have believed that himself; when he started going to trivia nights and told people he would win the million dollars one day, it was a laughable prospect, even to Martin himself.

'I don't think anyone believed me,' he says. 'And I didn't quite. Actually at the time I thought, "I'm about 1 per cent at the moment believing it." And I thought to myself at the time, "All I've got to do is get to 100 per cent and I'll win it." Something about the universe will provide, all that sort of crap, if I can get myself to that point where I know I'm going to win, I'll win it. I've just got to go from 1 per cent to 100 per cent.'

It is written. You could picture a *Slumdog*-style film about Martin Flood. There he is, flicking channels—'They're spraying the Mumm.' Now he walks past his globe, spins it to find the Caspian Sea and stares at it mysteriously. Here he is at Hornsby RSL, scoffing at the idea that Adolf Hitler was *Time*'s Man of the Year. Now he sits in the hot seat, his self-belief at 100 per cent. It is not all or nothing. It is all.

The reality is not nearly so mystical. Martin made his own luck. For every topic he studied that came up in his fifteen questions, there must have been hundreds if not thousands that didn't, but which he had also studied. That's not luck. That's hard work.

His reward? Martin hasn't had a regular job since. He hasn't needed one. He stayed on at the bank for six months before quitting for good. Since then he has invested, played the stock market and generally built on his success. In 2006, he was cast as *The Master* in the Channel Seven quiz show of that name, in which ordinary contestants competed against each other for the right to play against Martin. Unfortunately, the show is most famous for its short lifespan: it is now immortalised on the Wikipedia page titled 'List of television series cancelled after one episode'. Martin hasn't actively studied trivia since then, but he retains the curiosity that is the keystone of any good quizzer. During our chat, he remembers that the *Mastermind* grand final is on in a few hours and quickly flicks the television on to record it. Later, he enjoys trying to trip me up on quirky, trick questions. One that he asks is an old favourite of mine: Which two Australian states share the shortest land border[1]?

After a couple of Martin and Robyn's friends arrive, including phone-a-friend Dave, I ask a question I've been dying to ask all night: 'Who's the table-tennis player?' A table-tennis table is set

---

[1] Victoria and Tasmania, which share an 85-metre boundary on a two-hectare rocky outcrop in Bass Strait named Boundary Islet. In the early nineteenth century, the border was set as a straight line at 39°12'S, which authorities believed did not touch any land. But a surveying error was later discovered: the border did indeed bisect the tiny islet then named North East Islet. It was renamed Boundary Islet, and it remains the site of the shortest and least-known Australian state border.

up next to the kitchen, where you'd expect to see a dining table in most houses. I'm a table-tennis player from way back and am thrilled to find that the same is true of everyone in the room: Martin, Robyn, Dave and their friend Matt. Several hours of round-robin action follows, mostly featuring me, Robyn, Dave and Matt. Martin jumps in for just one game, playing with me in a doubles match. We win a tense battle, 24–22. The rest of us play on all night, but Martin is happy with his achievement and calls it quits.

Always the winner. Always unbeaten.

▼

When I appeared on *Millionaire*, Rob Fulton and Martin Flood were still two years away from becoming the show's first seven-figure winners. I find Martin's self-assurance remarkable; the fact that he would have been disappointed with anything less than a million dollars is hard to comprehend. But, had I put in five years of relentless study, I might have felt the same.

I had barely studied for *Millionaire* at all. I thought I had pretty good general knowledge and was prepared to rely on that. I tried to memorise some lists when I knew I was going to be on—British monarchs, major Oscar winners, that sort of thing—but it was fairly basic. I also ensured that my phone-a-friends had some of those lists on hand. The show allowed you to nominate three phone-a-friend options, and you could choose which one to use when you were in the hot seat. I picked three people whose knowledge bases, I hoped, wouldn't overlap too much. My older brother, Chris, was strong in areas in which I was weak, such as science, mythology and astronomy. Ian, the father of my then-girlfriend Kirsty, was well versed in cars, musical theatre and a few other fields that were similarly poor areas for me. But I would only call Chris or Ian if I got stuck on a question that I knew fell in their wheelhouse. For all other enquiries, I would press one: my brother-in-law Paul, who had a broader range of knowledge than anyone I knew, and whom I had trained to appear on *Sale of the Century.*

With three phone-a-friends in place, my major aim was to reach $32,000, the second of the two 'safe levels' designed to encourage contestants to play on. The first safe level was $1000, a consolation prize really, which you reached after answering five easy questions. A further five correct answers earned you $32,000, and five more would win you the million. Contestants could walk away at any time with the money they had won so far; if they played on and answered incorrectly, they fell back to the highest safe level they had reached. This meant that plenty of contestants won $32,000, many crashed back down to $1000 and an unlucky few—*Survivor*'s Richard Hatch, for example— failed to reach the first safe level. Even at twenty-one years of age, I was not prepared to walk away with $4000, or $8000, or $16,000. This was a rare opportunity to win a life-changing amount of money. I had to get to $32,000; after that, who knew what could happen? On the episode in which I stupidly placed Boy George in Wham!, a woman had been asked, for $64,000, in which year Paul Keating became Australia's prime minister[1]. I could have answered that in my sleep. Everything depended on what questions came my way.

It's an interesting experience watching tapes of myself from twenty years ago, and not only because of my fashion and hair—in this case, a messy spike of early 2000s gel. Even watching a VHS tape is nostalgic—I'd forgotten what it was like to physically fast forward or rewind a video. Then there are the ads that take you back to another era: Steve Irwin advertising the Ghan railway, a little girl saying, 'Don't chop the dinosaur, Daddy!' The most unexpected blast from the past was the discovery, on the same tape as *Millionaire*, of a program called *Newsline*, which my university journalism class produced for community television station Channel 31. It reminded me that you can pick up information anywhere: after I was part of a live panel interview, we cut to a story by my classmate, Jason Om, who covered the Dalai Lama's visit to Melbourne and used a caption that said, 'Tenzin Gyatso, 14th Dalai Lama'. Back in 2002, I had never stopped to think about how many men had held the title Dalai Lama, but I filed it away in my brain as something that was worth knowing.

As I sat down in the hot seat opposite Eddie McGuire, I felt quite calm. I was by now a veteran of television game shows, having added *Wheel of Fortune* and *Burgo's Catch Phrase* to *Sale of the Century*, *The Weakest Link* and *Pass the Buck*. On some shows I had won, on some I had lost. You can't win them all.

---

[1] 1991

I hit no stumbling blocks in the first five questions, comfortably reaching the $1000 safe level. For $2000, I was asked a rugby league question, which could easily have stumped someone from Victoria: Which of Warriors, Cowboys, Bulldogs and Roosters is the only non-Australian team in the NRL[1]? Fortunately, a couple of years earlier, I had taken part in an online footy tipping competition that involved both AFL and NRL, so this was one of the few rugby league facts of which I was confident. For $4000, I was asked who played Ellen Ripley in the *Alien* films[2] — so far so good. My next question, for $8000, asked whether it was a roller-coaster, lightning, killer whale or jetski that injured four spectators during a September 2002 show at Seaworld on the Gold Coast[3]. As a recent journalism graduate I was well across current events. So, $8000 and I hadn't broken a sweat.

Having all three lifelines in hand was useful, but there wasn't much point holding on to 'Ask the Audience' beyond the next couple of questions. When a contestant used that lifeline, every member of the studio audience was asked to vote for answer A, B, C or D and the contestant was told what percentage of people chose each response. To be of any value, Ask the Audience generally had to be used early, for a question that most average people would know. Sure, there might have been a few people in

---

[1] New Zealand Warriors

[2] Sigourney Weaver

[3] An out-of-control jetski flew out of the water and careened into spectators; a week after my episode went to air, the incident was back in the news again when charges were laid over alleged breaches of workplace health and safety.

the studio audience who would know the answer to a $64,000 or $125,000 question or higher, but the majority would not, so the data would be fairly useless. It might even lead you the wrong way; as Martin Flood noted, at the higher levels the obvious answer was often the wrong one, but would likely be the one that uncertain audience members would pick.

An opportunity to ask the audience came on my $16,000 question, when I was asked whether the latissimus dorsi was a muscle in the leg, chest, back or arm. I had no idea. I had never heard of it and didn't spot the hint in the word 'dorsi'[1]. So, I asked the audience: 57 per cent said 'back', 20 per cent said 'chest', 14 per cent said 'arm' and 9 per cent said 'leg'. Such a majority suggested this was a well-known fact to the average person, and Eddie emphasised the figure a couple of times: 57 per cent! That was enough of a sign for me. Prior to the show, contestants were advised that Eddie was not told the answers in advance; the producers wanted to ensure that we didn't read too much into anything Eddie said. But I was sure that, as a sports journalist, Eddie would know this answer. I felt that, without saying as much, he was discouraging me from wasting another lifeline. I correctly locked in back—these were the 'lats', Eddie explained when he revealed the answer. It still meant nothing to me. I should have spent more time on that home gym I'd won on *Pass the Buck*. Or, indeed, any time.

---

[1] A dorsal fin is on a fish's back. You'd be surprised how often answers are discernible from word origins, if you can spot the connections.

One more question and $32,000 was mine. From 1969 to 1985, Spain closed its border with which neighbour? France, Gibraltar, Andorra or Portugal. Damn. I didn't know this. Didn't know it at all. The extent of my logic was to think that Andorra and Gibraltar were tiny, so those borders would be easier to close. But on the other hand, why would Spain have a problem with such minor territories? Was there not more chance of tension with a larger neighbour such as France or Portugal? I wondered if this was reasonably common knowledge, or if I had struck it unlucky and drawn a tough $32,000 question. I had no choice but to use a lifeline; I would still only be guessing if I used 50-50, so I decided to call Paul. 'Not really sure but possibly Gibraltar,' he said, with what he called 50 per cent or 60 per cent confidence. He later told me that once he'd had more thinking time, he was actually less confident—perhaps as low as 20 per cent. But at the time, I believed he had probably been conservative, and might have been more certain than he let on. So I felt okay about Gibraltar, but I didn't want to leave anything to chance. I used my 50-50, which eliminated France and Andorra, leaving Gibraltar and Portugal. With no knowledge of my own, and both lifelines steering me towards Gibraltar, I locked it in.

'Like a good journo,' Eddie said, 'you've sucked the goodness out of everyone else around you and you've won $32,000!'

I was ecstatic, and I looked it. Unlike *Pass the Buck*, there was no retake needed here. Partly that was because I had a lot to lose: until Eddie revealed the answer, I had no idea if I had won $32,000 or lost $15,000. Now I had made it to the safe level.

That $32,000 would give me a terrific kick-start as my working life began, and nobody could take it away. You can sense the relief, you can see the pressure lift as Eddie asks me how I'd like to win $64,000. 'I'd love it,' I say, smiling.

To double my money, I was asked: 'Brontosaurus is properly known as which dinosaur? Allosaurus, apatosaurus, stegosaurus or styracosaurus.'

Ouch. I would never have thought to study up on dinosaurs. All I could do was rule out stegosaurus—I knew what one of those looked like, and it certainly wasn't a brontosaurus. I was pretty good at real names—I could tell you which celebrities were born Maurice Micklewhite or Richard Starkey or Betty Joan Perske[1]—but I was miffed to discover that even the brontosaurus used a stage name. With nothing to lose, I took a stab at 'styra-cosaurus', for no other reason than it was difficult to pronounce and I thought perhaps that's why it was given an easier-to-say name. After all, that had worked for Volodymyr Palahniuk, who won an Oscar as Jack Palance. But there wasn't much logic in my logic—the correct answer was apatosaurus. Oh, well, I hadn't lost anything, except the chance to win more money.

Success on *Who Wants To Be a Millionaire?* was part skill and part luck, although, as Martin Flood proved, you could change the ratio with hard work. I would have known Martin's $64,000 question straight off—which of thug, lout, brute and hoon is derived

---

[1]   Michael Caine, Ringo Starr and Lauren Bacall (three more people who have never been in my kitchen).

from a former confederacy of assassins in India?[1]—because I had written the same question in my *Sale* practice for Paul. But there were plenty of occasions when I would have struck a hurdle at $4000 or $8000 as well. That's the luck of the question draw, and I was happy with my $32,000. I felt even better about it when I discovered that the only person I knew who would have nailed apatosaurus was my six-year-old nephew.

Watching the episode back, I note how little I give Eddie to work with: short answers to his questions, not much discussion, at least a little excitement by the end. I didn't throw a crutch at him, like AFL legend Tony Lockett in a famous incident, but I was about as interested in conversation with Eddie as Plugger had been. That was nothing against Eddie, but I simply had to stay focused. Burgo could have given Eddie the heads-up on that. These days, on *The Chase*, I'm far more adept at mixing banter and serious quiz play without getting distracted. But at 21, playing for big money, I had to concentrate.

A counter-example came straight after my exit, when a young dad named Troy was the next to play. Troy had a bubbly, infectious personality and was always smiling. He brought in a photo of his baby to show off, and was chatting to Eddie about wanting to win money to visit his wife's family in Argentina. He was terrific television. But before even reaching the $1000 safe level, he was gone. When asked on which continent you would find the world's ten highest peaks, he convinced himself the answer

---

[1] Thug

was South America, locked it in and was devastated to walk away with nothing. I felt terrible for Troy. It seemed like all the chat with Eddie had distracted him, and I wondered if he simply had South America on the brain because he wanted to visit Argentina. The question boiled down to something simple: Where is Mount Everest? I'm sure Troy would have known that Everest was in Asia, but he didn't take the time to think it through. It was an object lesson in focus.

Troy's early departure, right before the end of the episode, allowed the show to scrape in one more Fastest Finger question. A New Zealander, librarian Andrew Lockett, was victorious, and the following week went on to become the sixth contestant on the Australian show to win $500,000. I can't remember all of Andrew's questions, nor whether I would have known them. But I certainly recall the million-dollar question, which he chose not to answer: Have 13, 14, 15 or 16 Dalai Lamas ruled Tibet?

'Fourteen!' I shouted at the screen.

But of course by now I was at home in front of the television, and Andrew Lockett couldn't hear me. I was an ex-contestant, another in a long line of players who had won middling amounts on *Who Wants To Be a Millionaire?* I couldn't help but imagine it was me being asked that question for a million dollars. I hadn't become a legend of the show like Andrew, but nor had I crashed out like Troy. I had won a terrific chunk of money for a 21-year-old, and I'll never know how the butterfly effect would have changed my life had I won a million dollars.

I look back on all these game show experiences—the wins and the losses—with gratitude, knowing they have all led me to this wonderful point in my life: chaser, husband, father of three. Similarly, that job with *Stock & Land* that I didn't really want led to my career as a cricket journalist, as it was through my *Stock & Land* colleague Gregor and his cricket-writing friend Jenny that I learnt Cricinfo was hiring and landed my dream job in 2006. As the fourteenth Dalai Lama once said, 'Not getting what you want is sometimes a wonderful stroke of luck.'

CHAPTER 8

A STEP BACK

I'M NOT A RELIGIOUS PERSON, BUT AS I SAT IN THE STANDS AT KENSINGTON Oval in Barbados, watching Adam Gilchrist smash Sri Lanka around the park as Australia won the final of the 2007 Cricket World Cup, I silently said a prayer of thanks to my holy trinity: Eddie McGuire, my brother-in-law Paul and the late Spanish dictator Francisco Franco, who ordered the closure of his country's border with Gibraltar in 1969. Without them, I wouldn't have won $32,000 on *Who Wants To Be a Millionaire?* and I wouldn't be sipping rum on a luxury cricket cruise of the Caribbean watching Australia win its third consecutive World Cup.

I didn't rush out and spend my winnings after the cheque turned up in the mail—I put it in the bank and left it there for several years. But I always wanted to spend it on something specific, something I could point to and say, 'Millionaire paid for that.' So when my oldest friend Ben and I floated the idea of travelling together to the World Cup in the West Indies, I decided it was the perfect opportunity to spend a chunk of my $32,000.

It was also a way to relive a little of my game show glory, because by 2007 I was well out of that world. For four intensive years from 2000 to 2003, I tried my hand at pretty much any game show that would have me. I had a crack at *Burgo's Catch Phrase* after it came back to replace *Pass the Buck*, but like going back to an old flame on the rebound I couldn't rekindle the magic with Burgo and failed to win my episode.

I tried *Wheel of Fortune* when it was hosted by Rob Elliott. Keeping up with *Wheel*'s hosts was like trying to keep track of recent Australian prime ministers—it seemed like every year there was a coup and someone else was brought in until he too spun up 'Lose a Turn'. I grew up with the John Burgess version of *Wheel*, in which the camera panned over a mesmerising 'prize shop', laid out like some sort of dream-like department store, where contestants could spend their winnings on as many prizes as they could afford. 'I'll have the luggage, thanks, John. And the power tools. Hmm, and the men's socks, please.' By the time I was on the show, that wonderland was gone and contestants who won each round made a prosaic choice from three prizes. I took home a Telefunken stereo for winning one round, but overconfidence cost me a more impressive prize.

By spinning up the 'Surprise' wedge, I was guaranteed a bonus prize if I solved that round's puzzle, whose category was 'clue'.

I could see where the puzzle was going and cockily decided to answer with plenty of letters still to fill in:

```
TH_  Y_N  _S
TH_  __RR_N_Y
     __  TH_S
     ___NTRY
```

'The yen is the currency in this country,' I said. Instantly I realised my mistake and heard the 'wrong answer' buzzer. The sixth word was 'of', not 'in'. It was a stupid, lazy error. 'Might have been a bit nervous,' Rob Elliott wondered out loud. He was wrong. I wasn't nervous enough. And then, when I found out what the prize was, I kicked myself even harder: one little word had cost me a trip to Japan. Still, I enjoyed the show, spinning that big iconic wheel and calling out the letters. I didn't want to be like every other contestant, guessing 'N for Nelly' and 'S for Sam'. For my own amusement, I decided to use country names: 'N for Norway', 'D for Denmark', 'H for Hungary', though I stopped short of 'Y for Yemen'—I wasn't *that* much of a smart-arse. I also didn't take it as far as comedian and maths expert Adam Spencer, who became a carry-over champion on *Wheel* a year or two after my appearance and chose letters such as 'T for trigonometry' and 'H for hypotenuse'.

In 2004, I tried my luck at *Deal or No Deal*, but I didn't get the chance to be the main contestant and simply opened a briefcase like 25 other random faces. And with that, I had pretty much exhausted my game show options. I deliberately avoided

Shafted, was too slow to apply for a few programs that were quickly axed and didn't bother with *The Price Is Right*. That was no reflection on the show; I would very happily have putted a golf ball for a chance to win a car, and having worked in a supermarket as a teenager I'd have been quite good at guessing prices. But *The Price Is Right* didn't hold auditions like other game shows. Instead, the producers chatted backstage to the audience members and the most extroverted, the most gregarious, the most outrageous were then asked to 'Come on down!' I could have been the only member of the audience and still wouldn't have been extroverted, gregarious or outrageous enough for *The Price Is Right*.

And so, that was that. On most game shows, losing players were allowed to re-audition after a couple of years but contestants who had won an episode were generally precluded from ever coming back. Unfortunately, when *Temptation* began in 2005 with Ed Phillips and Livinia Nixon hosting, it was considered a continuation of *Sale of the Century* for the purposes of filtering out past winners. So I was done with game shows until something else came along. That was okay, because in 2006 I started writing for Cricinfo, the world's largest cricket website, and I had plenty to keep me occupied. I was certainly more excited about the job than I had been at *Stock & Land*. No more would I have to report on the cattle competitions at the Royal Melbourne Show, hear a judge say something like, 'This cow has excellent udder placement' and wonder if there's an alternative. What, do some cows have them on their back?

This fallow television period for me coincided with the end of a golden game-show era. Perhaps I was nostalgic, but I felt the 1980s and '90s had been a wonderful time for the genre. I had enjoyed game shows aimed at kids: *Vidiot*, *Double Dare*, *Now You See It*, *Blockbusters*, *Big Square Eye*, *A*Mazing*. I had loved *It's a Knockout* with its zany games and golf carts[1] and *The Krypton Factor* with its mixture of quizzing and obstacle course. I enjoyed the wackiness of *Supermarket Sweep* and *The Price Is Right*[2]. I liked *The Main Event*—my favourite segment was where they showed you inside a celebrity's house and you had to guess who lived there. I even occasionally watched dating-style game shows such as *Man O Man*, which is best remembered for the eliminated male suitors being shoved into a swimming pool fully clothed. When we started filming *The Chase Australia* in 2015, I was thrilled to learn that the *Man O Man* pool still existed

---

[1] A man from Camperdown, Finley Lucas, had been a contestant on *It's a Knockout* when I was very young. I got to know Finley when I was a teenager and started playing competitive table-tennis; Finley was the driving force behind the town's table-tennis league and coached the junior players. To know someone from my small country town who had been a contestant on a national game show was an inspiration to me and showed me what was possible.

[2] Likewise I knew someone who had appeared on both of these shows when I was a kid. Kaye Hanvin, a cousin of my brother-in-law Paul, and whom I had met at Lindy and Paul's wedding, was a serial game show contestant—she later won an episode of *The Weakest Link*. As with Finley, knowing that I had a personal connection to Kaye, and knowing that she too was a normal, everyday person, further made me realise that my dreams of becoming a contestant were absolutely achievable.

underneath the floor of our studio. It felt like we were working at a television archaeological site.

I don't mean to say that all these shows were quality, but they were fun. By the mid-2000s, it felt as though the genre was dying. *Sale of the Century* had ended in 2001 and its revival as *Temptation* in 2005 never hit the heights of the original, lasting four seasons. *The Price Is Right*, cancelled in 1998, briefly returned from 2003 to 2005 before Cliff the yodelling alpine hiker tumbled off his mountain and into oblivion. *Family Feud*, so popular with host Rob Brough in the 1990s, was tried once more in 2006 with four-time Gold Logie–winning legend Bert Newton at the helm, but lasted only two seasons. Rob Brough might have been no Bert Newton, but it turned out Bert Newton was no Rob Brough either. *Wheel of Fortune* continued to spin up new hosts—Steve Oemcke, Larry Emdur, Tim Campbell—and was even rebranded as *Million Dollar Wheel of Fortune* for its final season in 2008.

The iconic hosts moved on as well. John Burgess drifted off to the game show host's version of a retirement home: easy listening radio. Larry Emdur switched gears to host *The Morning Show*. Eddie McGuire became CEO of the Nine Network, and, as his off-screen duties increased, his on-screen flagship show *Who Wants To Be a Millionaire?* ended. He turned up now and again to host new prime-time quiz shows such as *The Million Dollar Drop* and *1 vs 100*, but neither lasted long. When *Millionaire Hot Seat* began as an afternoon show, Eddie was back on a winner.

Andrew O'Keefe, whose television career started with impersonations of Eddie McGuire on the sketch comedy series *Big*

Bite, found that life imitated art when he turned game show host himself, fronting the most successful and long-lasting game show of the mid-2000s era: *Deal or No Deal*. Andrew was given another prime-time shot with the big-money quiz show *The Rich List* in 2007; I liked the concept of this show, building lists of answers to questions like 'Countries beginning with A' or 'The fifty highest wicket-takers in Test cricket'. *The Rich List* may be the only show I auditioned for but never appeared on; it lasted only 40 episodes spread across three years. It's no coincidence that this era in which classic game shows struggled was also when reality television hit giddy heights. Millions watched *Australian Idol*, *The Block*, *MasterChef*, *Dancing with the Stars* and *The Biggest Loser*. Tastes had changed, but I still believed there was a place for the game show. To put it in *MasterChef* terms, television needed a balance of flavours.

One show I could have attempted was *The Einstein Factor*, which ticked along on the ABC during the mid-2000s, but it required contestants to have a special subject and I was a jack of all trivia trades. I sometimes watched *The Einstein Factor*, though not to see how Joe Bloggs did with his special topic of Dickens novels or Danish monarchs or dung beetles. I was more interested in the show's 'Brains Trust', the rotating panel of three experts who nominally competed with and against the contestants, but also offered background discussion and humour along with host Peter Berner. The Brains Trust included quiz-show winning comedians such as Matt Parkinson and Stephen Hall, television presenters like Jennifer Byrne and Red Symons, as well as the most iconic quiz-show figure Australia has ever seen: Barry Jones.

To watch Barry Jones on *The Einstein Factor* was a beautiful thing. In one episode, Barry was joined in the Brains Trust by Byrne and also Symons, who leaned across comically to Barry when a question asked about an intended eighteenth-century marriage between Frederick the Great and Princess Amelia of Britain. Of course, Barry knew all the intimate details. A few minutes later, when asked if the famous surname of siblings Ahmet, Diva and Dweezil is Zane, Zappa or Zellweger, Barry wryly admitted: 'I fear it's out of my comfort zone.' Naturally, Jennifer and Red both knew the answer[1] to this classic pop culture question—as did all three contestants. I have on my bookshelf the 1998 edition of the *Dictionary of World Biography*, written by Barry Jones, which runs to 828 pages profiling roughly 8500 notable figures. Frank Zappa, the father of Ahmet, Diva and Dweezil, is included, but his entry is only 35 words long and certainly doesn't mention his children.

▼

I doubt anyone but Barry Jones could have written such a detailed tome. His knowledge is the definition of encyclopedic. In 2020, when Barry was 88, his latest book was published, an important, ambitious work titled *What Is to Be Done: Political engagement*

---

[1] Zappa. They are children of rock legend Frank Zappa. Another of his daughters is named Moon Unit.

and saving the planet. He analyses the fundamental problems facing humanity: climate change, population growth exacerbated by resource use, pandemics, and racism and state violence. As a voracious reader and acquirer of knowledge, he understands the way these issues are inextricably connected. He worked as a teacher, lawyer and historian before entering politics, and became Australia's Minister for Science for most of the 1980s. He describes himself as obsessive about finding linkages, which is key to understanding large, complex problems.

Jones warned of climate change as far back as the early 1980s, but his argument was dismissed as alarmist and premature. His political colleagues were not ready to listen, hardly surprising given that 35 years later, politicians were fondling coal in parliament. On understanding weighty issues and trends, Barry has been decades ahead of most people. His influential 1982 book *Sleepers, Wake!*, which explored the approaching changes in technology and work, and Australia's inevitable transition to a post-industrial society, was read and admired by figures as disparate as Bill Gates and Deng Xiaoping. In *What Is to Be Done*, Barry notes with apparent frustration that in the digital age, mainstream and social media are focused not on long-term, universal issues, but on short-term, personal ones. As, to a large degree, is politics, where all that seems to matter is winning the next election. Barry Jones was that rarest of politicians, one who genuinely wanted to use his position to improve the world. He was a passionate campaigner against the death penalty during the 1960s and regards his role in its abolition as one of his finest achievements.

So who cares if Barry Jones doesn't know the names of Frank Zappa's children?

If it seems hard to reconcile all of Barry Jones' important works with his role as a television quizzer, that is likely because television quizzes have changed so much since he became a household name on *Pick a Box*. Consider the current quiz shows on Australian television: *The Chase, Hot Seat, Mastermind, Hard Quiz*. Contestants might be asked questions on ancient history or classical music or world affairs, but these subjects are now considered quite highbrow and are offset by pop culture, sport and the minutiae of day-to-day life. I have no problem with that. In fact, I enjoy racking my brain to try to picture what year is printed on the logo of Schweppes soft drinks[1] or showing off that I know what animal Helen is in the *Spot* series of children's books[2]. But these topics are unquestionably 'trivia' in the traditional sense—pieces of information with little value or importance.

Now consider the questions Barry Jones was asked on an episode of *Pick a Box* from the early 1960s, in which he was competing against South African champion Henry Springer. After what pagan goddess is the day Friday named? What was the name of the emperor who abdicated in 1814 and again in 1815? What

---

[1] 1783

[2] Helen is a hippopotamus. Spot's friends also include Steve the Monkey and Tom the Alligator.

instrument is used for measuring the speed and strength of wind and air? What is the highest rank in the British Army? What country was inhabited by the Incas before the Spaniards reached South America? What name is given to the distilled cider brandy produced in a part of Normandy? What name was given to the period of rule in France between 1795 and Napoleon's consulate in 1799? From which country was the Louisiana Purchase made by the United States? In what village in Germany is the famous passion play enacted every ten years? In Greek mythology who were the creatures who were part man and part horse? Excluding the Australian continent, which is the largest island in the world?[1]

The only one Barry missed was the brandy. Henry Springer knew it, but the best that teetotaller Barry could come up with was a throwaway answer of 'champagne'. Some of these questions are quite straightforward—there were easy questions on *Pick a Box*—but they all require rather traditional knowledge. From what I can tell, *Pick a Box* covered little popular culture of the era. The show started on radio in 1948 and then ran on television until 1971, but contestants weren't inundated with questions about The Beatles and *Gilligan's Island* and Morris West novels. Instead they were expected to name Alfred the Great's father[2], or the country in which poets Robert Browning and Elizabeth

---

[1] The answers: Frigg, Napoleon I (aka Napoleon Bonaparte), anemometer, field marshal, Peru, calvados, the Directory, France, Oberammergau, centaurs, Greenland.

[2] Aethelwulf

Barrett Browning spent most of their married life[1], or the British suffragist and composer who was made a dame in 1922[2]. In many cases, the contestants did know these answers—and not just Barry Jones.

When he first appeared on *Pick a Box* in 1960, Barry Jones was a 28-year-old teacher at Dandenong High School but already a veteran of broadcast quizzes. In his 2006 book *A Thinking Reed*, he recalls that his first experience of winning a quiz took place at age ten, on the Geelong radio station 3GL, when he correctly identified the pen-name of the American author Samuel Langhorne Clemens[3] and won a threepenny bit. In 1944, he was a finalist on a Melbourne radio quiz called *Junior Information*, and a few years later he featured as a Melbourne panellist on the radio show *Quiz Kids*, whose Sydney panel had included future New South Wales premier Neville Wran.

In 1955, Barry won money on the radio show *Give It a Go*, hosted by Jack Davey, and he was an unsuccessful contestant on the early television quiz show *Tic Tac Dough*—he could answer the questions, no problem, but the secondary part of the show, playing noughts and crosses, proved harder. He won a first-class round-the-world airfare on another Jack Davey production, *The Dulux Show*, and after these performances Barry travelled to the United States in the hopes of auditioning for the American

---

[1] Italy

[2] Dame Ethel Smyth

[3] Mark Twain, which you may remember from Chapter 7.

shows *Twenty One* and *Tic Tac Dough*. Not long afterwards, the American quiz show scandals came to light. As depicted in the 1994 film *Quiz Show*, directed by Robert Redford, contestants on *Twenty One* were variously fed the answers or told to take a fall.

Barry was already politically active before his *Pick a Box* fame—on the morning of his first appearance, he handed out how-to-vote cards for the Labor Party in a by-election for the federal seat of La Trobe. The seat had been vacated by Richard Casey, who later became Australia's governor-general, and, in a connection of sorts to Barry Jones' most famous *Pick a Box* moment, had also served as governor of Bengal during the 1940s.

Pick a Box was the baby of presenters Bob and Dolly Dyer, the married couple who had launched the show on radio in 1948 and transitioned smoothly to television in 1957. A half-hour *Pick a Box* episode generally consisted of two sections. In the first half, two contestants would play head-to-head, answering the same five questions individually. The winner picked a numbered box that contained a mystery prize. Bob Dyer would then offer the contestant a cash payment instead of the mystery prize, which led to his catchphrase: 'The money or the box?' The winning contestant could keep returning until he or she was beaten, or claimed all 40 boxes. The second half of the show typically involved a battle between former champions, or international champions, for a cash prize. These would be epic ten-week contests, with the scores building cumulatively, and they became must-watch television.

Barry Jones soon became known for making clarifications and corrections to the show's questions while a contestant. In his second episode, he was asked by Bob Dyer for the name of the battle fought on the Plains of Abraham in 1739. Barry suggested to Bob that he must be referring to the Battle of Quebec, but that it was fought in 1759, not 1739. Bob seemed to take such corrections in good humour, no doubt realising it made excellent television.

Barry became the first contestant to win all 40 boxes, his prizes including a Morris Major car (which he described as the worst car he ever owned) and a caravan, which he never saw, instead organising for a friend to sell it for charity, because, to Barry, towing a caravan would have been the holiday from hell. He became a fixture on the show, appearing in 208 episodes and often featuring in ten-week battles against other champions such as Frank Partridge and George Black. Partridge was an extraordinary figure who had been born into a poor farming family, left school at thirteen, was awarded the Victoria Cross during World War II and after returning from the war devoted himself to reading the *Encyclopaedia Britannica* by kerosene lamp in the dirt-floored farmhouse. In *A Thinking Reed*, Barry wrote that he felt uneasy competing against a genuine hero like Frank Partridge, who had had none of the advantages in life that Barry had.

'I felt like a smart arse in Frank's company,' Barry wrote.

Pick a Box champions had acquired their knowledge via different methods. For Frank Partridge, it was reading the encyclopedia. George Black used complex memory systems and mnemonics. But Barry Jones was simply interested in the world. By his own description, each book he read, each place he visited, each piece of music he heard, each person he talked to, added to the information in his brain. He does not believe he has a full photographic memory, although he can recall precisely where certain information is found on a page, a trait shared by my *Chase* colleague Issa Schultz. But for Barry Jones, the information needed to be of intrinsic interest in the first place. If he tried to learn a list of Melbourne Cup winners, for example, he would likely have been unsuccessful, because he had no interest in horseracing.

Fortunately for Barry, the questions on *Pick a Box* tended to stay within his areas of interest. Bob Dyer was American and wasn't about to ask questions on Australian sport. Many of the show's questions related to world history, which was a great strength for Barry, as he demonstrated in *Pick a Box*'s most famous incident. During Barry's tenth episode, he was asked who was the first British governor-general of India. He knew that the expected answer was Warren Hastings, as per *Britannica* and other sources. Barry also knew this was incorrect. He launched into an extended monologue explaining that, while Hastings was usually described as the first British governor-general of India, his title was in fact governor-general of Bengal. This put Dyer in an awkward position, and he decided that the following week he would devote an entire half-hour of television to discussing the Hastings question, featuring a panel of experts. In *A Thinking Reed*, Barry wrote: 'Bob's experiment with the Warren Hastings question was significant. He challenged the assumption that the mass media had to appeal to the lowest common denominator, the phenomenon now called "dumbing down". He demonstrated, although his initial position may have been instinctive rather than considered, that an obscure esoteric issue could capture public interest provided that it was handled effectively. I was grateful to him for that.'

Over eight years, Barry Jones won approximately $55,000 on *Pick a Box* and became a household name, so much so that when seeking election to parliament in the early 1970s he grew a beard to distance himself from the quiz show fame. He might have been the most recognisable quiz-winning politician in Australia, but he wasn't the first.

▼

In 1972, Barry Jones was elected to the Victorian parliament for the seat of Melbourne; later that year Australians elevated Gough Whitlam to the prime ministership, ending 23 years of Liberal Party rule. Most Victorians knew Barry Jones was a quiz champion; few Australians had any idea their new prime minister was as well. Whitlam had won the Australian National Quiz Championship in 1948 and 1949, and was runner-up in 1950. The popular radio competition was broadcast on the ABC on Friday nights and was sponsored by the federal Treasury to promote the use of government security loans to encourage post-war nation-building. In her biography *Gough Whitlam: A Moment in History*, historian Jenny Hocking wrote that Ben

Chifley was a devoted listener to the quiz and believed that Whitlam was the kind of professional, intelligent and articulate person the Labor Party needed to take it forward. Neither man could have imagined that after Chifley's electoral defeat in 1949, Whitlam would be the country's next Labor prime minister more than two decades later.

A fascinating newspaper article in 1949 profiled Australia's 'quiz kings', including '32-year-old barrister Edward Whitlam' (Gough was his middle name). The article reads: 'Whitlam, with two young babies, says he can never get a chance of listening to radio quiz sessions because they're always on the air when he is either washing the dishes or changing the baby's diapers.'

As a contestant, Whitlam was asked questions such as 'Who composed the opera *The Daughter of the Regiment*?[1]' and 'Who was the king who reigned from about 115–63 BC, who fortified himself so strongly against poison by the use of antidotes that he could not kill himself and had to get a Gallic mercenary soldier to stab him, as he preferred death to captivity?[2]' The learned future prime minister knew both of those answers.

Less successful was Liberal prime minister John Howard, who, at the age of sixteen, while a student at Canterbury Boys' High School, appeared on Jack Davey's radio show *Give It a Go*. He won 100 bars of Velvet soap, due more to Davey's generosity than Howard's correct answers. Listening to the audio 65 years

---

[1] Donizetti
[2] Mithridates

later is a hilarious experience. I laughed out loud a number of times—as did the studio audience—as Davey expertly steered the clueless teenage Howard, with a broad Australian accent, through a series of questions.

JD: 'Where do you find a mezzanine floor?'[1]

JH: 'Oh, on the floor of a, a house in, ah, in, in an Eastern country?'

JD: 'What is an abigail?'[2]

JH: 'Oh it's a sort of an, ah, sort of a minor gale, sort of thing.'

JD: 'What is the unusual characteristic of a kiwi?'[3]

JH: 'It's on the face of a tin of boot polish.'

JD: 'What is mimosa?'[4]

JH: 'Oh, it's the name of a sort of a native tribal dance.'

JD: 'This fella would have the most colossal imagination I have ever heard! I don't know whether he's right or wrong, but if he's making these up, he's not bad!'

I have omitted a few questions and Howard did correctly answer a couple (Who wrote the oratorio *The Messiah*?[5] What is the near side of a horse?[6]), but the above exchanges highlight

---

[1]   Between the ground floor and the first floor of a building.

[2]   It's an old-fashioned term for a female servant or lady's maid.

[3]   The answer wasn't revealed, but it could have been as simple as that the kiwi can't fly. Two interesting facts about the kiwi: it is the only bird with nostrils at the tip of its beak, and it lays the largest egg relative to body size of any bird.

[4]   Another name for a type of wattle, although 'a mimosa' is a cocktail of champagne and orange juice.

[5]   Handel

[6]   The left side

what an entertaining guest, perhaps unwittingly so, the sixteen-year-old Howard was. I couldn't help but notice that even as a teenager, Howard instinctively pretended to know what he was talking about even when he didn't—a skill that successful politicians of all persuasions tend to master.

▼

John Howard's appearance on *Give It a Go* came in 1955, the year before television began in Australia. That same year, a survey by market research firm McNair Anderson found that quiz shows were Australia's most popular type of radio program. The comperes of radio quizzes were the most famous entertainers in Australia during that era, and the two biggest were the American-born Dyer and the New Zealander Davey. They engaged in a well-publicised friendly rivalry but were distinctly different personalities.

Bob Dyer was a self-styled 'hillbilly' entertainer and vaudevillian from Tennessee, whose early radio shows relied on stunts involving audience members. Think of the classic 'pie in the face' routine and you'll get the gist. Jack Davey's gift was his lightning wit and ability to ad lib. His first radio quiz was *That's What You Think*, broadcast on 2GB in Sydney in 1934. By the mid-1950s, Davey was hosting four different prime-time shows on radio every week, all variations on the quiz theme.

In early 1957, many of the radio quiz shows transitioned to television via simulcast, and a week of such premieres was promoted as the greatest television event since the 1956 Olympics. On Monday night, Davey hosted *Give It a Go*. On Tuesday, Dyer had *It Pays to Be Funny*. Davey was back on Wednesday with *The Dulux Show*. On Thursday was the *Pantomime Quiz*, hosted by Harry Dearth and George Foster. The *Pressure Pak Programme* with Davey was on Friday night. On Saturday evening, Dyer's *Pick a Box* made its television debut. And on Sunday night there was *The Quiz Kids* with John Dease, a highly successful format on radio, where it ran for twenty years and featured a panel of eleven- to fifteen-year-olds trying to answer questions sent in by listeners.

Dyer took the transition to television seriously, reportedly losing nearly 20 kilograms to make himself presentable. He listened to television experts, was prepared to learn new ways and worked out how best to make his radio format of *Pick a Box* work on camera. It was highly successful, and the show ran until he retired in 1971. Davey, on the other hand, seemed to believe that adding some cameras to his successful radio shows would be sufficient, and his programs barely lasted a year.

Davey's other problem was his ill health. An extravagant spender who worked hard and played even harder, Davey died from cancer in 1959, at 52. More than 100,000 people stood in the rain in Sydney to pay tribute to him after a memorial service. To these people he would always be 'Mr Radio', and a golden age of wireless broadcasting died with him.

▼

There was, however, more to Australia's pioneering television quiz and game show days than Bob Dyer and Jack Davey.

Another long-running quiz show was the *Coles £3000 Question*, which ran from 1960 to 1971 and became the *Coles $6000 Question* when Australia switched to decimal currency[1]. Hosted first by Malcolm Searle and then Roland Strong, it was Australia's version of the hit American show *The $64,000 Question* and provided the lure of a big cash prize. An early episode available on YouTube features a contestant strolling on holding a pipe; he is noted puppeteer F.W. Parry Marshall, who correctly names the instrument used to measure the height of an aircraft above the ground[2] but bombs out when unable to recall what the acronym Anzac stands for[3]. Old 'Parry', as he was known, was no Barry Jones. The next contestant is Mr Stanley Hampson, a blacksmith from the now wealthy Melbourne suburb of Kew, who cannot name the bill confirmed by William and Mary in 1689 that affirmed the liberties of their subjects and settled the issue of succession to the throne[4]. A blacksmith, a man with a pipe, prize money in pounds—it truly was another time.

Australia's first television game show was *Name That Tune*, hosted by Bruce Gyngell, the man who had welcomed Australia to television in 1956[5]. The National Film and Sound Archive

---

[1]   14 February 1966

[2]   Altimeter

[3]   Australian and New Zealand Army Corps

[4]   The Bill of Rights

[5]   Footage also exists of a 1953 television recording of Jack Davey hosting a panel game show called *Ask Me Another*, recorded as part of the Macquarie radio network's bid to gain a television licence.

holds a 1957 clip of future television star and Gold Logie winner Jimmy Hannan competing as a regular contestant on *Name That Tune*, where he had to identify snippets of popular songs played live in the studio by the Gus Merzi Quintette. Among the songs Hannan named were the 1930s tunes 'Anything Goes' and 'Let's Fall in Love', but also some that were recent hits at the time: 1954's 'Mr Sandman' and the 1955 Gogi Grant hit 'Suddenly There's a Valley'. Modern pop culture *did* appear on game shows in the 1950s after all.

Some early game shows aired in only one Australian city, due to the localised nature of the television industry. Some are considered 'lost', with no recordings having survived, while others live on. The titles are evocative. There was *Do You Trust Your Wife?*, hosted by ventriloquist Ron Blaskett and his puppet Gerry Gee. There was *Balance Your Budget*, about which little is known other than its riveting title. And there was *Lady for a Day*[1], an afternoon favourite with Melbourne housewives, presented by the American comedian Larry K. Nixon. On ABC radio in 2011, comedian Trent McCarthy recalled that his grandmother had appeared on *Lady for a Day*, where she won some rubbish bins and a sponge cake.

---

[1]   *Lady for a Day* shared its title with a 1933 Hollywood film that starred May Robson, who had been born in the Murray River town of Moama in 1858. Many Australians would be aware of our own Errol Flynn making his mark in Hollywood in the 1930s, but precious few would remember Robson, who was the earliest-born person to be nominated for an Academy Award, as well as the first Australian.

Others had a lasting impact. One was *Wheel of Fortune*, which shares its title with the long-running game show from a later era, but had a different format. This *Wheel of Fortune* was a quiz show; the titular wheel served only to determine prizes. It too had started on radio before moving to television but did not enjoy a long run. It is notable mostly for introducing Australian audiences to the man who would arguably become the most important figure in Australian television over the next few decades: Reg Grundy.

Reg Grundy had started his media career as a boxing commentator on Sydney radio, where he also came up with the *Wheel of Fortune* concept. He hosted the show on radio and television but soon moved behind the camera to focus on his eponymous production company, which became a national powerhouse and a significant presence overseas as well. Grundy's company was responsible for some of Australia's most successful television soaps—*Neighbours*, *Prisoner*, *Sons and Daughters*, *The Young Doctors*—as well as game shows such as *Family Feud*, the later *Wheel of Fortune* and *Blankety Blanks*, which nominally involved contestants but was mostly a vehicle for jokes and innuendo from host Graham Kennedy and his panellists, including Ugly Dave Gray, Noeline Brown and Stuart Wagstaff. Perhaps the greatest indication of Reg Grundy's fame in Australia is that his name entered the vernacular—and the *Macquarie Dictionary*—as rhyming slang for undies.

The longest-running game show for Grundy was *Sale of the Century*, which started in 1980 but had its origins ten years earlier.

In 1970, Grundy introduced *Temptation*, which aired at 1.30 p.m.
on Channel Seven and was hosted by a then 30-year-old Tony
Barber. Sponsored by a supermarket chain, it was stereotypical
daytime television but proved such a ratings winner that its
half-hour timeslot was increased to one hour.

In 1971, when Bob and Dolly Dyer announced they were
retiring themselves and their iconic *Pick a Box* from the Monday 7
p.m. timeslot, Grundy's and Channel Seven decided *Temptation* was
the natural replacement. All it needed was a bit of extra pizzazz to
become a prime-time show, and thus the *$25,000 Great Temptation*
was born. Soon, it also replaced the *Coles $6000 Question* on
Wednesday nights, and by 1973 the *Great Temptation* was on five
nights a week. This meant a staggering workload for Tony Barber
and his co-host Barbie Rogers, because the daytime show was still
in production as well. The shows were so successful that Barber
won the Gold Logie in 1973. But the following year, Seven made
the bold move to switch the *Great Temptation* to the 8.30 p.m.
timeslot in Melbourne and Sydney, to tackle the ratings juggernaut
of the raunchy soap *Number 96* on Channel 0 (which later became
Channel 10). Viewers preferred titillation to information, and
neither *Temptation* nor the *Great Temptation* returned in 1975.

In 1980, the show was revived with even more glitz and
glamour and a new title: *Sale of the Century*. Tony Barber was
back in the host's position, this time on Channel Nine, with
bigger and better prizes. For twenty-one years *Sale* reigned,
occupying the important 7 p.m. timeslot (although in the country
area where I grew up, it was on at 5.30 p.m., because an extra

half-hour had to be found for the local Ballarat news bulletin). *Sale* was the ultimate in family television: all ages could watch and get something out of it. I have heard many stories of people watching it with their grandparents.

In his autobiography, Tony Barber observed that the success of *Sale* was due to its straddling the line between the quiz and game genres. It was a quiz show, but variables such as speed on the buzzer, the temptation of spending money to buy prizes in the gift shop and the element of luck from the Fame Game board meant the smartest player didn't always win and the underdog could get up. Thanks for rubbing it in, Tony.

The premiere episode of *Sale* was won by a bearded, long-haired student teacher from Adelaide by the name of Grant Hare (or Hair). He also had the distinction of answering the first question in the show's two-decade run, buzzing in after 'Eva Braun had a famous boyfriend' to give the correct name[1]. As was the case with *Pick a Box*, the questions were classical, covering topics such as Dante's *Divine Comedy*, the US Civil War, the Hanseatic League, Mozart and British history. There was not a single question about television or popular music, and the nearest thing to a film question asked who wrote the musical *My Fair Lady*[2].

It is also notable that there were almost no questions about Australia, the only exceptions being a 'Who Am I?' on Gough Whitlam, and the rather oddly phrased 'What disability do the

---

[1]   Adolf Hitler
[2]   Lerner and Loewe

emu and cassowary have in common?[1]' This shortage of local content is an interesting phenomenon, and one that I observed in most of the older quiz shows. That may in part be due to the sources, such as *Britannica*, having a worldwide focus. These older shows tended to include vast numbers of questions about classical history, which probably reflected school learning of the time. But I wonder if there was also an element of cultural cringe, the belief that Australian history and arts were unworthy of a quiz show. I'm pleased to say quiz shows today include far more local content. SBS's *Mastermind* also ensures a higher representation of questions relating to the culture and history of First Nations Australians, which is another important step.

The first contestant to win the Mercedes on *Sale of the Century* was Vincent Smith, a school teacher from the appropriately named Victorian town of Sale. Over the years, the show's champions became well-known names. But gradually, the questions changed a little. Barber suggested that this was due in part to a dwindling pool of high-calibre contestants, but also the changing nature of school education. Questions became easier, with far more covering movies and music, and topics that could be considered 'trivia' in the dictionary sense. There was also a tendency to ask questions that gave part of the answer and simply required the contestant to finish the sentence: 'A common proverb states that a penny saved is a penny what?[2]'

---

[1]   They can't fly
[2]   Earned

The issue of 'dumbing down' quiz shows is an interesting one. I could imagine Barry Jones scoffing at $1 million being given away to a contestant who guessed which of *Bewitched*, *Get Smart*, *I Dream of Jeannie* and *Hogan's Heroes* premiered first, as Rob Fulton did on *Who Wants To Be a Millionaire?* Are such questions asked because viewers enjoy them, or do viewers enjoy them because that's what gets asked? What is worthy knowledge and what is trivia? Jones had such a voracious appetite to understand the world that he read widely on history, science, politics and geography, and has applied that knowledge to the most important issues facing humanity. As a by-product, he did well at quiz shows along the way. But it's clear that Barry Jones' mind operates at a higher level, and that Australia—and the world—is lucky to have him.

For the rest of us, I think the modern quiz show balance is about right. On *The Chase*, I may be asked the names of Frank Zappa's children, or Taylor Swift's new album, or who starred in *Kath & Kim*. But I'll also be asked in which century the War of the Spanish Succession took place[1], or which Ancient Greek wrote the play *Oedipus at Colonus*[2]. To me, that balance makes for more inclusive television viewing, because there's something for everyone. It also means that today's quiz shows tick the most important box: they're fun to play along with while watching at home.

---

[1]   The eighteenth century (1701–14)

[2]   Sophocles

CHAPTER 9

TRIVIAL PURSUITS

THE WORLD IS A SMALL PLACE THESE DAYS. IF YOU HAD AN INTEREST IN quizzing in the 1950s or 1960s, your options as an Australian were limited. You could watch shows like *Pick a Box*, listen to radio quizzes or ... or what? Not much. Trivia board games were a thing of the future. So were pub quizzes. As late as the 1990s, I was calling up Tony Delroy's midnight quiz because it was one of the few things that scratched my quizzing itch. These days, as with all forms of media, you can consume trivia anywhere and everywhere.

Whenever I'm out for a walk, or hanging up washing, or doing some gardening, I'll stick my headphones in and listen to a trivia podcast. My favourites are both American productions: *Trivial Warfare* and *Triviality*, both of which re-create the experience of pub trivia. They're not major media productions but were started by amateurs who enjoyed trivia and wanted to share their passion. Listeners are invited on as guests, which builds a community feel, and hundreds of listeners support the shows with a monthly donation. In 2019, I guest-hosted an episode of *Triviality* via Skype, sitting in my house in Melbourne, quizzing three young guys in Chicago—the show's regular hosts, whom I had come to think of as friends. Globalisation may have its downsides, but it has its joys as well.

You really can provide trivia from anywhere. Miles Glaspole, a young Melbourne man who has appeared on *The Chase* and *Hard Quiz*, gained popularity on TikTok in 2021 by creating what he calls the TikTok10, a daily ten-question quiz that Miles reads out rapid-fire from the front seat of his car. Viewers are encouraged to 'blind react' and say whatever answer comes to mind in the roughly one second between Miles finishing the question and giving the answer. The whole quiz lasts one minute, but has often gone viral due to viewers creating what TikTok calls 'Duets': a split-screen video where a user reacts to another video—of themselves answering the questions. TikTok's Duets had been popular with users creating vocal harmonies or reacting to funny videos, but Miles saw a gap in the market. Within months, the TikTok10 was reaching 200,000 to 300,000 users per day.

I'm a 40-year-old man, not a social media influencer, so to me the TikTok10 sounds more like a full packet of Arnott's biscuits than a quiz show. More my speed is a daily online quiz called Learned League, run by Seattle man Shayne Bushfield. Learned League is a bit like a private members' club for trivia. It has several thousand participants but is invitation-only. The league had its origins as a pen-and-paper competition in an office in the late 1990s before Bushfield transferred it online in 2000. It is divided into hundreds of groups of 26 players each, with promotion and relegation and head-to-head battles. Each day, you play against another player in your division, each answering the same six questions and assigning points based on whether you think your opponent will know the answer.

Of course, with an online league it is entirely possible to cheat, which is why the competition is invitation only—another player has to vouch for your trustworthiness. Personally, I don't care about winning or losing in Learned League (there are no prizes anyway)—I just love the style of the questions. They are interesting, meticulously crafted and often include little clues that, if spotted, point you in the right direction. Some questions are so chewy that I'll ponder them for hours, first reading them when they are posted at around 5 p.m. Melbourne time, and thinking them over as I put the kids to bed.

Often, they resemble puzzles. '*Hackbraten, Pieczeń rzymska,* רשב ייצק and *Pain de viande* are names of dishes that can be translated into English as the name of what musical artist?' I spent hours working that one out, starting with the assumption that it must be a bread-related name because 'pain' means bread in French. But 'viande' wasn't clicking for me—and the other languages were no help. I ruled out the band Bread, because the wording was 'musical artist' singular. But what singer or musician had a name that was the same as a food with a bready connection? The correct answer[1] eventually popped into my brain while I was changing a nappy, and the satisfaction was immense.

Sometimes the answer to a Learned League question will immediately occur to me, but it's still satisfying because I have learnt a fascinating fact. 'Kiwi Caleb Shepherd made history on July 30 as the first male to win a women's Olympic Games medal, earning a silver in what sport (while facing his eight fellow New Zealand teammates)?' This was not something I had heard about during the Tokyo Games; while I knew that several sports featured men and women competing together—equestrian, sailing, swimming and athletics—the question specified that Shepherd won a *women's* medal. The correct answer[2] came to me quickly thanks to the clue—while facing his eight fellow New Zealand teammates. But the Learned League message boards showed that others took this clue in a different way: someone wrote that they thought he might have been the catcher in a softball team. Part of Learned League's appeal is the depth of question data and statistics that it keeps: I can therefore tell you that 49 per cent of players answered this question correctly, and the most common wrong answer was rugby.

---

[1] Meat Loaf

[2] Rowing. Caleb Shepherd was the cox in the New Zealand women's rowing eight. In 2017, the international governing body of rowing declared that the role of coxswain was gender neutral.

Learned League has fostered a quirky online community, and the divisions allow a wide range of skills. Players include trivia professionals such as Chasers and Eggheads, former *Jeopardy!* champions and everyday quizzers. Occasionally, I'll discover that someone totally unexpected is a Learned League player, such as Paris Themmen, who as a child actor starred as Mike Teavee in a classic 1971 film[1] and, as a 58-year-old, competed on *Jeopardy!* in 2018. For me, Learned League is a wonderful diversion, one of the most enjoyable parts of my day. I can be sitting at the computer late in the afternoon, working, and an email will land in my inbox telling me the day's questions are now available. On a bad day, I might only get two of the six correct. Rarely, I'll get all six, and the league has its own terminology for that: beer (as in, a six-pack). For me, it provides nothing but internal pleasure.

'There's also no need to be able to throw a wad of paper into a wastebasket twenty feet away,' Shayne Bushfield told the *Washington Post* in a 2014 interview, but 'it feels awesome when it goes in—in a totally meaningless but still fulfilling way.'

Like many quiz nerds, Bushfield grew up playing Trivial Pursuit—and memorising the answers. His family loved the game; so did mine. The Coverdales played all sorts of board and card games when I was young—Scrabble, Trouble, Monopoly, Uno—and as the youngest of four siblings by six years, I was always punching up, trying to be competitive. Sometimes I was easy pickings:

---

[1]   *Willy Wonka & the Chocolate Factory*

I remember my sister once getting bored during Monopoly, selling me all her holdings for $1 and then declaring that each player had to pack up their own cash and properties. I quickly learnt to say no when asked if I wanted to play 'Fifty-two pick-up'.

When we did play, I wanted to *win*. And trivia was the one set of games in which I could actively train and improve on my own. We had several trivia games in our house, and I tried to memorise the questions and answers, desperate to give myself an advantage. There was Oz Quiz, a stereotypically Aussie trivia game that came not in a box but a Styrofoam esky and featured a penalty category called 'Up the Creek', printed on brown cards. There was the Sale of the Century board game; even today I recall the specific wording of some of its questions and answers ('What do the initials S.O.S. stand for?[1]').

And, of course, there was Trivial Pursuit, which was much harder for me as a young child. There were more than 6000 questions in Trivial Pursuit, far too many to memorise, and largely targeted to a North American Baby Boomer audience. But certain facts did stick (Where did Maxwell Smart keep his telephone?[2] What was the name of the lioness in *Born Free*?[3]) and I still enjoyed it. As I got older, I liked Trivial Pursuit more and more. It was hard and it stretched my knowledge, but I loved

---

[1]   'Save our souls or ships'. That's exactly how the answer was phrased, and therefore exactly how six-year-old me answered when we played. 'Save our souls or ships.'

[2]   In his shoe

[3]   Which, as you may recall, helped me on *The Weakest Link*.

the thrill of getting a big run of correct answers. I don't recall many specific questions, but one from my later teenage years has stuck in my head: 'How big was Kim Beazley's black hole?'

▼

Bruce Elder lets out a big laugh.

'That's a classic!' he says. 'I don't know whether I was responsible for that or not!'

Chances are he probably was, because for more than twenty years Bruce was the main writer and editor of the Australian questions for local editions of Trivial Pursuit. The size of Kim Beazley's black hole, for the record, was measured not in diameter but in dollars: $8 billion, if memory serves. Beazley had been Labor's finance minister and his so-called 'black hole' was the budget gap new Liberal federal treasurer Peter Costello claimed to have found after taking over the nation's books in 1996. It was also, to my teenage mind, a first-rate double entendre.

'Well, that was part of the deal,' Bruce says. 'You would love to have been able to have written 3000 questions like that, but you never could . . . The silly one was "Where does a Vietnamese put his đồng?" And of course the đồng was the currency[1], and the answer in theory was "In his wallet."'

---

[1]   I remember the Vietnamese currency thanks to an incident at a family board game night. My dad, who is smart but not wild, played the word 'dong' in Scrabble. I asked him what a 'dong' was. He said 'Isn't it what they use to smoke marijuana?' No, Dad, that's a bong. We looked up dong in the dictionary and found that it was nevertheless a legal word: the currency of Vietnam.

It is difficult to convey what a cultural phenomenon Trivial Pursuit was when it arrived in stores in the early 1980s. The game was conceived by two Canadians: Chris Haney, a photo editor for the *Montreal Gazette*, and his friend Scott Abbott, a sportswriter. The creation of the game is the subject of much mythology, but all versions have the same elements: Haney and Abbott decided to play Scrabble one day and either couldn't find the board or couldn't find all the pieces. In some versions, Haney set off to the shops to buy a new set and, upon returning, commented to Abbott that the makers of Scrabble must have made a fortune.

The pair started wondering if they could come up with a board game of their own. Abbott observed that nobody had made a really great trivia game, and they brainstormed some ideas. Within 45 minutes, they had sketched up a prototype of what would become Trivial Pursuit, based around a circular board like a ship's wheel and six question categories. The year was 1979 and they thought they were onto a winner. Two years later, they had written the questions and attracted just enough investors to produce 1000 copies of the game. It was hardly an economy of scale, except in the sense that it cost a lot. The game's high-quality board, cards, box and design meant each copy cost an eye-watering $75 (Canadian) to make. That would be a loss-making operation in 2021, let alone 1981. The investors might have been staring at a budget black hole of their own.

Everything was against Haney and Abbott. The game's cost was outrageous—even selling at a loss, with a $40 price-tag, it was still more than five times dearer than Scrabble. They were rejected at the major toy fairs because video games, not board games, were seen as the future. And anyway, what adult would buy a board game for themselves? With a few older exceptions, such as Scrabble, board games were by 1981 viewed as primarily entertainment for children. But slowly, the initial run of a thousand games sold. And, out of the blue, a Canadian bank manager who played the game and became addicted offered them a loan. Suddenly they could produce another 20,000 copies. And they could make a profit. A huge profit. The cast of the 1983 film *The Big Chill*, the archetypal Baby Boomer ensemble movie, were said to play the game obsessively on set. In 1984, it sold 20 million copies. In the United States, the combined sales of all adult board games in 1983 totalled $142 million. The following year, it was $598 million. That was entirely down to Trivial Pursuit, which tapped into Baby Boomers' craving for nostalgia. Pop culture questions were Trivial Pursuit's bread and butter.

In one famous instance, Trivial Pursuit asked for the first name of the television detective Columbo, played by Peter Falk. The answer: Philip. Haney and Abbott had sourced the information from a popular trivia encyclopedia compiled by American Fred L. Worth. The only problem was, it was wrong[1]. Worth had simply

---

[1]   What was Columbo's real first name? It is generally said that he didn't have one, although in one episode his badge is fleetingly shown and the name scrawled next to it looks like 'Frank Columbo'.

made up the name Philip and planted it deliberately because he was worried someone would steal his trivia and use it for their own profit. A similar idea is used by cartographers, who might insert what is known as a 'trap street' in a city map—a street that does not exist, but which, if reproduced by another map-maker, would prove copyright infringement. Worth took Haney and Abbott to court in California, suing for $300 million, only to have his case thrown out after the judge stated that Trivial Pursuit was 'substantially different' from Worth's encyclopedia. Haney and Abbott did not deny using Worth's book as a source—but then, they used hundreds of sources to compile their 6000 questions. The case was, more or less, a legal confirmation that while a particular presentation or trivia format could be copyrighted, the facts themselves could not.

Nothing could stop Trivial Pursuit, and soon international editions were on the cards, literally. That's where Bruce Elder came in. An Australian who had been the London correspondent for both radio station Double Jay and *Rolling Stone* magazine, Bruce had moved back home to Australia in 1980 and continued to work for Double Jay (by then rebranded as Triple J), doing interviews and generally being part of the furniture of the station. He also continued to write articles and music reviews for *Rolling Stone*; years later, after moving to the *Sydney Morning Herald*, he became the first rock critic to win the Pascall Prize for criticism. But his other main job was teaching English and communication

at TAFE (pop quiz: For what do the initials TAFE stand?[1]),
where he worked with an expat Canadian teacher named Bob
Neilson. Bob was an old friend of Chris Haney and, by a quirk
of fate, ran into Haney again while he and Abbott were writing
the questions for their original version of the game. So, when
they needed content for an Australian release, they asked their
Canadian-Australian buddy, Bob, to write the questions. But Bob
knew his limitations as a relatively new arrival Down Under:
great swathes of Australian history and pop culture were not
part of his knowledge base. But his friend Bruce Elder knew
Australian pop culture back to front and was happy to contribute
questions. Soon, Bob returned to Canada to work on the North
American versions of the game, and Bruce became the main
Australian writer.

When a fresh edition was required, Bruce would be sent
the questions from the new American or British versions. He
would painstakingly read through every question and determine
whether it was suitable for an Australian audience. The process
was computerised from the outset—Bruce would be air-mailed
the questions on five-and-a-half-inch floppy disks and trawl
through them on his Kaypro computer. A high percentage of
the 'Sports and Leisure' questions had to be axed, because they
focused on either North American sports or British soccer. Some
geography questions were too locally American or British, or too

---

[1] Technical and Further Education

easy for an Australian audience (What country would you be in if you whiled away time playing a didjeridoo in Wagga Wagga?[1]). Plenty of the television questions didn't translate. Consider this question from the original edition: 'Who played Mr Peepers?' That's it. No context, no clue to help the player make a plausible guess. For the record, *Mister Peepers* was an American sitcom that centred on a science teacher named Robinson J. Peepers. He was played by Wally Cox. Ever heard of him? Me neither. The show ran from 1952 to 1955; television didn't arrive in Australia until 1956. It was this kind of question Bruce had to cull.

Trivial Pursuit featured six question categories: Geography; Entertainment; History; Arts and Literature; Science and Nature; and Sports and Leisure. Bruce found Science and Nature more difficult to find topics that had not already been covered. I too find science the most challenging subject to write, partly because of the finite number of topics the average person can answer. Often, science enthusiasts find the questions too easy while the rest of the population finds them very hard. Sports and Leisure is also fraught for Australian audiences, which may seem counterintuitive given Australia's famous love of sport.

---

[1] For a city of roughly 70,000 people, Wagga Wagga more than pulls its cultural weight. The Chiko Roll was first sold at the Wagga show in 1951; Dame Edna Everage was supposedly born there; the Eurythmics formed in a Wagga hotel room when Annie Lennox and Dave Stewart, touring with British band The Tourists, decided to become a duo; Australian cricket's opening batters for most of the 1990s, Mark Taylor and Michael Slater, were both from Wagga.

But the split between the rugby league states and the Australian Rules football regions[1] makes it almost impossible to ask about either code.

'Fortunately it was "sport and leisure",' Bruce says, 'so always there were lots of grog questions. How do you make a cocktail, that sort of thing.'

Contrary to popular belief, the point of writing trivia questions is not to stump the audience. Where's the fun in that? The easiest thing for a trivia writer is producing hard questions. The hardest thing is hitting the sweet spot, that zone in which players think, 'I should know this . . .'

'One of my favourites,' Bruce says, 'and this probably sums the process up: What line followed "Goodbye Yellow Brick Road" in Elton John's hit? And people are sitting there going "doo doo doo doo doo dah". And it's such a weird line: "Where the dogs of society howl". And you sort-of know it and you should know it, but you don't know it. I think the great joy is in sort of knowing and saying to yourself that you should know.'

---

[1]   Historian Ian Turner came up with a way of demarcating the zones of Australia by dominant football code: the Barassi Line, named after Aussie rules legend Ron Barassi. It's roughly a straight line from the border of Queensland and the Northern Territory on the Gulf of Carpentaria to the border of Victoria and New South Wales on the Tasman Sea, and while it's not perfect it pretty neatly captures the divide: the territory north-east of the Barassi Line favours rugby league, the land to the south and west prefers Australian rules. Wagga Wagga, incidentally, is smack bang on the Barassi line and thus has produced countless champions of both codes.

Bruce wrote for Trivial Pursuit until 2008, when Haney and Abbott sold the game to the global toy giant Hasbro for $80 million. At the time of the sale, Bruce and all the game's question writers from around the world were invited to the German city of Essen, home of an annual board game fair called Spiel (play), and were asked for ideas about how to take the product forward. But Hasbro decided not to continue with separate national editions of the game. To a multinational company this might have made sense, but Bruce saw the move as folly: how could the same set of questions challenge everyone equally?

That was the end of Bruce's involvement with Trivial Pursuit, a role he had enjoyed for two decades despite being, by his own admission, not a 'trivia person', but his eye for the quirky, his knack for finding useful titbits in sources as diverse as *Encyclopaedia Britannica* and *Who Weekly*, helped make Trivial Pursuit accessible to Australians. Perhaps Bruce's greatest asset was the way he balanced attention to detail and intellectual rigour with not taking the content too seriously. He knows serious topics intimately: he is the author of the highly respected 1988 nonfiction book *Blood on the Wattle*, which drew together all the known details of the massacres of Aboriginal Australians since 1788. That is a subject of such weight that it's hard to imagine the same person pulling questions like 'Who was Princess Diana's secret lover?' from gossip magazines. Bruce sees the value in trivia but is wise enough not to overvalue it.

'Of itself trivia is fun, obviously, people love it,' Bruce says. 'It's become obsessive. I find it very distressing when people want to argue with you about answers and god knows what. You think to yourself, for god's sake, mate, it's trivia, let's not get too worked up about this. And it is essentially useless information, but it's also a very essential aspect of your life. I grew up in the 1950s, and I can still sing an awful lot of the pop songs of that time. And that's part of who I am, and I'm very happy. And if somebody wants to ask me about the next line to "Rock Around the Clock", I'm happy to answer it. It's not terribly important and one should never think that it is important. But it is fun.'

▼

It's not terribly important, but it is fun. They are wise words. Whenever someone asks me if I enjoy working on *The Chase*, my standard response is: 'Of course—I get to play games for a living!' Never in my wildest dreams would I have imagined I could be paid to play trivia. The fact that such a job does exist is faintly ridiculous. But, then, is it any more preposterous than two Canadian guys making tens of millions from asking 'What colour is Mr Spock's blood?[1]'

Trivial Pursuit made quizzing accessible to the average person. You didn't have to be Barry Jones. In fact, it helped *not* to be Barry Jones—I'm not sure how he'd go at the entertainment and sports and leisure categories. The game redefined the term 'general

---

[1]   Green

knowledge' to refer to the everyday memories and minutiae that the average person picks up just from living in the modern world. Haney and Abbott helped introduce pop culture to quizzing, and the genre has not been the same since. I don't see that as quizzing being dumbed down, but rather opened up.

CHAPTER 10

PUB SCRAWL

'STELLA LASHES. WHAT DO WE THINK, TEAM?'

I'm sitting at the Skinny Dog Hotel in Kew, sipping a pint of beer, discussing an important pub trivia question with my team-mates: my then-girlfriend-now-wife Zoe, my oldest mate Ben, and his then-girlfriend-now-wife Louise. The year is 2011. We're all in our late twenties. It's more than a decade since I won three nights on *Sale of the Century*, eight years since I scored $32,000 on *Who Wants To Be a Millionaire?* And now here I am, trying to decide whether Stella Lashes is the name of a porn star or a My Little Pony. How has my quizzing career come to this? What am I doing here? At least I can answer that question. I'm having fun. Lots and lots of fun.

▼

I might have a pretty good quizzing résumé, but it also contains a large gap. For eight years after my *Who Wants To Be a Millionaire?* experience in 2003, I didn't do much quizzing at all. At least, not much organised quizzing. I still played trivia board games with my family, and I remember one Christmas gathering was dominated by *Buzz!*, the PlayStation quiz show game where the host was voiced by Jason Donovan. One year, I joined Ben's team at his cricket club trivia night and, in a round where we had to match celebrities with their real names, I nailed twenty out of twenty. The host must have thought I was cheating.

In 2011, Ben, Louise, Zoe and I started catching up semi-regularly for pub trivia at the Skinny Dog Hotel. The host was an entertaining character named Rob Coslovich, and we often got chatting after the quiz was over. Rob knew that I had a background as both a game show winner and journalist, so when I showed some interest in contributing questions, he put in a good word for me with Pete Curry, the co-founder of Quiz Meisters, the company that ran the Skinny Dog quiz. It was the beginning of a two-and-a-half-year sideline for me as a pub quiz writer. Roughly once a month, Pete would ask me for a batch of 100 questions, which Quiz Meisters would put into their trivia nights. I loved the work, because it didn't feel like work. The only downside was I had torpedoed our weekly social catch-ups. We couldn't very well play the quizzes if I was writing them.

Not surprisingly, pub trivia has its origins in the UK. In his excellent 2016 book *The Joy of Quiz*, British television quiz show writer Alan Connor dates it to the 1940s, when women's institutes and mothers' unions would organise wholesome quiz events at local halls, probably inspired by the popular radio quiz shows. Quizzes found their way into pubs, where publicans were keen to bring in patrons on quieter nights. The idea became big business in the 1980s when publicans Sharon Burns and Tom Porter started supplying questions for pubs all over Britain. At their peak, more than 10,000 teams across the country were answering questions by Burns and Porter. The organised pub league concept has remained popular in Britain, although there are also vast numbers of more casual pub quizzes, as is the norm in Australia.

'If the British style was brought in here, I think a lot of Aussies would get quite a shock,' says my *Chase* colleague Issa Schultz, who grew up in the UK. 'It's quite formal. There are many, many leagues all over the country that have a formal structure: this many weeks, turn up on time, four players a side. It would be quite alarming. Here it's play with your mates at the pub, chime in with an answer.'

One of the oldest pub trivia companies in Australia, Fame Trivia, started in 1988, and by the early 1990s pub trivia had become a fad. A 1994 article in the *Sydney Morning Herald* explored the trend, noting that, 'This new form of nightlife is attracting all types of people, from children to grandparents to high level executives.' A 1995 episode of the ABC medical drama *G.P.* showed the doctors and practice staff competing in a pub trivia competition under the team name Neo Cortex. Clearly it was a big part of the urban culture of the era.

These days, Fame Trivia boasts not only 100-plus shows every week across Australia, but responsibility for more than thirty marriages of couples who met at Fame Trivia nights. For the venues and the trivia companies, pub quizzes are good business; for the punters who come along to play, it's a fun social event and an excuse to catch up with friends. It can also be profitable: some Fame venues offer a jackpot in the hundreds of dollars, which can be collected by any team that correctly answers one final series of three difficult questions.

Quiz Meisters was born out of Fame Trivia. Melbourne mates Pete Curry and Steffan van Lint were hosting pub quizzes for Fame and, while the events brought in plenty of business—the whole point from the pubs' perspective—Pete and Steffan felt a little out of touch with some of the content. They were only 23 years old, yet found themselves asking questions about music and pop culture from the 1960s and 1970s to people who had lived through that era. It was the equivalent of me at nine years old reading 'Who played Mister Peepers?' off a Trivial Pursuit card. Inspiration struck. Why couldn't they start their own pub trivia business aimed at a younger audience?

Pete and Steffan set out to bring pub trivia into the twenty-first century. There was—and still is—a high degree of audiovisual content involved in Quiz Meisters nights, and I don't mean the typical printed sheet where you name the famous faces. Every third question was an audiovisual one that appeared on a television screen in the venue, and these were inventive, unique concepts that could only have been conjured by creative minds. Quiz Meisters redefined the pub trivia experience.

As a punter, one of my favourite rounds was 'Opera Boy', which featured video of actor Chris Ryan (who later played the key role of Jack Driscoll in the world premiere of the *King Kong* musical) singing the lyrics to a pop song in operatic style. Teams had to guess the song—and it's surprisingly hard to identify Justin Timberlake's 'SexyBack' or LMFAO's 'Party Rock Anthem' when performed as if by Pavarotti. There was also 'Name These Films', in which Quiz Meisters staff dressed in neutral, everyday clothes and re-enacted a famous film scene deliberately poorly. Dolly Parton once said 'It costs a lot of money to look this cheap'; likewise, I think it took a lot of talent for the Quiz Meisters crew to make slick content like 'Name These Films' appear amateurish.

In another popular round, video footage of a small Daewoo Matiz car was shown on screen. As the Matiz drove past the stationary camera, you heard a song blaring from the car radio, and then the music faded out again as the car disappeared. The question was, could you pick the song from that brief and bizarre snippet? Then there was Porn Star or Pony—you'd be amazed how many My Little Pony characters sound like they should be porn stars. Rodger Doger. Ruby Splash. Steel Buns. And, yes, Stella Lashes. Eschewing things like the traditional pub trivia 'heads or tails' event, Quiz Meisters secured the non-exclusive rights from Nintendo to use Mario Kart footage in their quizzes;

teams had to bet on which character they thought would win the pre-recorded race.

It was, in essence, closer to a television show than traditional pub trivia. Some of the rounds you could have imagined featuring in a comedy quiz show like *Spicks and Specks*. The high ratio of this creative content also made cheating hard, which could be an issue in pub trivia in the smartphone era. How could you cheat with Opera Boy? You certainly couldn't Shazam the song. Maybe you could write down the lyrics and try to google them, but by the time you went to the trouble, the host and other teams would have moved on. There was no possible way to cheat with a game called Jacko Surgery, in which Michael Jackson's face slowly morphed into that of another mystery celebrity and the first team to text the correct name to the host's phone won a prize.

Of course, there was also plenty of regular trivia. Quiz Meisters deliberately avoided themed rounds such as sport or geography or film, knowing that some patrons tended to switch off if they had no interest in a particular topic. Steffan and Pete wanted their punters to stay engaged. And their offbeat content was perfect for engaging the gap in the pub trivia market: the eighteen- to thirty-year-olds.

Another key was finding the right hosts, and Quiz Meisters presenters tended to be young aspiring comedians, actors and entertainers—people for whom a paid gig hosting live trivia was more valuable experience than stacking shelves or waiting tables. Comedian Dave Warneke, who created and co-hosts one of my favourite podcasts, the hilarious and informative *Do Go On*, cut his teeth hosting more than a thousand trivia nights for Quiz Meisters over a six-year period starting when he was twenty. Many were pub quizzes but there were also corporate trivia events, including one for the Hawthorn Football Club, and another in front of 600 chartered accountants at Crown Casino. Dave says these experiences greatly improved his stage presence and gave him the confidence to stand up with a microphone in front of anyone.

Quiz Meisters became more popular than Steffan and Pete could ever have imagined, and by 2019 they were the biggest pub trivia operator in Australia, with 130 shows across all eight states and territories. They even expanded to Penang and Boston.

Competitors emerged. One is QuizzaMe, whose quizzes don't require pen and paper. Instead, teams are provided with an electronic device with buttons labelled A, B, C, D and E, and answer multiple-choice questions each worth 1000 points—the faster you lock in a correct answer, the more points you earn, but the faster you lock in an incorrect answer, the more points you lose. The concept has been successful: in 2019, QuizzaMe held an end-of-year final in which more than 380 players across 76 teams competed for a pool of $10,000. The winning team, who called themselves Vandelay Industries (a reference from which television show?[1]), collected a cool $3000.

---

[1] *Seinfeld*. George's regular alias when he was up to some questionable scheme was Art Vandelay, who of course ran Vandelay Industries.

The QuizzaMe approach strikes me as a tempting concept, because I love buzzer quizzes. But the need for speed, and the fact that one person per table is most likely holding the buzzer and doing the answering, means that questions can't be discussed at length. In my opinion, the fun of a trivia night is figuring out an answer together. As Bruce Elder noted, one of the great joys of trivia is thinking 'I should know this', and gradually working it out.

Finding the right balance of questions is one of the challenges in any quiz. You can barrage punters with impossible questions that make them feel dumb, but they won't come back. When I started writing for Quiz Meisters, I was told about the 70 per cent rule: if teams were getting about 70 per cent of answers correct, the quiz universe was in perfect equilibrium. Not that I had to worry about that per se; I just sent in what I thought were fun questions for the audience (Who are the only two people mentioned in the first line of the first Harry Potter book[1]? What is the only James Bond film with a six-word title?[2]) and Quiz Meisters did the rest.

There is one experience that Quiz Meisters brought me for which I'm especially grateful. In 2017, I introduced Pete and Steffan to my then nineteen-year-old nephew Ben, who was studying journalism like I had, and was keen to host pub trivia for extra pocket money. Ben was soon writing questions and in

---

[1]   Mr and Mrs Dursley, Harry's aunt and uncle

[2]   *The Man with the Golden Gun*

2019 he, Quiz Meisters and I worked together on a very cool project: we provided the trivia questions for the bottle caps of Carlton Draught beer. It was great fun working with my nephew on a trivia job, and it gave me a buzz to be able to flick the top off a cold beer and see our questions. The project also highlighted the importance of proofreading. When I gave the caps one final check before they were printed, I found that the answers to two questions had been accidentally transposed. As a result, 'Morphine is derived from what natural source?' had the answer 'Baking soda'[1]. No wonder I always felt sleepy after a big afternoon tea of cake and biscuits.

The Carlton Draught project came shortly before COVID-19 reshaped the world, and, like all industries based around hospitality, pub trivia suffered tremendously. Many pub trivia operators tried to take their shows online, but it was hard to make money that way. The typical pub trivia business model is that a venue pays the quiz provider for putting on a show that will bring in punters on an otherwise quiet night. Online shows did, however, have the potential to broaden the audience, because people could play from anywhere.

Many quizzes found enormous audiences online. Melbourne couple Michael and Erin Nunan created 'Locked Down Trivia', which ran online each week that Melbourne was under lockdown

---

[1]   Baking soda was the answer to the question: 'Sodium bicarbonate is better known as what?' The answer to the morphine question should have been 'Opium poppies'.

during 2020 and 2021. At its peak, the quiz had 670 households from around the world logging in. It was initially conceived as a one-off fundraising project for the Nunans' local childcare centre, but quickly ballooned. Over 42 weeks of lockdowns, the Nunans raised a phenomenal $287,000 through voluntary donations, which they distributed among more than 100 charities and organisations. Their local council named the Nunans the Darebin Community Group of the Year.

'I don't think it really occurred to us until the final few weeks, when we started to get messages, how much it had meant to people,' Michael Nunan said on ABC Radio Melbourne in October 2021. 'We knew that a lot of families were playing as families, and this was their way of catching up for the week. There might be ten houses all joined together as a team. Some of the messages we've had in the last few weeks have been so amazing and unexpected—people who were struggling with their mental health, or who had kids that were missing school so much.'

Meanwhile, for professional trivia operators, there was still *some* money to be made, because companies were looking for morale-boosting team-building activities that could be done remotely. The big pub quiz operators run one-off corporate events and fundraisers in addition to weekly pub trivia, and this could be transferred online in some capacity, at least. Quizzing as a pastime seemed to boom during lockdowns, with trivia apps such as Kahoot becoming popular to use for Zoom parties and get-togethers.

Trivia is always evolving for new media and fresh ideas, but I don't see the various parts of the industry cannibalising each other. New parents are often told that sleep promotes sleep. I suspect that quiz promotes quiz. I hope that pub quiz companies not only survive but thrive after the massive interruptions caused by COVID-19. And I hope that quiz fans find the format that suits them best. For me, in my late twenties, that was Quiz Meisters. For some it will be QuizzaMe. For others it will be classic pub quizzes. Whatever form it takes, call your friends, put together a team, and get out there and have some fun.

CHAPTER 11

ANOTHER SHOT AT A MILLION

NOT FOR A MOMENT DO I FORGET HOW FORTUNATE I WAS TO LAND MY dream job as a cricket reporter. Within a month of starting at Cricinfo, I was playing beach cricket in Goa with Greg Chappell, who was a guest at a Cricinfo editorial conference. I once answered my phone to hear, in that iconic voice, 'Hello Brydon, it's Richie Benaud here.' In Abu Dhabi, I saw Pakistan's Misbah-ul-Haq equal Viv Richards' 30-year-old record for the fastest Test hundred, and a year later I was in Christchurch to witness Brendon McCullum break that record. Cricket tours allowed me to see some of the world's most incredible sights: the Taj Mahal, Cape Town's Table Mountain, the Red Fort in Delhi.

Which brings me to Northampton's three-star Park Inn by Radisson, a middling hotel in a middle-sized town in the middle of the Midlands of England: as well as the killer sights, cricket tours also offered plenty of filler. I was there in the middle of an Ashes series in August 2013 to watch Australia play a practice match that was as pointless as a broken pencil: England was 3–0 up and had already won the Ashes. Still, I enjoyed the atmosphere of a quiet county cricket ground and the camaraderie of the other Australian reporters on tour. One of the great things about the cricket media is that, despite working for competing news organisations, the journalists inevitably help each other out and enjoy a convivial drink together at the end of the day. When I returned to my room at the Park Inn one evening, a couple of beers worse for wear, I was jolted out of my mid-tour reverie when I checked my email: a new quiz show was coming to Australian television, and I had an audition date.

It had been ten years since I had appeared on a quiz show, but that was through lack of opportunity, not lack of interest. The only game show that I had competed on was *Letters and Numbers*, the SBS adaptation of the long-running British show *Countdown*. In terms of prizes, if *Who Wants To Be a Millionaire?* was a quiz show on steroids then *Letters and Numbers* was a game show on Valium. The only prize was a *Macquarie Dictionary* signed by the show's hosts, and every contestant received one whether they won or lost. But to be fair, I've used the *Macquarie Dictionary* a hell of a lot more than that box of wet tyre shine from *Pass the Buck*.

The show was based around anagrams and basic algebra. Contestants had to find the longest word they could from a set of nine letters, and then hit a random numerical target using only six specific numbers and the four basic maths operations: addition, subtraction, multiplication and division. That was it. Letters. And numbers. It did what it said on the tin. I decided to have a crack in 2011 because I enjoyed wordplay and anagrams. I was only average at maths but hoped for a passable performance in the numbers games. As it happened, I won six consecutive episodes to become a 'retiring champion'. My abiding memory after retiring was nipping off to the toilets backstage where, as I washed my hands, the host Richard Morecroft came in, stepped up to the urinal and said over his shoulder: 'Ah, Brydon. Congratulations. I hope we'll see you again in a champions' tournament at the end of the season.' He said it in such a perfectly modulated newsreader voice that I had to double-check there was no autocue and camera in the men's room.

Richard was joined on the show by co-hosts Lily Serna, a mathematician who could manipulate the numbers in ways my mind couldn't comprehend, and wordsmith David Astle, a cruciverbalist[1] whose cryptic crosswords in *The Age* and the *Sydney Morning Herald* were so dastardly that for readers his by-line initials, DA, were said to stand for 'Don't Attempt'. In recent years, David has hosted the evening show on ABC Radio Melbourne, and I have been a semi-regular guest, sharing our interest in quirky stories from history.

I should have known that someone with David's curiosity would also have been a quizzer and, indeed, he had been a *Sale*

---

[1]   Aka a crossword compiler.

of the Century contestant in his youth. In 1981, when he was nineteen or twenty, David had flown from Sydney to Melbourne to compete on the show, despite looking, in his own words, 'like Frankenstein's monster fresh off the slab' after suffering a nasty facial injury playing rugby. David was vanquished by Vincent Smith, the school teacher from Sale (not *Sale*) who was the first contestant to win the lot. Unable to match the buzzer speed of such a champion, David finished on $15—quite an effort, since the starting score was $20.

'I felt a bit like roadkill,' David says. 'And I looked like roadkill, too.'

That wasn't David's only quiz show experience. At forty, he was one of the brave souls who risked losing dignity on *Shafted* with Red Symons, again winning no money. At the time of writing, they are David Astle's only game show appearances as a contestant, although he must be due for his vicennial[1] attempt to win big on television. See how useful that *Letters and Numbers* prize has been: I can use big words like 'vicennial' because I can look them up in a *Macquarie Dictionary* signed by David Astle.

Letters and Numbers gave me a glimpse of how tricky it could be to juggle game show appearances and a full-time job (which might also explain why many people turn up for quiz shows having done little preparation). As foreshadowed by Richard Morecroft at the urinal (one of the strangest things I've ever typed), I was invited back for a champions' tournament. But

---

[1]   Occurring every twenty years.

it was filmed on 19 August, the day Cricket Australia released findings from the so-called Argus Report into the failings of the national team. It was a major cricket news story happening in Melbourne, and I was Cricinfo's Melbourne correspondent. I called in a favour from my Sydney-based colleague Daniel Brettig, who agreed to cover the news conference off television. But I was utterly distracted on the morning of my *Letters and Numbers* quarterfinal, knowing that if I won the game and had to stay for a semifinal I would certainly miss the afternoon news conference. Not surprisingly, I played a fairly mediocre game and lost—but at least it allowed me time to do my job.

Cricket also got in the way of me auditioning for *Million Dollar Minute*, the show that popped up in my email when I was in Northampton. I had seen Channel Seven advertise a 'brand new quiz show' before I flew to England, so I sent off an email expressing interest. But I couldn't audition until I was back in Melbourne, so I had to decline the first invitation. Then a second. And a third. With every missed audition, I became more and more worried I would miss out. New game shows in Australia had an unfortunate habit of disappearing quickly and if I didn't get to an audition soon, I might be too late. Zoe and I were also planning our October wedding and a month-long honeymoon in North America, so my *Million Dollar Minute* window was very narrow. For years I had waited for a show that combined my quizzing strength—buzzer speed and anticipation—with a huge cash jackpot. *Million Dollar Minute* was that show; to miss out would have been devastating.

In early September, shortly before the show premiered, I made it to an audition and did well, but there was no chance I would be called up until after our honeymoon. On its debut night, 16 September, *Million Dollar Minute* rated extremely well, but the numbers dropped sharply on night two, and by its third night it was being beaten by Channel Nine's *Millionaire Hot Seat*. This was a worrying sign, but the show ticked over for a few months, even surviving the early resignation of the host, Grant Denyer, who was replaced by Simon Reeve. And then, in early January, I got the call-up. For the first time in more than a decade, I would be on a show that offered greater reward than a dictionary. I was pleased I hadn't made it on earlier, because a tweak to the rules had made it a lot easier to win big money.

The basic premise was similar to *Sale*: three contestants, buzzers, five points for a correct answer and five points off for a wrong answer. In the final 'Double-Points Decider' round, correct answers earned ten points and incorrect answers resulted in being locked out from the next question. The key difference from *Sale* was that cash was the only prize. The leading player after round one was offered $2000, but they had to give up their lead, their score dropping to that of their nearest opponent. A similar offer was made after round two, but for $5000. Each episode also included two multiple-choice 'Snapshot' questions that allowed a player the choice between $1500 cash and 15 points onto their score.

The winning contestant played one final solo round, in which five multiple-choice questions were asked in 60 seconds—the titular million-dollar minute. Should a contestant answer all five correctly, he or she advanced up the cash jackpot ladder: $20,000 on the first night, then $50,000; $75,000; $100,000; $200,000; $300,000; $500,000; and $1,000,000. Theoretically, it could take as few as eight nights to win $1 million. But here was the catch: a single incorrect answer among those final five questions meant you stayed in your current position on the cash ladder. And you could only choose to walk away immediately after securing one of the cash amounts. So for example, if I won the $50,000 I could take my cash and leave, but if I chose to play on, I was locked in for as long as it took to either win the $75,000 or get beaten. It was entirely possible for a contestant to win episode after episode after episode, yet advance nowhere.

To me, the cash ladder idea seemed flawed, because without any safe level, there was too much risk involved in playing for the higher amounts. At any time, you could crash back down to zero. Not surprisingly, in the first few months, nobody went further than the $100,000 level. The producers realised they would never give away a million dollars with the existing format. So they turned $75,000 into a safe level, much like the $32,000 on *Who Wants To Be a Millionaire?* I couldn't believe my luck: if I could reach the third step on the ladder, the minimum I would win was $75,000.

I arrived at the studio in a confident frame of mind. I had done minimal preparation, although I refreshed my buzzer skills by recording *Million Dollar Minute* at home and pressing pause when I would have buzzed in. If the lights on the contestant podiums hadn't come on, I had beaten them. I'm hopeless at long-view strategy games like chess, and even Connect Four, because I can't see further ahead than the current move. But I have a well-honed sense for where a question is going. These traits also manifest themselves away from quizzing: if Zoe tries to explain how we might renovate our house, I can never picture her grand vision, but I will jump in and try to finish her sentences, often incorrectly.

As with *Sale*, I didn't film my first episode until late in the afternoon, the fourth of five shows filmed that day. But there was no studio audience and waiting contestants were sequestered in a green room without television screens and thus no idea of how episodes were playing out. Losing contestants came back to collect their things and gave a brief update to everyone else. It meant the carry-over champion had the advantage of feeling at home while the challengers came in cold—literally. I walked into the freezing, cavernous studio, along with my fellow challenger, a middle-aged woman named Pat, to face a young carry-over champion named Anthony, who had won the $20,000 and was playing for $50,000. As I sat down and placed my hands on the buzzer, I felt completely in my element.

Watching the episode back, I'm struck by how often I was able to buzz in early and correctly judge what was about to be asked. When Simon Reeve began, 'The early stages of Dan Brown's novel *The Da Vinci Code* are set—', I buzzed, recalling the book that I had read ten years earlier. The novel opened with the discovery of a body in the Louvre, but the question might have asked for the museum, the city or the country. In a split second, I reasoned that if I was asking this question, Paris and France would be less interesting answers, so I correctly answered 'Louvre'. Likewise, 'Which former Beatle narrated TV's—' had to be referring to *Thomas the Tank Engine*, so I buzzed and nailed the answer[1].

On *Million Dollar Minute*, my anticipation didn't always pay off. When asked 'What was the maiden name of Sarah Murdoch?[2]' I buzzed as Simon said 'Sarah Murdoch', confident that I would probably know the maiden surname of any woman famous enough to be the subject of a question. And I did know it, deep down, but I couldn't unlock the correct drawer from my memory. Many contestants are too worried about looking silly to take a risk unless they are certain of the answer, and that's understandable. Nobody *wants* to look silly on national television. But that has never concerned me. I know the viewers will simply move on to the next question, so I do, too. As ice hockey great Wayne Gretzky once said, you miss 100 per cent of the shots you don't take.

Occasionally my timing was off, as when Simon began a question with: 'The line "Out, damned spot!"—'. I buzzed, then realised that I didn't know if he wanted the name of the character or the play. So, I gave him both, by answering: 'Spoken by Lady Macbeth in *Macbeth*', and was marked correct. Despite being agnostic, I nailed 'What name applies to the Biblical land Cain

---

[1] Ringo Starr

[2] O'Hare

was exiled to—'[1] because I remembered having written the same question as *Sale* practice for Paul, thirteen years earlier.

I won the episode on a score of 130 points, to Anthony on 50 and Pat on 45. I had taken the $2000 as the leader after the first round; I wanted to make sure I left with *something*. The five questions in the million-dollar minute proved no problem, and $20,000 was mine. But my goal was the safe level, so I risked my $20,000 to come back and play the final episode of the filming day.

Facing me was one of my toughest challengers, Kirsty Seebeck, who was quick on the buzzer and very knowledgeable. The scores were up and down—Kirsty took the $2000 as the leader after the first round, and I took the $5000 after the second, to give me $7000 of safe money. I won the game on a score of 140, with Kirsty on 90 and the third contestant, Michael, on 25. That may look convincing; in reality, the scoreline gave me a scare. In the double-points round, Kirsty and I had often pressed our buzzers at much the same time; had she pipped me three more times, I would have finished on 110 to her 120. I had effectively only won by three questions, which was too close for comfort[2].

---

[1] The Land of Nod. The remainder of the *Million Dollar Minute* question, which Simon completed after I had given the correct answer, was: '. . . and a mythical land of sleep?'

[2] I made a mistake by answering 'Two' when asked how many humps a dromedary camel has, and I've since learnt an easy memory tool: dromedary camels have one hump, and their body resembles a D standing on its side, whereas Bactrian camels have two humps, and their body looks like a sideways B.

As I walked out of the studio that evening, having secured $50,000 and chosen to play on, Zoe was waiting to pick me up on her way home from work. The contestant coordinator, Ben, walked me to the car. 'I think your husband is going to win a lot of money,' he told her. I hoped he was right. But Zoe and I had some decisions to make. I would be back in the studio the next morning, and I needed a plan. The burning question was this: How far was I prepared to go?

▼

Lisa Paton still remembers her regret at knocking back $50,000 on *Million Dollar Minute*.

'I didn't have a lot of money,' Lisa recalls. 'I had debt, and I'd turned down the $50,000. I was lying in bed [a few hours later] thinking, "Oh, $50,000 would actually solve all my problems. I'm such an idiot. I've fluked getting this far, but what was I thinking?"'

A few days later, Lisa passed the $75,000 safe level and then turned down $100,000. Also $200,000. Then $300,000. In less than a week of filming, she became the first contestant in the short history of the show to reject half-a-million dollars, in order to play on for the chance at a million.

'I got past the safe stage of the $75,000,' Lisa says, 'and kind of thought, "Oh, well, may as well keep going."'

It took incredible courage for Lisa to break new ground as the first contestant to play for $1 million, even with the safety

net. Rob Fulton and Martin Flood had won the top prize on
Who Wants To Be a Millionaire?, but they took that risk having
seen a single million-dollar question, with the option to pull out
at any stage. A buzzer quiz against unknown opponents was
completely different, and nobody had yet won a million dollars
in such circumstances. There was no way for Lisa to know who
might be coming through the studio door: it could have been
the next Barry Jones or Cary Young. She couldn't know how
many attempts she might need to win the million: it might take
two or three or four or five episodes. It could take twenty. But
just as Martin Flood applied an unusual method to *Millionaire*
by studying the show for five years, Lisa's approach to *Million
Dollar Minute* was equally remarkable: when she was called up,
she had never even watched an episode.

'It was interesting on the first day,' Lisa says. 'All the contestants came in at some ridiculously early hour, and they're all
talking about all the planning they've done and the training,
and they're all sitting there reading their reference books and
looking at things on their phone. I remember then thinking,
"Oh, maybe I should have done a bit more. Oh, well. It doesn't
really matter. I'm doing it for fun." It was all a bit silly really
that I hadn't considered doing any work. Before I auditioned,
I'd never even watched the show. I didn't really know it at all.
After the audition, after they contacted me to say, "Could you
come in for a filming?" I watched two episodes then.'

Lisa only auditioned because a friend was trying out, and
she thought she might as well come along and have a go. She

had been a contestant on *Temptation* five or six years earlier, but had been very nervous and finished third. *Million Dollar Minute* wasn't on her radar. But in a strange way, the absence of preparation and lack of emotional energy helped her relax. She won her first episode in a close finish, and secured the $20,000. Then she won her second and the $50,000. Then what she was risking started to sink in.

Unusually, Lisa's entire run of thirteen episodes was filmed in a week. The effect of this was twofold. It meant she didn't have much time to think about her strategy. It also left her exhausted. A full day of quiz show filming is completely draining, physically, mentally and emotionally. Lisa had two full days of five episodes each, bookended by two days on which she filmed one or two episodes. It was like having thirteen high school exams back-to-back. Could she win the million before the adrenaline ran out?

The big-money decisions occurred on Lisa's third day of filming. After winning the third episode of that day, she secured $500,000 and could have quit, as former Models bassist Pierre Sutcliffe had done a few weeks earlier. But Lisa, riding the wave and treating every win as a bonus, played on. Why not? While she won the next episode, she couldn't nail all five questions in the minute. The same thing happened in the final episode of the day. Two shots at the million; two wins; two missed opportunities. She was stuck in a loop: playing, winning, missing. Not surprisingly, that night Lisa hardly slept.

Lisa's journey towards $1 million made for compelling television, not just because she was the first to take the plunge, but because nearly all the biggest winners on *Million Dollar Minute* were men. The same was true of *Who Wants To Be a Millionaire?* and *Sale of the Century*, although its twenty-year run gave it time to find plenty of legendary female players as well. But there was no doubt that Lisa Paton, a 38-year-old single mother, was far from a typical champion. Not surprisingly, Channel Seven gave heavy promotion to her push for the million, and the fact that her eleven-year-old daughter Caitlin had encouraged her to go all the way.

'I'm a single parent,' Lisa says. 'Most of my life has been the two of us. We're kind of a bit of a team. She was certainly in my mind. I was also thinking about things like financial security for us and what we could do with the money together. She was definitely part of the motivation, but I do think it was probably overplayed, which is fine, because I also understood that it's unusual for a woman to get that far. They loved the story of this single mother overcoming the odds. I can see how that was appealing and kind of inspirational for the audience … That's probably a big part of why I was so popular on the show, and why they pumped up the advertising: because I wasn't a middle-aged man. It was different, which I think is interesting, because they obviously struggle to get women to audition, or women just aren't interested in it. I don't know what it is.'

▼

The contestant mix at quiz show auditions is not a 50-50 split and never has been. When I first tried out for *Sale of the Century* in 2000, more than 100 people auditioned, and I counted only ten women. Surprisingly, when I auditioned for *Million Dollar Minute* in 2013, the numbers were much the same. To a female family member who was thinking about applying, I emailed: 'You definitely should have a go. It was about 90% men at my audition so they might fast-track women on to the show.'

Why should this be? I can't answer that, but the gender mix at my regular Quiz Meisters pub trivia nights had always seemed fairly even. So why do men apply for quiz shows in far greater numbers? Research has found that men tend to overestimate their skills more than women, and I wonder if that plays some role. There is also the question of spare time. The most recent 'How Australians Use Their Time' survey by the Australian Bureau of Statistics revealed that in 2006, women spent far more time than men on domestic tasks such as housework and caring for children, whereas men devoted, on average, 32 more minutes per day to leisure activities than women. That imbalance equates to nearly four fewer hours per week that women were spending on leisure activities than men.

My fellow Chaser Cheryl Toh, known as the 'Tiger Mum', a long-time player of pub trivia in Sydney, has observed that men tend to outnumber women two to one at the venues she has frequented.

'Speaking very generally, my experience is that many men tend to be more interested in things and facts,' Cheryl says, 'while many women tend to be more interested in people and relationships—an observation which is consistent with data from studies conducted by psychologists and social scientists. Most men also gravitate towards "shoulder-to-shoulder" activities[1] and team trivia is an excellent example. It's not a question of intelligence or ability but rather interest. Based on my experience, I also think there is still a "confidence gap" between men and women. I have noticed in various workplaces and also on *The Chase Australia* that many extremely capable women are prone to underplaying their talents, performance and achievements—I've seen less of that with men.'

Of course, the issue of whether women are less likely to show off their intellect is a much bigger question than just quiz shows. According to the 2016 census, women accounted for only 15 per cent of Australia's CEOs and one-third of the nation's politicians. And consider game show hosts: it took until 2001 for women—Kerri-Anne Kennerley on *Greed* and Cornelia Frances on *The Weakest Link*—to finally host a quiz show, as opposed to being the co-host (think Dolly Dyer helping her husband Bob with the prizes on *Pick a Box*, or Adriana Xenides turning the letters on *Wheel of Fortune*).

There have always been champion female contestants—in 1959, Leah Andrew, described as a 'Melbourne housewife', became one of the earliest long-running *Pick a Box* winners on television.

---

[1]   Examples of shoulder-to-shoulder friendship activities include watching a football game or playing in a team—things that men have traditionally done. The focus is the activity more than the other person. By comparison, face-to-face activities are literally that—looking at the other person and talking to them about life, feelings and all that stuff from which men stereotypically shy away.

When I think of the great champions on *Sale* and *Temptation*, many outstanding women come to mind: Virginia Noel, Fran Powell, Maria McCabe, Kate Buckingham, Sandra Oxley, Louise Williams, Brigid O'Connor, Yolanda Stopar and many others. But the numbers have never been even. A 1998 *Sydney Morning Herald* article titled 'It's almost male of the Century' quoted *Sale* producer Michael Whyte as saying that only 35 per cent of the show's applicants were women. The article also noted that of the 142 grand champions during its then eighteen-year run, only 32 were women.

Anecdotally, I've heard from female contestant coordinators that women have traditionally been more likely to audition for less serious 'game shows' as opposed to quiz shows. A show like *The Price Is Right*, for example, was all about household products and some women have historically felt more comfortable in that space. A former *Deal or No Deal* producer told me that roughly three-quarters of applicants for that show were women. That was a virtual mirror image of quiz show auditions, although contestant coordinators are seeing a change in the demographic, observing greater numbers of women—particularly younger women—applying for quiz shows. Again, that reflects societal trends, with the gender balance slowly closing in some traditionally male-dominated industries, such as STEM (science, technology, engineering and mathematics).

Of course, there is more to representation on quiz and game shows than the male–female divide. These shows are a microcosm of society, and ours is a society that has been inevitably

shaped by the White Australia policy, which for most of the twentieth century restricted non-white people from immigrating to
Australia. It was only in the late 1960s and early 1970s that these
policies were gradually dismantled, leading to far greater immi-
gration diversity. Naturally, the make-up of Australia's society
has historically been reflected on television, which meant that
quiz and game shows were mostly populated by white contestants
for the first few decades.

'Going on a TV show can be a daunting experience, akin to
public speaking,' Cheryl Toh says. 'Many early migrants would
have spoken English as a second, third or fourth language—this
might have put some of them off applying to appear on TV. Even
migrants with perfect English were probably not initially well
versed in Aussie pop culture, sports, politics, slang and other
topics that come up on Australian quiz shows.

'But I think the main reason is best illustrated by my father's
example and a hierarchy of priorities. He arrived in Australia
speaking the Queen's English, having been taught by British
teachers in Malaya. A Fulbright Scholar and very well read, he
has always been extremely knowledgeable. However, he had
three main goals upon migrating: to establish his career here,
provide well for his family and ensure that his children received
an excellent education. I say with immense gratitude and admir-
ation that he successfully achieved all three. For Dad and most
migrants of his era, I don't think going on quiz shows, or any
TV shows, was on the radar—explaining the rarity of non-white
contestants in the 1970s and 1980s.'

Things started to change in the late 1990s, when some second-generation Australians began to appear on the shows they had grown up watching. Cheryl Toh was one such contestant, winning $75,000 on *Million Dollar Minute* before joining the cast of *The Chase Australia*.

'For these contestants there's no language barrier and no problem with knowledge of Australiana,' Cheryl says. 'Their outlook is also usually a little different from their parents' or grandparents'. I hope that one day Australian quizzers of all races and cultural backgrounds will feel equally confident in applying for quiz shows, and I also hope to see more Indigenous contestants on our quiz shows.'

Cheryl believes that Australia has made significant progress in better representing a diverse society in the mainstream media. Roughly half of Australia's population are either born overseas or have at least one parent who was born overseas.

'I was a teenager before I saw an Asian on an Australian TV show—Ling-Hsueh Tang on *All Saints* in 1998,' Cheryl says. 'Chris Ho was the first Asian contestant I saw on an Australian quiz show, back in 1999. I remember these moments clearly because these trailblazers made a deep impression on me. It's human nature to want acceptance, acknowledgement and a sense of belonging in the community or country that you live in. Representation in the media reinforces all of these concepts. Currently I am the only chaser who is an Australian woman, a mother and of non-Anglo-Celtic descent. So if my work on *The Chase Australia* has made any girl, woman, mother or non-white

Australian feel more included in our wonderful society, or inspired to give trivia and quiz shows a go, that's a great honour and one for which I'm grateful.'

I was in awe of Cheryl's performance on *Beat the Chasers*, particularly in the high-stakes grand final, when David Poltorak returned for a second shot against all four Chasers for $250,000 and Cheryl demolished him almost single-handedly. It was one of the finest high-pressure quizzing performances I've seen: Matt, Issa and I could barely get a word in. It's that kind of display that has made Cheryl such a wonderful role model, not only for her own children, but for viewers such as Jennifer Ong, a Melbourne teenager who has been a vocal supporter of Cheryl on social media. Jennifer says that Cheryl's presence on television is a constant reminder to be proud of her Chinese and Malaysian heritage and has helped inspire her to one day apply to become a quiz show contestant.

'As a young Asian woman, I feel that it is important to see people like myself reflected on television as smart, classy, independent and capable human beings, as equals to white men,' Jennifer says. 'I say this because historically, white men have dominated the quizzing sphere, and they have long been considered as the "superior" race, whilst unhealthy and diminishing stereotypes about Asians have been ingrained into society.'

Fortunately, in quizzing at least, things seem to be heading in a positive direction. Anecdotally, I have heard of increased cultural diversity among pub trivia patrons, particularly among those with heritage in South Asian countries such as India, where quizzing is a popular pastime. While some critics may argue that television quiz shows have been 'dumbed down' by including more pop culture, they have also broadened their remit to include far more questions that reflect a truly global view. More women, greater cultural diversity and more inclusive questions can only broaden quizzing as a hobby. And that is a wonderful thing.

▼

Lisa Paton, exhausted after a sleepless night, has her hands on the buzzer and stares straight ahead, trying to focus on the question Simon Reeve is delivering. Backstage, her father and Caitlin are waiting nervously. Also waiting is a bottle of champagne and a big bunch of flowers. Twice already, in yesterday's last games, she missed questions in the million-dollar minute. Now, in her first episode on day four of her massive filming week, she simply has to stay focused.

'In the 1963 film *Cleopatra*, who plays Mark Antony?[1]'

The contestants—Lisa, Mark and Derek—are in a three-way tie on 45 points in the dying seconds of the Double-Points Decider round. But none of them knows it, because they cannot see the scores. Neither do they know how long is left in the game. All three slam their buzzers, milliseconds separating them. Mark is in first, correctly answers the question, and the siren sounds to end the game. As Simon Reeve pauses to collect his thoughts, you can see the panic on Lisa's face: she fears she has lost, yet

---

[1]   Richard Burton

hopes she has sneaked through. But as Simon announces the result—'Mark, you are our new champion on *Million Dollar Minute*'—the gravity of the moment sinks in. Lisa's dream is over.

'I feel terrible. I'm so sorry, Lisa,' Mark says.

'They were all really lovely and kind,' Lisa says seven years later. 'I didn't get shoved out the door. Simon came down and talked to my dad, who was a mad fan of anyone on television. They were really friendly and took photos. They still gave me the big bunch of flowers and the bottle of champagne. And then it was like, "Yeah, I guess I'll go home now."'

As simple as that. I remember watching on television and wondering how she would process the loss. She walked away with $77,000, a life-changing amount of money but not a million dollars. Mark, Mark Antony and milliseconds had cost her $425,000. I recall only too well my salad days, when I was green in judgement and had lost the chance at a quarter of a million on *Sale*. It plagued me for years. I wondered if Lisa would be similarly haunted. But a fundamental difference helped Lisa move on: I was obsessed with *Sale* and certain I would win; Lisa had no expectations.

'None of it was real money,' Lisa says. 'I didn't have any of it in my hand. It all seemed pretend in a lot of ways. I think in the moment I was a bit shocked. Then quite quickly it was kind of like, "Oh, well. I never had it." It wasn't like something got taken away from me, because it was all theoretical money.'

It's a remarkable attitude. And there was one more significant difference. When I lost on *Sale*, I was nineteen years old and had all the spare time in the world to mull over my failure. Lisa, a 38-year-old single parent, didn't have that luxury—and is all the better for it.

'I just had to get on with life,' Lisa says. 'I still had to work and raise my daughter. I was busy. Otherwise, my concerns were not necessarily about this kind of weird chapter in my life. It definitely hasn't weighed on me in that way, but it does fleetingly every now and again, particularly when I've struggled with other challenges, being like, "Oh, yeah. Well, it could have been easier."'

The hardest part for Lisa was watching the episodes, because they aired across a three-week period and she knew how it was going to end. Still, she was justifiably proud of herself: winning twelve episodes and having the guts to play for the million was a massive achievement. The day after her final episode aired, Lisa was approached outside a supermarket by a sobbing woman who had been so invested in the show that she just wanted to give Lisa a hug. Lisa occasionally runs into Mark, the contestant who defeated her, because their workplaces happen to be near each other. They sometimes say a polite hello on the street during their lunch breaks, forever linked by Mark Antony and a million dollars.

Still, $77,000 was a major windfall for Lisa. She says it saved her bacon, financially. When she filmed the episodes, she was looking for work, having left a career in kindergarten management. After her win, she paid off her credit card, bought a new car and took her time to find a job that suited her. Now she works in environmental sustainability for a local council. Occasionally, she still gets recognised on the street, and there are moments when she wonders what life would have been like had she walked away with the $500,000. But it doesn't haunt her.

'Obviously I was disappointed that I didn't win the million dollars,' Lisa says. 'But overall, I still recall the whole experience as being really positive. The people were lovely. It was kind of fun, although stressful and nerve-racking, and it was lovely seeing strangers supporting me. That was a beautiful thing. I don't regret doing it. It's mostly positive in my mind.'

▼

John from Langwarrin. Ho Chi Minh. Suzie Wilks. $25.

These were the flashbacks that I couldn't escape after recording my first two episodes of *Million Dollar Minute*.

I had gone into the first day's filming with two goals: walk away if I reached the $100,000 level on the cash ladder and take a little safe money on the way. This plan was based on what I thought I knew: there was no safe level and there was too much to lose if I pushed on beyond $100,000. I didn't know about the new $75,000 safe level until it was explained to us in the green room that morning, and it left my head spinning. It was like Willy Wonka's golden ticket had just landed in my lap. Suddenly, I was unsure of my tactics. I quickly set my new goal at $200,000, and I took $7000 in safe money across my first two shows so I would go home with something.

But now, discussing the situation with Zoe after the first day of filming, I had to make an adjustment. It had been thirteen years since playing the Cash Card on *Sale of the Century* had cost me the game, but it felt like yesterday. I knew that if I lost *Million Dollar Minute* in similar circumstances, it would be even harder to take. So then and there, I made a commitment to myself: I would accept no more safe money during episodes, at all. My goal was $75,000 and beyond; it was not worth risking that for $2000 here or $5000 there. Homer Simpson once observed that cold turkey isn't as delicious as it sounds, and the cash-for-lead offers that I was quitting were mouth-watering. If I was only a question or two ahead, surely it was worth conceding such a small lead for $5000? No. Because if my lead was so small, my opponents must be a threat. And if my lead was large, it was too great a buffer to give up. I considered relaxing my stance for the two 'Snapshot' questions per game, the multiple-choice ones that offered either $1500 cash or 15 points. It might be safe to take that money if I had a huge lead. But I ruled it out. For my own peace of mind, I needed a strict system that I would follow no matter what. I wanted these decisions made ahead of time, rather than occupying my mental space during the pressure of a game.

My resolve was tested almost to breaking point in my first episode the next morning. I was so fast on the buzzer that my two opponents, Helen and Greg, were shaking their heads and laughing in resignation. They must have wondered what on earth they had walked into. I was buzzing in after question introductions as brief as 'Former footballer Sam Kekovich is associated with—'[1], 'Children's author Theodor Geisel—'[2], 'Jim Davis is the creator—'[3]

I was 30 points ahead after the first round, 75 points in front after the second. I had taken the 15 points instead of $1500 at the start of round two, and was starting to feel so embarrassed by the scoreline that I hoped Helen or Greg would pick up the $1500 in the third round. I wanted at least one of them to go home with something and knew that if I took the points it would look like an egotistical move to crush them even more. Displayed on the screen were pictures of a bear, a chimpanzee and a tiger. The question began: 'A toy version of which of these—' and Greg buzzed in, taking a stab at the bear. Wrong. Helen buzzed in right on the back of Greg's miss and guessed chimp. Wrong[4]. I could only shake my head as, by default, the cash or points choice fell to me again. It was the ultimate test of my self-discipline.

Sheepishly, I took the points.

To the viewers at home, it must have seemed a ridiculous decision. It *was* a ridiculous decision. It took my score to 130, a full 100 points ahead. I could have had $1500 cash in my pocket for virtually no risk. But I had a system, and for my own sanity

---

[1] Lamb (the rest of the question was '... the promotion of which Australian food product?')

[2] Dr Seuss ('... is best known by what doctorial pen-name?')

[3] *Garfield* ('... of which well-known comic strip about a fat orange cat?')

[4] The full question was: 'A toy version of which of these features in the comic strip *Calvin & Hobbes*?'

I couldn't bend from it. Making that rigid rule ensured I would have no regrets. If I was beaten by a better player, so be it. But I refused to open the door, even a sliver, to the possibility of losing due to my own choices. That was the result of a thirteen-year *Sale* hangover. Not for a moment have I regretted giving up that $1500, but I would never have forgiven myself if I lost a game because I took a cash offer. I finished on a record score of 220 points, to Helen on 40 and Greg on 30. Forty questions had been asked: I had answered 30, for 29 correct and 1 wrong.

And it was all for nothing, because in the million-dollar minute round I missed one of the five questions and failed to secure the safe $75,000. The question that tripped me up was 'For which band did drummer Keith Moon play?' The options were The Kinks, Pink Floyd and The Who. I was a big fan of The Kinks, and knew them well, but couldn't say the same about Pink Floyd and The Who. Under the pressure of a ticking clock, with only a couple of seconds to answer, I pressed Pink Floyd. Moments later, I realised my mistake. It was a matter of word association. Pink Floyd's most famous album was *Dark Side of the Moon*; in the absence of definite knowledge, my brain had sensed a connection between Pink Floyd and the word 'Moon'. But it was the wrong connection.

Missing the $75,000 was deflating, but I secured it in the next episode. That episode also confirmed my belief that, even though I was well suited to the show, my fortunes could change at any moment. One opponent proved a serious threat, Michael Risby, who shot to a 10-point lead at the end of the first round and signalled his intentions by turning down the $2000 to keep his advantage. I edged back to lead by 5 points after the second round and likewise turned down $5000. We each sat on 45 points after the third round, and I breathed a sigh of relief to secure the extra 15 points from the Snapshot question. Michael and I were both buzzing early in the Double-Points Decider, desperate to shut each other out, and I gained enough momentum to win by 45 points. But it was tense. A fraction of a second here, a momentary hesitation there, and it could have been a different result.

Then, as I played for the money in the million-dollar minute, one question highlighted my weakness in observation and visual cues. Asked which of red, blue and violet was not one of the colours of the Olympic rings, I didn't have the foggiest idea. I couldn't have told you with confidence what colour *any* of them were. I guessed violet, only because blue and red were such basic colours. I could imagine viewers being amazed that I would struggle with a question like that, but different people learn in different ways. While I had seen the Olympic rings countless times, I had never actively processed the information. My strength is recalling facts that I have seen written down.

When violet was confirmed as correct, meaning I had $75,000 that couldn't be taken away, I put my head in my hands, almost shaking with relief. It's hard to believe the same person had given John Burgess so little reaction upon winning a car, but by now I was older and understood that this was a life-changing moment. Despite winning most of my episodes by reasonable margins, playing for big money was highly stressful.

My fifth game was a comfortable 100-point victory, but I missed the $100,000 level by failing to identify which of Los Angeles, Detroit or Seattle provided the futuristic setting for the film *Blade Runner*[1]. In game six, a contestant named Lyndal McKenzie gave me a red-hot run for my money, leading through much of the game and taking the $2000 and $5000 safe money before I slipped away to win by 55 points.

The Double-Points Decider round was always my greatest strength. The momentum of a faster-paced round suited my focus level and ability to mentally discard a question as soon as it was done and concentrate immediately on the next one. I sensed that some contestants were still thinking about the last question, which also happens on *The Chase*. This round was also different because incorrect answers didn't cost you money; they just locked you out from the next question. This meant that only one opponent could possibly gain on me by getting the next question right, whereas if I had lost points both contestants would gain on me. So buzzing in early was worth the risk. I nearly always ran away by the end of the Double-Points Decider round, but if an opponent nailed a couple of questions in a row I became nervous because the scores could change so quickly.

I won the $100,000 in that sixth episode, and won my seventh episode, but again missed a question in the final minute that cost me the $200,000, wrongly guessing which of scurvy, shingles or

---

[1] It was Los Angeles. At the time, I hadn't seen the film and guessed Detroit because I felt *Blade Runner* might have had an industrial feel to it.

beri-beri was caused by a deficiency of vitamin B1[1]. That was the last episode of the day, and as I played that final solo round the vanquished contestants, Karyn and Shane, walked out of the studio. Zoe, waiting in the car for me, overheard them commiserating with each other about how fast I was on the buzzer.

Now I had some breathing space. I had secured the safe $75,000 and reached the next level of $100,000. And I had two weeks before the next filming date to regroup and refresh—I don't know how I would have coped with a hectic week of recording like Lisa Paton. Unfortunately, by the time I would next film, Zoe would be in London on a work trip. She was a music publishing executive for Michael Gudinski's Mushroom Group and usually took three overseas trips per year to musical festivals and industry events in London, Cannes, New York, Austin and all sorts of other places. And I thought cricket writer was a dream job.

Before she flew out, we needed to talk over what my opportunity meant for us. We had only been married three months, and you can often see me on *Million Dollar Minute* fidgeting with my wedding ring. Since finding out about the $75,000 safe level, I had thought $200,000 would be my upper limit, because playing on any further meant risking $125,000. Had I won $200,000 at the first attempt, I would already have walked away with it. But one summer evening, Zoe and I took a walk around Essendon and

---

[1]   I answered shingles; the answer was beri-beri. I knew scurvy was caused by a lack of vitamin C—that was why British sailors were nicknamed Limeys, because of the citrus fruits they were made to eat at sea to ward off scurvy.

Moonee Ponds, where we lived, and talked it over. She floated the idea of trying for the $300,000. That was an amount that would pay off our mortgage completely, and, at 32, owning our home outright would give us an incredible kick-start at the beginning of our married lives.

We agreed that I would make the decision based on how I felt in the studio on the day but that I would most likely have a crack at the $300,000. The only reason I might walk away with $200,000 would be if it took me too many episodes to lock it in, and I was becoming exhausted. I never realistically considered pushing for the $500,000 or $1,000,000. You may wonder why, if I was winning my episodes comfortably. But I was the first contestant to play for the $200,000 level; everything after that was uncharted territory. I suspected the difficulty level of the questions in the million-dollar minute would be ratcheted up if I played for the big bucks, and watching later players go for it confirmed this. I also wondered whether the producers would actually want me to win the million. The show had only been on air for four months. It took *Millionaire* six years to give away the top prize, and I wasn't convinced it would be good for *Million Dollar Minute* to do so this soon. I wondered whether some seriously high-calibre challengers would be lined up to play against me. And the fact that you were locked in after choosing to play on worried me as well. It could take weeks to secure the big amounts, and any good opponent might take me down. There was just too much uncertainty.

I was relieved to win my first episode on the third filming day—and eighth episode overall—by one of my biggest margins, 130 points. But once more a question stumped me in the final minute. Asked whether the distributor, carburettor or condenser was the car part that had been made obsolete by fuel injection[1], I didn't have a clue. Never mechanically minded, I generally thought I was doing well to remember where the lever was to open my bonnet. Not that there was any point opening it: you might as well have asked me to perform heart surgery. Knowledge does not equal intelligence. If a game show ever found a way to reward useful life skills instead of recalling obscure facts, 20 million Australians would beat me comfortably.

Twice now I had missed the $200,000, and I faced two strong opponents in my next game. One of them I recognised immediately: Alex, the young woman I had played against on *The Weakest Link* and who had been the final person Simon and I voted off before the prize round. The quiz show contestant pool is not a large one. Although Australians enjoy watching quiz shows, only a tiny percentage of the country's 25 million people consider applying to become a contestant. And only a portion of those follow through—I'm sure many people are put off by the fear of looking silly on television. The list further reduces when some fail to pass the general knowledge test at an audition. Of those who remain, contenders with bright, outgoing personalities are

---

[1]   The answer was carburettor. I guessed distributor, on the basis that injecting and distributing sounded vaguely synonymous.

likely to be selected. On top of that, most Australian quiz shows have been filmed in Melbourne (although *The Chase* moved to Sydney in 2020), and production budgets are often too small to pay for interstate contestants to fly in. Because there are so many boxes a contestant must tick before making it to air, it's not surprising that we see the same people popping up on different shows—myself included.

Alex isn't the only person I've competed against on multiple shows. Rodney, the school teacher whom I had beaten in the final seconds of my second *Sale of the Century* episode, later appeared against me on *The Chase*. I felt extra bad knocking him out in the head-to-head round, given our history. He must curse the sight of me now. Alex probably does too because I beat her on *Million Dollar Minute* as well as *The Weakest Link*. But she was a strong competitor on *Million Dollar Minute*, and only 10 points separated all three players at the end of the third round, before I picked up 15 points from the final Snapshot and got away in the Double-Points Decider.

At my third attempt, I secured the $200,000 prize, confidently answering four questions and taking a successful guess at the fifth: Are there 56, 206 or 406 bones in the adult human body[1]? Another wave of relief washed over me, but now I had a decision to make. Would I walk away with $200,000 or play on for $300,000? I took the gamble, willing to push slightly beyond my comfort zone with a guaranteed $75,000 to fall back on.

---

[1]   206

During my tenth episode, I regretted it. Not because I was under threat—I led consistently and ended up winning by 125 points—but because I was worried about how many episodes it might take to secure the $300,000. Midway through that episode, a realisation dawned on me: I was no longer enjoying the experience, because I had too much to lose. I remembered the anti-gambling slogan: 'When it's no longer fun, walk away'. *Million Dollar Minute* was no longer fun, but I was locked in until I either won the $300,000 or was beaten. Lisa Paton viewed it as 'theoretical money', but to me it was very real. *Million Dollar Minute* no longer felt like a game. It felt like work. If I needed confirmation that playing on for the half million was not for me, that was it.

I was desperate to nail the final five questions and get the hell out of there. The first asked whether cycling, athletics or swimming had provided Australia with the most Olympic gold medals. It had to be swimming—all our greatest Olympians were swimmers and there were so many events. Next, I was asked if ichthyology was the study of birds, fish or insects[1]—I knew this one for certain. Did Mickey Rourke star in a film called *The Swimmer, The Wrestler* or *The Dancer*[2]? Easy, I had seen it when it came out in 2008. Are espadrilles worn on the feet, head or arms? This one caused me some angst. My initial thought was shoes, but something nagged in the back of my mind. What were

---

[1]   Fish. The study of birds is ornithology and the study of insects is entomology.

[2]   *The Wrestler*

those things that soldiers wore on their shoulders? I was sure it was a word like 'espadrille'. Would the shoulders count as the arms? All of this ran through my brain in a matter of seconds, and I pressed my answer. Finally, did Australia introduce the GST in 1995, 2000 or 2004? I was comfortable with 2000. John Howard brought in the GST and I knew he was not yet prime minister in 1995. And I recalled writing a news story about the GST for one of my first-year journalism classes in 2000. I believed I had nailed four out of five. But what about those damned espadrilles?

Naturally, knowing that was the question I was least confident about, Simon Reeve revealed that answer last. I'm not a religious person, but as I waited for that answer to be revealed I put my hands together as if in prayer and touched them to my nose. I just wanted it to be over. I had stuck with my gut and said espadrilles were worn on the feet. And as the big golden tick appeared on the screen, I felt the kind of relief I've never felt before or since[1]. I had done it! Ten episodes, twenty opponents, $307,000 including the safe money I had taken in my first two shows. I'm not naturally an emotional person, but I instinctively gave Simon a big hug and, when he asked if I would come back to play for $500,000, my voice was noticeably shaky: 'Simon, my nerves are shot. I'm going to go.'

And with that, it was all over. After I left the studio, I called Zoe in London, where it was about 5 a.m. Her first words were: 'Is it 200 or 300?' Her confidence in me was so great that she

---

[1]   Epaulettes are the things on the shoulders.

couldn't envisage me having been beaten. We could write off our mortgage in one hit. We had the sort of financial breathing space that people our age could only dream of. On the way home, I picked up a six-pack of Cooper's Celebration Ale—I wasn't about to drink a bottle of champagne by myself. I sat alone in our Essendon townhouse, with only our cat, Ruby, for company, had a couple of beers and went over the whole experience again.

Across my ten episodes, I had turned down $62,000 in safe money. But I didn't regret a single decision. Some of my opponents had been very strong, and had I conceded my leads I might not be sitting here with 300 grand. I could have safely taken $1500 here or there, but my strict system helped me remain focused. It felt like this triumph was redemption for my *Sale* failing—even though nobody else remembered. A few weeks after my episodes aired, the cheque arrived in the mail—not registered post, no bells and whistles, just a simple, regular envelope that contained $307,000.

Million Dollar Minute had been the perfect show for my skill set. It rewarded speed, anticipation, focus and breadth rather than depth of knowledge. On *Who Wants To Be a Millionaire?* a single question might stop you, but on *Million Dollar Minute* the odd incorrect answer could be offset by enough correct ones. And unlike *Sale*, *Million Dollar Minute* broadened its question base to include plenty of pop culture, which suited me: I had questions about *Cheers*, Simon and Garfunkel, *The Nanny*, *Roseanne*, *Perfect Match*, the *American Pie* films, *Harry Potter* and many others, alongside questions on more 'classic' categories.

Emboldened by the new safe level, I had stuck my neck out further than any previous contestant, and over the next few months others pushed further still. Several players won the $500,000 and Lisa Paton tried for the million, but the show didn't give away its million-dollar prize until March 2015, when Andrew Skarbek played a remarkable 23 episodes to secure the money. An outstanding performance, it came only after the producers added a second safety net to lure contestants higher: $300,000 was made a safe level, while an extra step on the ladder—$750,000— was added. Had the $300,000 safety net been in play for me, I would have pushed on for the million, even with my shot nerves.

A little part of me will always wonder whether I could have won the million dollars. But a big part of me is pleased that I never put myself under that stress. Never have I felt as tense as I was playing for that life-changing $300,000. Compared to that, *The Chase* is a walk in the park.

CHAPTER 12

THE CHASE IS ON

WHAT THE HELL AM I GOING TO WRITE? IT'S A QUESTION EVERY JOURNALIST asks themselves frequently. Daily. I'm asking it of myself now, as I write this book. See all those words in the next paragraph? I haven't come up with them yet. I'll be interested to see where this chapter goes. I was certainly asking myself the question one sunny day in March 2015, as I sat in the press box at Hobart's Bellerive Oval, watching two of the lowest-ranked teams, Ireland and Zimbabwe, train the day before their World Cup cricket match. I had a responsibility to readers all over the world to make the match sound interesting. It was a tall order. What the hell was I going to write?

And then my phone rang. It wasn't my editor asking for all my good story ideas, which was fortunate as I didn't even have bad story ideas. It was, unexpectedly, a producer for the Australian arm of ITV Studios, sounding out my interest in a new quiz show the company would be making for a major network. That was all the information I was given, but it was all I needed. I had watched enough of the UK version of *The Chase* to know it was produced by ITV, and I knew that in 2014, soon after my *Million Dollar Minute* success, a casting call had been put out for a possible Australian version of *The Chase*. I had applied to be on the show and inserted a cheeky suggestion that I be considered as a chaser. Now, nearly a year later, ITV was calling me out of the blue. The name of the show was not mentioned but it had to be *The Chase*—but was I being considered as a contestant or chaser?

I found myself walking around the picturesque Bellerive Oval, not really watching Ireland's George Dockrell practise his spin bowling or Zimbabwe's Brendan Taylor work on his wicketkeeping, but staring out at the River Derwent estuary, answering a 20-question quiz on the phone with a television producer in Sydney. I recall nothing except that one concerned a favourite sitcom of mine, *Frasier* (maybe it asked the name of the coffee shop that Frasier frequents[1], or what city the show was set in[2]—I can't remember). But I do recall my surprise at the way the questions kept landing in areas that I knew. After hanging up, I mentally debriefed, and while the producer had not given any indication of whether my answers were correct, I was pretty

---

[1]   Café Nervosa

[2]   Seattle

sure they were. All of them. This was as unexpected to me as it probably was to the producer. Had I been lucky? Or did I just know more than I realised? Whatever the case, a week later I was on a plane to Sydney, auditioning to be a chaser.

The call at Bellerive Oval had happened so quickly that there was no chance to get nervous, but now I had too much time to think about this incredible opportunity. Inevitably, self-doubt kicked in. 'What the hell am I going to write?' was replaced by 'What on earth am I going to say?' My most vivid memory of this first in-person audition was waiting in a small room at ITV headquarters—it felt like a disused storeroom—and seeing a Logie Award for *Talkin' 'Bout Your Generation*, the Shaun Micallef comedy panel show that ITV had produced. I once read that Kate Winslet keeps her Oscar in her bathroom, so that guests can pose with it in front of the mirror when they go to the toilet. I thought about picking up the Logie, propped up inconspicuously against a dark window, but decided it would be bad luck to touch a television award when I hadn't even got a job in television yet. At the time, I worked from home for a Mickey Mouse organisation[1] and here I was trying out for a role with a company that could leave Logies lying around in storerooms. The audition itself, in which a producer asked me some trivia questions to see how I would respond in person, remains a blur.

---

[1]   By which I mean Mickey Mouse's company, Disney, which owned ESPN, which in turn owned ESPNcricinfo. But, working from home for a small, niche offshoot of an offshoot, I never felt part of the global mega-brand.

The only question I recall is 'Which actor is married to *Modern Family* star Sofia Vergara?'[1] I got it wrong, but was clever enough that when the producer gave the correct answer, I nodded sagely as if to say, 'I should have known that', instead of giving the true response: 'Never heard of him.'

I must have done enough, because I was invited to a more serious audition in Sydney the following week. This time there was a rolling camera and a mock-up of the set, with me sitting in a lofty position to look down upon a real-life host and contestant. It felt surreal for a mild-mannered reporter to sit there pretending to be a superman, but I took comfort from the fact that I would remember the audition for the rest of my life even if I didn't get the job. While there was a host and contestant, there was no 'Shark'. There was just me, an introvert trying to prove to the producers—and to myself—that I not only had the knowledge and fast recall to be a chaser but also the personality. I had seen what worked for the British chasers—the cocky swagger of Mark Labbett, the clinical coldness of Shaun Wallace, the frightening sternness of Anne Hegerty, the fun and humour of Paul Sinha—and I knew that key to my chances would be to combine some of those traits with my own natural, but often hidden, smart-aleck personality. I had to have fun, crack a few jokes, give extra information about the answers, banter with the host and contestant. I needed to be intimidating but not a monster; to respect the contestant if they played well.

---

[1] Joe Manganiello

More than anything, I had to look like I belonged at the top of that podium. This was the greatest challenge, because I felt I had bluffed my way this far, but surely there were others more qualified and better equipped than me. I hadn't won a million dollars, or the *Sale of the Century* jackpot. I had no background in performance or comedy. I was no Cary Young, or Barry Jones, or Martin Flood.

But then I added up everything I *had* achieved in quizzing and game shows. I had defeated roughly 90 contestants, and fewer than ten had beaten me. Given all the different skills required, this struck me as a solid strike-rate. Maybe I was good enough. And when it came to performing, my background as a writer and journalist could come in handy when trying to find the right words for the right situation. At least, that was what I told myself. Mostly, I was determined to leave the studio with no regrets.

So there I sat at the top of a makeshift podium, staring down a young bloke brought in to act as the contestant. He worked in finance and wanted to expand his collection of vintage luxury cars. I made some crack about me being the most popular man in Australia if I could beat him, and may have inadvertently spawned The Shark character in that moment. I didn't get all the questions right in the multiple-choice round. I wrongly guessed that *Charlie's Country* had been the film that tied with *The Water Diviner* for Best Picture at the AACTA Awards in 2014 (a horror film was the correct answer[1]), explaining that I had confused Best

---

[1]   *The Babadook*

Picture with Best Actor, which David Gulpilil did indeed win for *Charlie's Country*. So at least I proved I had some knowledge of the subject. There was also a question about who succeeded Karl Lagerfeld as creative director of the fashion house Chloé[1]; whether I guessed correctly I don't remember. I couldn't even tell you if I won the game. But it all felt surprisingly natural.

I flew home to Melbourne to an empty house—Zoe was on a work trip to New York—and I rushed off to Rod Laver Arena to fill her seat at a Rod Stewart concert; she had organised for her mum, a big fan of Rod, to meet him before the show. I arrived too late for the meet-and-greet and barely even paid attention to the concert, instead mentally dissecting my performance in Sydney with fifty years' worth of Rod Stewart hits as my live background music. I was happy with how it had gone, and Rod's lyrics proved apposite: I couldn't have tried any more and felt that if given the chance to be a chaser I could wear it well.

The Cricket World Cup continued, but I found it difficult to switch my brain out of *Chase* mode. I was inordinately excited when Paul Sinha started following me on Twitter after I made a *Chase*-related cricket reference. Andy Zaltzman, the British comedian and cricket statistician, was part of ESPNcricinfo's team for the World Cup, and one night as we chatted in a Melbourne pub about quiz shows he mentioned that he was a good friend of Paul Sinha. These unexpected connections helped me see that chasers were regular people with normal lives.

---

[1] Stella McCartney

I carried on with my own normal life; nobody but Zoe knew I had been auditioning for *The Chase*. Even after the World Cup there was plenty to keep me busy as we were preparing for the birth of our first child, due on 14 June. I had already arranged time off from my cricket-writing job around the birth, and, I hoped that, if I did score the gig, filming wouldn't take place in June. The last thing either of us wanted was for Zoe to go into labour while I was halfway through an episode. And then, on 1 May, an official offer came from ITV headquarters: the job was mine.

Oh, yes!

Filming would begin on 9 June and continue until 8 July, with only weekends off.

Oh, shit!

▼

I learnt to walk when I was ten months old. I've never had any trouble with it. One foot in front of the other, repeat as required. I can even run if the need arises. So you can imagine my surprise when I started working with a producer to prepare me for *The Chase* and one of my first training tasks was walking practice. I could amble. I could wander. I was a master of the sidle. But could I strut? Could I swagger? Could I stride in such a way as to convey self-assurance and power and menace? If you've ever watched *The Chase*, you'll know that when the chaser is revealed they walk down a tunnel-like bridge to their seat. It's a moment of pantomime drama as we impose ourselves onto a team of four nervous contestants, and it doesn't work if the chaser shuffles along sheepishly. Dragging this physical display of confidence out of me was one of the many tasks of producer Anthony Watt.

There could hardly have been a better person for the job. Anthony had been executive producer of *Spicks and Specks*, which mixed music trivia with the panel comedy format, and he had worked on sketch comedy shows such as *Full Frontal*. He had a deep knowledge of both trivia and comedy, and he was passionate about *The Chase*. Together we worked on turning me from a quiz contestant into an intimidating trivia machine.

Anthony put a timer on his phone and threw questions at me for 2 minutes, simulating the final chase. He showed me clips from the British version and paused them just before the chaser spoke, prompting me to come up with extra information or a humorous line. The 'Shark' persona had its origins when Anthony observed that I could be cast as something 'like a card shark'. Other names were considered—'The Hustler' was a strong candidate—but 'The Shark' got the nod. Anthony saw that I treated quizzing like a sport; I viewed him like a coach, preparing me for the Quizzing Olympics.

With his comedy background, Anthony instinctively understood what was funny; if I made him laugh, I knew it was genuine. Humour would be a key to *The Chase* succeeding in Australia. On the UK version, apart from Paul Sinha, the humour often came from host Bradley Walsh, whose fits of uncontrollable laughter were YouTube legend. The most memorable incident occurred when he asked which sport Germany's Fanny Chmelar competed in[1]; to see Bradley's contorted face as he tried not to lose control upon hearing her name, you'd think he'd just eaten six lemons. Australian viewers would react against the chasers if we took ourselves too seriously, but it was also clear that, no matter how much we fooled around on the job, we wouldn't get away with double entendres. The show was based around a three-way (get your mind out of the gutter) conversation between host, chaser and contestant, which would only make interesting viewing if the chasers had a sense of humour.

I was therefore thrilled to learn that one of my fellow chasers would be Matt Parkinson, a regular performer on the live television comedy show *The Big Gig* in the 1980s and '90s, and who had also hosted commercial breakfast radio. I remembered Matt winning the lot on *Sale of the Century* in the early '90s, and I had seen him pop up occasionally as part of the celebrity brains trust on *The Einstein Factor*. Only once had I seen Matt in person, as he sneaked into a side door of the studio foyer when I was a contestant on *Million Dollar Minute*; I later found out that Matt was in charge of the question-writing team on that show. It was in that same foyer eighteen months later that I officially met Matt for the first time as Anthony showed the three Australian chasers—Matt, me and Issa Schultz—through the studio to see the set and meet the then-host, Andrew O'Keefe. I knew Issa as the regular winner of the Australian leg of the World Quizzing Championship, and it was immediately clear

---

[1] Skiing

that he was a delightful person who would likely be the show's breakout star. Combined with the comedic instincts of Andrew, who had a background in improv and sketch comedy, and Matt, I was confident the show could achieve the right blend of serious quizzing and clever humour.

▼

Perth, 1978

Three Year 10 boys sit, stony-faced, deadly serious. This is not an end-of-year exam. It's more important than that. They are the chosen ones, the best and brightest, the representatives of Scotch College. The pride of their school is at stake. They sit in a television studio, cameras trained on them, as host Jeff Newman—Mr Newman to these boys—fires questions at them. The show is It's Academic, *and the atmosphere is tense. Mr Newman asks his next question: How many engines did the Spitfire fighter plane have? One of the boys, young in this group at just fourteen, is a World War II buff. He loves fighter planes. He knows the Spitfire inside out. He's so into this stuff that he once made a model Spitfire. He knows it has one engine. He assumes that everyone knows it has one engine. To him, it is the easiest question in the world. His teammate buzzes in ahead of him and answers: 'Two'.*

The memory is vivid. More than four decades later, that fourteen-year-old World War II buff is now in his late fifties. He recalls the incident in detail. 'It was the very early days of video

recording,' he says, 'and some of the nerdier boys from school
. . . would record our appearances on *It's Academic* and then we
would review them as part of our training session. What I didn't
notice until I saw it back on the video was when he said "Two"
both my eyebrows shot up about six inches. And as we were
sitting around watching it—me, the rest of the team, the teacher
who coached us and the guys who'd made the video—really big,
booming laughs from everyone. That was the first time I went,
"These two things go together really well." The seriousness, that's
actually the best position to launch your joke into. That wasn't
a joke that I'd come up with, but the laugh sat really well in the
background of seriousness.'

That boy was Matt Parkinson, now known to quiz show
viewers as 'Goliath' on *The Chase Australia*. His team reached
the state finals of *It's Academic*, but it's the eyebrow incident that
stands out. It was a seminal moment for Matt, who would go on
to make a career out of comedy and quizzing. I remember as a
kid in 1992 watching him blitz *Sale of the Century*, and being
amazed that a comedian could switch gears so easily into serious
quizzing. Matt was known as one half of comedy duo The Empty
Pockets—as an eleven-year-old, all I knew was that they wore
blue singlets and hit each other a lot. I might have expected a
comedian like Andrew Denton to do well at quizzing—he wore
glasses, so he must have been smart—but an Empty Pocket? That
was a surprise. But the more time I've spent in the quizzing
world, the more comedy connections I see.

Stephen Hall, a comedy writer and performer who frequently works with Shaun Micallef, won the lot on *Temptation* in 2005 and went on the following year to win *Australia's Brainiest Quiz Master* on a one-off television special, defeating *Sale* icons Cary Young and Virginia Noel and *Millionaire* winners Rob Fulton and Martin Flood. Andrew Jones, a former *Sale* grand champion whom I later encountered in my journalism career when he was CEO of Cricket New South Wales, has been a comedy writer and co-created the sketch comedy *Big Bite*. The *Sale* legend David Poltorak has worked as a stand-up comedian. Rusty Berther of the Scared Weird Little Guys won money as a regular contestant on *The Chase*. So too did Ben Pobjie, the satirist and author, one of the funniest writers I have ever read. Behind the scenes, comedians frequently pop up as question writers. The 'Chaser producers', who work with each chaser as Anthony Watt had done, have all been either comedy writers or performers. The wonderful satirist Mark Humphries put his name forward to host the Australian version of the quiz show *Pointless* because he loved the UK show so much—and he got the job. Tom Gleeson has created an entire show—*Hard Quiz*—and won a Gold Logie out of combining comedy and quizzing. Comedy panel shows such as *Have You Been Paying Attention?* cover similar territory, though they feature only professional comedians rather than regular punters.

I've often wondered why quizzing and comedy fit so neatly; perhaps it is that both pick out life's quirky and interesting information. Comedy is frequently about making connections between different ideas and finding something entertaining in the mundanity of everyday life. Quizzing does not have to be funny, and often it isn't, but at its core is the same fundamental idea: finding things in day-to-day life that are, for one reason or another, noteworthy.

'I think that thing that the humorous brain picks up on . . . that quirk, is the same thing that triggers your memory to recall something,' Matt Parkinson says. 'I think there is a connection there. There are a million questions we could be asked in *The Chase*, but we know some questions, they're too boring. Like who won the high jump gold medal at Munich in 1972[1]. Unless there was an incident or it was someone really famous, that doesn't count as trivia . . . It has to be a moment that is, in some sense, memorable.'

There is also a natural and obvious connection between the performance aspect of comedy and the recall required for television quiz shows. Matt honed his memory as a teenager by performing in school plays and discovered that he was quite good at learning lines. His memory strengthened when he became a comedian who wrote his own material and had to perfect the precise wording for the punchline. From there, it was a short leap to recalling random pieces of trivial information. But whereas

---

[1] Jüri Tarmak of the Soviet Union won the men's gold and Ulrike Meyfarth of West Germany won the women's. Meyfarth set an interesting record: by winning in 1972 at age 16 and in 1984 at age 28, she became both the youngest and oldest woman to win Olympic gold in high jump.

some top-level quizzers recall facts having rote-learned lists of capital cities and Oscar winners and the periodic table, Matt's brain works best by making connections. There is an element of list learning to the way he trains, but it is just as much about keeping his neural pathways fit and firing.

'I'm a great believer in you're not really remembering fixed things the whole time you're training, you're making those pathways fluent,' Matt says, 'from idea to idea, making those connections. I think most people, when they say "I've got a bad memory", what's actually happening is they've just got out of the habit of creating pathways and they have a life where they just have a lot of routine, they go over the same stuff, and so their brain isn't creating those pathways all the time. That's why I find question writing so useful as a practice for this job, because each time you write a question, you're looking at your question and your answer and you're saying, "What's the pathway from the question to the answer?" You're grooving that pathway the whole time. I think that's really important.'

When Matt talks about question writing, he isn't just referring to the time he spent working on *Million Dollar Minute*. One of the many ways in which the chasers train is by writing practice questions for each other. Only one of us competes against contestants in any given episode, but we are a supportive group and consider ourselves a team when it comes to preparation and training. I have a Word document consisting of more than 200 pages of practice questions I have written to help the other chasers train. Matt, Issa and Cheryl Toh do the same.

The inspiration for questions comes from daily life, whether I'm actively studying or not. Recently I was playing 'Bug Bingo' with my kids, which made me realise how little I know about insects, so my current set of questions includes 'What insect is a sunset morpho?[1]' On a family holiday we drove along the Murchison Highway; I wrote a question asking which state it is in[2], so that I won't get it confused with Western Australia's Murchison region or the Victorian town of Murchison. Reading a *Play School* book together, Heidi, Fletcher and I tried to name all the toys in the illustrations but none of us could recall the name of *Play School*'s toy cat[3]. That became a question. At any given time I will have several hundred browser tabs on my phone open to facts I intend to get back to later to write a question about.

Actively learning and recalling facts is important, but just as crucial to a successful quizzing performance is the right mindset. As a sportsperson will generally perform better if they enter a match in a calm state of mind, a quizzer is unlikely to be at their peak if they are feeling too tense or distracted. For that reason, when filming *The Chase* I like to arrive at the studio well ahead of my scheduled time, giving me a chance to sit in a quiet space and prepare. The last thing I want is to hurry out of the house where three small children might have been competing for my attention or throwing tantrums or generally occupying

---

[1]   A butterfly

[2]   Tasmania

[3]   Diddle

my headspace, then struggle to find a parking spot at the studio and be frazzled upon arrival. Experience has shown me that if I feel rushed ahead of filming, my performance suffers. Likewise, Matt has learnt how to find the right mental state to perform as a chaser.

It wasn't always quite so straightforward. In the early days of *The Chase*, Matt sometimes found the experience tense and stressful—as we all did. It was new and we were feeling our way, wanting to prove we were good enough. None of us wanted to be the chaser who would miss too many questions or lose a record amount of money. For Matt, the fact that we were encouraged to have fun with the show, to make jokes, to lighten the mood—all of that helped diffuse his internal tension and allowed his memory to function more effectively.

'One of the ways that I used humour was I really wanted to show people that I'm not taking myself seriously here,' Matt says. 'I don't think that I'm the best quizzer in Australia. I know there are people who have more depth and breadth to their trivia knowledge . . . Back then, I worried a lot about what other people thought of the fact that I was there, which I don't worry about now. But back then, I was really worried that there were people at home going, "He shouldn't be there." I was really relieved to have the humour in place and to be encouraged to do that. And also, this is Australia, so I knew we weren't going to get away with just coming out and big-noting ourselves and putting people down. I knew we'd have to do it in a good-natured, humorous way. Otherwise, people would just reject us straight out as being up ourselves.'

Strange as it may seem, Matt wasn't gripped with tension when he played for $100,000 on *Sale* back in 1992. And that was all down to realistic goals and expectations. During his comedy career, Matt had a ritual of plonking himself in front of the television each evening to watch *Sale*, playing along against the contestants. One night, when a graphic came up calling for prospective contestants, Matt realised that if he could get on the show and plug *A Gift from the Gobs*, a CD he had recorded with some other stand-up comedians, a national audience was there for the taking.

'I wasn't really counting on winning any money,' Matt says. 'My main thing was "I'll plug the CD". And in fact, I had to spend money to meet the minimum dress code for appearing on camera, because I didn't have anything besides jeans and T-shirts.'

In the studio, everything clicked. Host Glenn Ridge gave Matt a chance to hold up the CD in his first episode, so that was goal number one achieved. Relaxed after ticking off that important task, back in the familiar environs of a television studio, Matt went on to win the game. On his second episode, he picked up $7000 by playing the Cash Card game, and from then on he felt anything was a bonus.

The rest is history. Matt Parkinson went on to line his empty pockets by winning the lot. To this day, he and his wife Maryanne still use the dining table and six chairs that was one of his major prizes. There was a Filofax, purchased in the *Sale* gift shop, which Matt still owns but doesn't use: he simply likes the fact that it once made him feel like a grown-up to own a Filofax. Problematically, the car prize was not a single car but two small Nissans, a Pulsar and an NX-R. Since Matt stands 198 centimetres tall and lacks the ability to split himself into two 99-centimetre Matts, this was less than ideal. When he went to pick up the vehicles from the dealership and a local newspaper photographer was on hand to capture the moment, Matt sat in the sporty NX-R, with its roof off, and his head stuck out the top, well above the windscreen. Imagine the BFG driving Noddy's car. Knowing this was not a good advertisement for the NX-R, the car dealer waved the photographer away and gave Matt his choice of any car on the lot, up to the value of the *Sale* prize cars.

'There was this beautiful Nissan Patrol sitting there,' Matt says. 'I ended up driving that off the lot the next day. And that gave me a great deal of joy. I crossed the Nullarbor many, many times in that, went to some really great places.'

And then, of course, there was the cash jackpot of $102,000.

'It was a very confusing amount of money, because I really wasn't sure what to do with it,' Matt says. 'I had a lot of different ideas about what to do with it, but what I should have done was just gone and bought a little flat somewhere. It was the ideal time to get into the property market, but me being me, did I do that? No, I did not do that.'

Significantly, the win gave Matt the confidence that he could pursue projects and goals all on his own, rather than needing to be surrounded by others—as, say, part of a comedy group.

Speaking of which, did *A Gift from the Gobs* at least sell well after being promoted on *Sale of the Century*?

'No,' Matt says, 'but that's not for want of plugging it.'

▼

Why did Matt's cash jackpot have to be $102,000? A slight nausea ran through my body when he mentioned that dollar figure. Someone had to lose a record amount on *The Chase* and that someone was me. And the amount was $102,000. At the time of writing, it remains the highest cash-pot ever won by a team on *The Chase Australia*. It was the first episode I ever lost. I entered that show feeling good, having won, if memory serves, the first four episodes that I filmed. Those victories showed me I was good enough to be a chaser. And then I came crashing back to earth.

I knew I was in trouble from the moment I saw the contestants. Three were unfamiliar to me, but the player in seat three I recognised from previous quiz-show victories as William Laing, a star of the quiz world who had won $500,000 on *Who Wants To Be a Millionaire?* by correctly identifying the early explorer of Australian waters who had the middle name Janszoon[1]. He chose not to play for the million dollars when asked how many humans had set foot on the moon[2], but when pressed on which answer he would have gone for, he picked correctly. I also knew he was among the select group of contestants who had played in

---

[1] Abel Tasman

[2] Twelve—as mentioned in Chapter 4. Did you remember it?

Australia's Brainiest Quiz Master, won by Stephen Hall. What I didn't know was that William was dominating on television quiz shows as far back as 1985, when he went within a single question of becoming a *Sale of the Century* grand champion. In his final episode, William and another contestant were tied. William answered the tie-break question incorrectly, handing victory to his opponent by default and missing out, by that one question, on a cash jackpot of $104,000. He wrote about the experience in his 2004 book *How to Win a Million*. Yes, William Laing literally wrote the book on winning quiz shows. This was the innocuous-looking smiling assassin facing me in that record-breaking episode of *The Chase Australia*.

I expected a proven champion like William to choose the high offer in the head-to-head round (taking an extra risk by starting one step closer to the chaser for a chance at greater winnings) and indeed he did. What I didn't anticipate was that the first player, a tattooed concreter from the Victorian city of Warrnambool, would also take the high offer. But that's what Scott O'Keefe did, cruising through the head-to-head questions to put $38,000 in the team's bank. Scott didn't make a single mistake in those multiple-choice questions, correctly naming the country in which Joanna Lumley was born[1] and the full title of the James Bond character known as 'Q'[2], and identifying what the Turing Test is used to determine[3].

---

[1] India
[2] Quartermaster
[3] Whether a computer's artificial intelligence is good enough to imitate a human.

The second player, a young teacher named Sally Gridley, added a further $16,000 to the team total in another strong performance. Sally correctly named the type of environment in which a speleologist works[1] and the island to which King Arthur was sent after being wounded in battle[2]. She did miss one question, though: 'Which car-maker developed the engine used in the British Spitfire aircraft?[3]' Matt Parkinson may be 198 centimetres tall, but his eyebrows probably hit 3 metres when he saw that.

Then came William, if not the Don Bradman of Australian quizzing then perhaps the Richie Benaud: erudite, polite and seemingly all-knowing. William's cash-builder round was one of the best that I've seen. He correctly answered 12 questions in 60 seconds (including some tricky ones, such as the German city in which the European Central Bank has its headquarters[4]) and was so fast that he earned a near-record $24,000 despite a couple of incorrect answers. Surprisingly, William was the player I came closest to eliminating in the head-to-head round as he incorrectly guessed that Buster Keaton's trademark hat was a fedora[5] and that Aaron Spelling had been executive producer of *Dynasty* and *Dallas* but not *Charmed*[6]. Because I answered

---

[1] Caves

[2] Avalon

[3] Rolls-Royce. I didn't know the answer outright like Matt would have, but I knew Rolls-Royce made aeroplane engines and my educated guess paid off.

[4] Frankfurt

[5] It was a porkpie.

[6] Of the three, *Dallas* was the show that Spelling did not produce.

those questions correctly, and William had taken the risk of only a two-step head start, it could have been enough to knock him out. Except that I let him off the hook by missing this question: 'According to their official product histories and storylines, which character has run for US president the most times?' The options were Homer Simpson, Barbie and Miss Piggy. I guessed Miss Piggy; William correctly chose Barbie.

The final contestant, a chef named Caron Wasserfall, added a further $12,000 to take the cash-pot to its eventual $102,000. And when the team put up a target of 25 in their two-minute final chase, I was sweating. William led the way, answering 10 questions correctly (The only country to share a border with Haiti?[1] The decade in which Old Parliament House opened?[2] The type of tower that is a campanile?[3]), but all four members of the team contributed greatly to the win. Caron scored six correct answers, including the man Jennifer Lopez married in 2004[4]; Sally added four, including the Hitchcock film whose soundtrack was composed entirely of string instruments[5]; and Scott identified the famous winged horse of Greek myth[6]. They were so scarily fast that they scored 25 despite getting a further eight wrong: this was a team who could have posted an unprecedented score

---

[1]   Dominican Republic
[2]   1920s
[3]   Bell tower
[4]   Marc Anthony
[5]   *Psycho*
[6]   Pegasus

of 30-plus. To catch them, I had to give a correct answer every 4.8 seconds during the two minutes of my final chase. And any errors would be incredibly costly, not only because I would lose time, but because the question would then be thrown to the team, who could push me back one step by providing the correct answer.

As it happened, I made seven mistakes, which meant a team victory was inevitable. I often found myself answering by way of word association, because my brain had no time to think answers through completely. For example, I was asked 'Beginning with C, what type of building is a motte and bailey?' In milliseconds, my brain took in the 'bailey' and the 'beginning with C', made a connection to London's Old Bailey, and I guessed 'court'. The team answered correctly[1] and pushed me back one step. Likewise, when asked which war featured the Battle of Guadalajara, my brain jumped to World War II as soon as it heard 'Guadal—', as my mental pathway led me to the Battle of Guadalcanal, in the Solomon Islands[2]. I also confused epaulettes and espadrilles (an ironic mistake given my *Million Dollar Minute* finale), missed the width of an Olympic balance beam by 5 centimetres[3], couldn't recall the New York hotel in which children's character Eloise

---

[1] Castle

[2] The correct answer was the Spanish Civil War, although the team guessed the Mexican–American War.

[3] I said 15 centimetres; the team talked out their answer, correctly thinking it might be around four inches or 10 centimetres.

lives[1] and had no idea in which video game you play as the character 'Master Chief'[2].

I finished my two minutes on 19, six short of defeating the team. In raw numbers, they answered 21 questions correctly during their own two minutes, while I answered 24 correctly during mine. But the final chase isn't about raw numbers. As well as having the chance to push the chaser back, the contestants begin with a head start based on how many players have reached the final. These advantages are a fair way of compensating them for the disadvantage of having to use buzzers and wait for their names before answering, which costs time. Scott, Sally, William and Caron played a near-perfect game and walked away with $25,500 each; at the time of writing, no other team on *The Chase Australia* has collectively won a six-figure sum.

Watching the episode six years later, I was struck by how serious I looked. I was still trying to prove I could be intimidating. But I was also learning how to balance concentration and recall, humour and entertainment. Of course, given the strength of the team, I also knew as the episode unfolded that my unbeaten streak was likely to end, which put me in a darker mood as well. These days, while I'm still highly competitive, I'm much more philosophical when I lose. *C'est la vie* and all that. And I take comfort from the knowledge that if I lose, the contestants have

---

[1] The Plaza; Caron knew this answer and pushed me back.

[2] Halo. Sally knew this one cold and as a teacher earned serious cred from her students.

had a life-changing day. Re-watching this episode also got me wondering: What was the experience like for the contestants?

For Scott O'Keefe, a father and stepfather of nine, appearing on a quiz show was the number one item on his bucket list. He was determined to make the most of it, and playing for the high offer was always his plan. Scott has always had a knack for trivia and fast recall of answers, honed by watching *Sale* when he was young, and when he was selected as a *Chase* contestant he hit the books.

'I trained real hard,' Scott says. 'Reading, googling . . . I had three or four different trivia apps on my phone and I'd swap from one to the other. Every newspaper or magazine I could get my hands on with a quiz in it—my wife was quiz master, reading the questions out.'

That sounds familiar. My wife Zoe and her mother, Margaret, are constantly cutting quizzes out of newspapers and magazines for me, and every now and then Zoe will play quiz master and test me while I'm washing dishes or folding washing, just to keep my brain ticking over.

Scott received his $25,500 just before Christmas—perfect timing, his kids thought—and it gave him and his wife Mel the breathing space to pursue a new path.

'We did have ambitions of investing towards a house,' Scott says. 'But around that time my wife was looking to go into mature-age study . . . It just kept us ticking on for a little while, while she returned to study.'

Sally Gridley was 29 when the show was filmed, and she had already tried her luck as a contestant on *Hot Seat* and *Million Dollar Minute*. But nothing quite prepared her for *The Chase*.

'*The Chase* was the most nerve-racking thing I have ever done,' Sally says. 'I've never been quite so nervous in all my life as when I was facing down you! That bit where you're going up against the chaser, I was so nervous that my hands stopped moving ... They had to re-film the bit where I walked back to my seat, twice, because I couldn't get back on the stool. My hands stopped working and I couldn't work out how to get on a barstool again!'

Of course, Sally and her teammates had the last laugh.

'It was pretty funny, right at the end when you came down to congratulate us, you were so grumpy!' she says. 'It was so funny. You were really angry at us! You were like, I can't believe it, grumble grumble!'

I must admit to feeling a little embarrassed and disappointed hearing this from Sally, even six years later. These days I always try to be humble and generous in defeat. If ever I seem too down on myself for losing, Zoe snaps me out of it by asking the most relevant question: 'But was it good television?' That first loss would have hit hard, not only because it was a new experience but also such a large amount of money. I was pleased to hear that the prize money had really made a difference for the contestants.

'I'd just come out of a really messy divorce, where I had about $20,000 in debt,' Sally says. 'So my $25,000 went to clearing the slate so I was debt free. And then I bought myself a PlayStation 4.'

For William Laing, the experience of winning money on television was old hat—his cash winnings total roughly $625,000. But that didn't make it any less special, and the prize money allowed him to visit his daughter, who was studying in Oregon.

'I saw a lot more of her after,' William says. 'I spent about six weeks in Oregon. It rained every single day. But that was really good. I went around the world visiting some people.'

Caron Wasserfall put her winnings towards the things that were important to her: helping out her family and starting a small business that prepared and delivered ready-made meals. Two years later, Caron won $100,000 on *Millionaire Hot Seat* and had a total career change: she qualified as an environmental health officer. And in her new role, I encountered Caron once again: she worked at the council immunisation sessions where I have taken my children for their regular vaccinations.

'It's been a really good career shift for me,' Caron says. 'Now I get to share my "fun facts" about health and food safety with the unsuspecting public!'

Four people—Scott, Sally, William and Caron—always linked by that victory, that $102,000. In all my game show experience, I've never won as part of a team. I think there would be something special about walking out of the studio together, all four of you having shared in the spoils.

'There was a little bar two or three doors down from the studio and it was not open for long,' Sally says. 'But we thought, let's go have a beer. And Caron's a chef, so she was like, "You should definitely try these truffle parmesan fries." So we all had truffle parmesan fries and beers and it was very nice.'

And then they went their separate ways. Sally went on to appear on *Hard Quiz* and *Mastermind* with her special subjects, the Harry Potter books and the television show *The IT Crowd*. She won both episodes. Caron cashed in on *Hot Seat*. In 2020, William faced me, Matt, Issa and Cheryl on our spin-off show *Beat the Chasers*, where we narrowly defeated him in his attempt to win $101,000 on his own. The following year, he was the overall champion of *Mastermind*. Of the four team members, Scott is the only one who hasn't appeared on a game show since. But given his success on *The Chase*, and the pedigree of his team, look out anyone who has to face him when he does.

▼

That episode was, I think, filmed in August 2015. The recording schedule I had been so concerned about, given the impending arrival of our first child, proved no issue at all, as the start of filming was pushed back by a few weeks. Zoe and I breathed a joint sigh of relief at the delay, which meant that throughout June we could focus entirely on the birth of our daughter Heidi. It truly was a defining few weeks in my life: suddenly I was a father and a television personality. Our sons, Fletcher and Avery, were born in 2017 and 2019 respectively, and our kids think nothing of their dad being on television, because they have never known anything else.

Sometimes I come home from the studio and tell Heidi and Fletcher that I had a 'kiddy question' today; they love being able to answer the occasional question from the show (Mr Smee works for which fictional pirate?[1] What is the name of Snow White's sister?[2]) They enjoy watching the show, and the language of *The Chase* sometimes creeps into regular life. When Heidi was four, she asked me how many hundreds and thousands were on the finger bun she was eating.

'I don't know, maybe fifty,' I said.

'Stop the clock!' she replied.

Dinner time is often punctuated by 'Chase questions' at the request of the kids—they get asked a child-friendly trivia question for each mouthful of vegetables. I don't view it as bribery; I think of it as training. My job makes it difficult to get away with answering 'I don't know' to some of the curly questions children ask of their parents. If I try to feign ignorance, Heidi hits back with 'But you're a chaser!'

My lifestyle means I have learnt to study in unusual ways. Although I have spent countless hours rocking babies to sleep, I developed a habit that allowed me to train my brain at the same time. I would set myself a mental challenge—name all the US states and their capitals, say—and I would silently tick them off in my head as Heidi, or Fletcher, or Avery drifted off to sleep in my arms. Then I would put the baby down and sneak out of

---

[1]   Captain Hook

[2]   Rose Red

the room while thinking to myself, 'Why can't I remember the capital of Connecticut?[1]'

I also use a website called Studystack to create my own sets of flashcards—obscure capital cities, world currencies, NRL players and coaches. I like to revise these in the days before filming, grooving those mental pathways again. If ever you see me in a final chase thump my fist in anger or shout at myself, it's probably because I've just missed a question that is covered in my flashcards. Like the time, late in a tense final chase, when I was asked which Pacific country had the capital city Funafuti. This was in my capital city flashcards, and I knew I knew it. But the pathways hadn't been grooved for a while, and half-heartedly I said Kiribati, knowing it was wrong, and as the team deliberated over what answer to give for their pushback opportunity, my brain belatedly came up with the correct country[2].

I have often heard cricketers say the key to a long innings is to constantly change mental gears: switch on their full focus when the bowler is running in; switch it off after each delivery is completed. Staying mentally 'up' for a sustained period is too taxing. I take a similar approach on *The Chase*: I treat each

---

[1] Hartford

[2] Tuvalu. The tiny island nation with roughly 12,000 people doesn't pop up much in trivia, but there is one particularly interesting fact about Tuvalu. For many years, Tuvalu couldn't afford the fee to join the United Nations, but they hit the jackpot when internet country codes were handed out. Tuvalu's code—.tv—was highly desirable, and the nation brought in US$50 million by leasing out the domain, allowing Tuvalu to finally join the UN.

question like a 'ball', focusing when the host delivers it and switching my focus off during any short breaks between questions. I've seen plenty of cricketers mouth the words 'Watch the ball' to themselves as the bowler approaches; the mantra I repeat to myself in a final chase is 'Listen to the question; jump in when I can.'

Why do I tell myself to listen to the question? Because it is surprisingly easy to answer the wrong question. There is nothing more frustrating than to be asked, say, 'Pandas are native to which continent?' and answer 'China' instead of 'Asia' because you weren't listening carefully. This high level of focus makes it a surprisingly draining job. My role is not physical but, at the end of a filming day, I am often completely and utterly exhausted.

It helps that we are encouraged to have fun with the game, to banter and throw in jokes. This relaxes everyone—host, chaser and contestants—and reduces to a manageable level the tension caused by playing for big money. Although we haven't had our own 'Fanny Chmelar' moment, the questions have thrown up some hilarious answers. It's hard to beat the young man who, in one of my first episodes, was asked in his cash-builder round: 'The sculpture Venus de Milo is renowned for missing which body part?' He answered 'penis', to which Andrew O'Keefe replied: 'To be fair, the Venus de Milo is missing a penis. But that's because it's a woman.' Then there are the plain bizarre answers, like the guy who was asked, 'FOMO stands for fear of missing . . . what?' and said: 'Octopuses'.

Within a month of the show being on air, Matt Parkinson and I flew to Perth to be part of Channel Seven's annual Telethon that raises money for charities including the city's children's hospital. Having grown up in Western Australia, Matt knew that Telethon was a truly massive event, but, as a Victorian, I had no concept of what I was flying into. I soon learnt that this was a weekend of fundraising that captivated the entire city.

Telethon began in 1968 and over the years some of the world's most famous entertainers had made appearances to help raise money: Stevie Wonder, Celine Dion, Tina Turner, Cliff Richard, Whitney Houston, Sammy Davis Jr. The biggest story in Telethon legend was the involvement of Michael Jackson in 1985. At the time, businessman Robert Holmes à Court owned both Channel Seven in Perth and ATV Music Publishing, the company whose assets included the rights to 250 songs by The Beatles. Jackson wanted The Beatles catalogue but it took ten months of negotiations to do the US$47.5 million deal (a process one of Jackson's lawyers called 'The Long and Winding Road'). As part of the contract, Holmes à Court required Jackson to fly to Perth and appear on Telethon. The world's biggest music star didn't sing but he did give his time, visiting children in hospital and being interviewed in the Telethon studio. It might have been a contractual obligation on Jackson's part, but it showed what the Telethon meant to Holmes à Court and Western Australia.

So when Matt and I joined an eclectic group of entertainers and Channel Seven figures for that 2015 Telethon, you can imagine my surprise when one of the event's two child mascots, the 'Little

Telethon Stars', told the audience that her highlight of the entire weekend was 'meeting Fat Cat and Goliath and The Shark'. *The Chase Australia* had only been on air for weeks, and we had spent much of the weekend explaining who we were. As I tagged along behind the actor Erik Thomson, visiting children and families at the hospital, people assumed I was his manager or publicist. But for the 'Little Telethon Star', then ten-year-old Alyssa Bolger, who is autistic, meeting people from *The Chase Australia* was of more interest than the stars of *Home and Away* or *800 Words* or *Sunrise*. A year later when my fellow chaser, The Governess, Anne Hegerty, spoke about her own experience with having Asperger's syndrome, Alyssa and her younger brother Lachlan (who is also autistic) were thrilled to add Anne to their list of 'awesome autistic heroes'.

While writing this chapter, I asked Alyssa, Lachlan and their parents, Rhona and Clay, what it was about *The Chase* that appealed to the kids.

Alyssa wrote: 'I loved *The Chase* from the first episode, because there were questions that only I knew the answers to! I also love all the chasers. I know I'm supposed to go for the contestants, but I prefer to see the chasers win! Especially my two friends, Goliath and Shark.'

Lachlan: 'I just love *The Chase*! I always have. I love watching quiz shows, and I love hosting family quizzes and I want to run pub quizzes when I'm 18.'

Rhona and Clay described the scene in their house when the show is on: '*Chase* Time in the Bolger house starts around 4.45

p.m. when at least one of us yells out 'Almost *Chase* Time!' from wherever we are in the house. No matter how busy or stressful the day has been, within 15 minutes the TV is on, the snacks/ drinks are prepared and we are all together on the couch. We make a guess as to who the chaser will be and settle in to see how many questions we can get right! Being a family of autistics, we all have strong special interests and just love researching things in general . . . so we make a pretty good team (if we do say so ourselves!). We sometimes are cheering for the contestants but usually we get a kick out of seeing the chaser win. *The Chase* has been a permanent favourite in our house for six years, and as long as it is on the air, the four of us will be on the couch at 5 p.m. to see how many questions we can answer correctly!'

Feedback doesn't get much better than that. Don't ever make the mistake of thinking trivia is worthless.

CHAPTER 13

THE WORLD QUIZZING CHAMPIONSHIP

'WHICH PERUVIAN-BORN AMERICAN ANTHROPOLOGIST—'

Okay, bad start, I don't know any Peruvian-born Americans and very few anthropologists.

'received widespread attention—'

Really?

'. . . and became an important influence on the New Age movement with his books describing his experience as the apprentice of a Yaqui Indian sorcerer named Don Juan Matus? He insisted Don Juan was a real person, but this is widely doubted by scholars.'

Cool, cool, cool. Let me just reach into my big bag of 'Peruvian-born American anthropologists who apprenticed to a Yaqui Indian sorcerer' names and hope I pick the right one. There are so many to choose from. Let's say . . . Sanchez. Is that a common Peruvian surname? I hope so, because that's my totally well-informed and 100 per cent reliable blind guess.

I'm sitting in a meeting room at the Holiday Inn Sydney Airport, hunched over a stack of papers, wondering why I bothered to fly to Sydney for the World Quizzing Championship, or the WQC to its friends. Have you ever watched the Olympics and thought, 'Meh, I could do that'? Yeah, yeah, Usain Bolt is fast, but he's not *that* much quicker than me.' Well, the WQC is the nearest thing the quiz world has to the Olympics, and woe betide anyone who thinks they will keep up with the likes of Kevin Ashman and Olav Bjortomt from Britain, Ronny Swiggers of Belgium, Steve Perry from the USA, Finland's Tero Kalliolevo and others—the Usain Bolts of the quizzing world. God forbid you even think you'll challenge Issa Schultz, the Supernerd from *The Chase Australia*, who has finished as high as 23rd in the world. For context, the first year I participated, I finished 310th and was happy with that. You might dominate your family's Trivial Pursuit evenings, but that's a gentle stroll. Perhaps you've even won big on a television quiz show. Irrelevant. Don't know your Slovakian politicians, or Panamanian songwriters, or nineteenth-century tunnels of Switzerland? Then don't expect to win the World Quizzing Championship.

The WQC is like a school exam on steroids. It is run by the International Quizzing Association once a year, simultaneously in forty-five countries, available in fifteen languages, with up to 3000 competitors. Australia is a minor player, with usually just a few dozen participants. Europe and the USA provide huge numbers, with India also bulking up in recent years. Of the top 100 scorers in 2018, 28 were from the UK, 20 from the USA, 12 from Belgium, 6 from Croatia, 6 from Norway, 5 from Estonia, 4 from Germany and 4 from Ireland. Two Australians were in the top 100: Issa Schultz, in position 57, and Ross Evans, who was 71st.

The event consists of 240 questions divided into eight categories: culture, entertainment, history, lifestyle, media, sciences, sport and games, and world. The scoring is out of 210, because a quirk of the rules is that each player's lowest-scoring category is ignored. That allows you to have one big weakness and still score highly. The winning score tends to be in the range of 160–170. As of 2021, Kevin Ashman, one of the panellists from the British quiz show *Eggheads*, has won the world title six times, his fellow Egghead Pat Gibson four times and Olav Bjortomt, who writes questions for *The Chase* in the UK and *The Times* newspaper, and joined the *Eggheads* panel in 2021, has also won on four occasions.

The international nature of the quiz means the questions must be accessible to a global audience. The test is sat in two hour-long halves, which averages out to 30 seconds per question. Usually, the nub of the question is highlighted in bold, to help focus your attention as you speed-read through. This is important, because in this style of highbrow quizzing even the simple questions tend to be wordy.

Coined using Greek words meaning 'running back again', **what name** is given to words, numbers, or other sequence of characters, or complete phrases, that are exactly the same when written backwards? Examples include the English word 'racecar', the Latin phrase 'Sator Arepo Tenet Opera Rotas', the German word 'reliefpfeiler', and in French, 'La mariée ira mal'?

Most people will know the answer to this question[1], which essentially asks 'What is the term for a word spelled the same forwards and backwards?' Half the challenge is wading through the detail to find the question. Sometimes, the questions are short, but that doesn't make them any easier.

Which **judoka from the Netherlands** is the only athlete to win two gold medals in Judo at one Olympics—in the heavyweight and open categories in 1972[2]?

There is no possibility of guessing the answer—you either know it or you don't. But there are some questions you can work out, and one of the most satisfying parts of quizzing is to come up with a correct guess through deduction. I can't believe I plucked the correct response to this question from the 'lifestyle' category in 2018:

---

[1] Palindrome

[2] Wim Ruska

One of Hungary's largest, oldest and internationally most prestigious firms, known for light bulbs and electronics, **which company** takes its name from a combination of the English and German names for the chemical element with atomic number 74?

I couldn't name a single company from Hungary, nor told you with confidence which chemical element was number 74. And I don't speak German. So how did I work out the answer? I started from a single piece of knowledge: that tungsten is commonly used in light bulbs due to its extremely high melting point. What else did I know about tungsten? That its chemical symbol is W, because it was historically called 'wolfram'. And wolfram does sound German. So, then what? Can I put tungsten and wolfram together to form a plausible name? Wolfsten? No, the question listed English first and German second, and I thought there would be a reason for that. I took a stab at Tungsram and was gobsmacked to discover that I had made up the correct name.

Most people don't want to think that deeply about trivia, so the World Quizzing Championship is not for everyone. Some come along once, can't wrap their head around the style of question and the depth of knowledge required and never return. Some, like me, sit there thinking, 'What the hell am I doing here?', but enjoy the experience enough to come back. For others, the WQC is not an experience but an obsession.

▼

You have probably heard of Issa Schultz—The Supernerd—on *The Chase Australia*. Issa is so recognisable that viewers sometimes literally shriek when they see him. You probably haven't heard of Ross Evans and wouldn't know him by his nickname, which I assume is something like 'Rosco' or 'Evo'. You wouldn't squeal if you saw Ross in the street, but maybe you would if you knew he was one of the two best quiz players in Australia. I mean, most people still wouldn't, but you've reached Chapter 13 in a book about Australian quizzing, so you're not most people.

Every year, at the Australian leg of the World Quizzing Championship, Issa and Ross fight it out for the title of Australian Quiz Champion. The rest of us make up the numbers. In the eleven years from 2011 to 2021, Issa has won eight Australian championships and Ross three. They are the kind of people who, when asked 'Which Peruvian-born American anthropologist', may *actually* have several to choose from[1].

Though they share some similarities, Issa and Ross are very different. Issa, 38 at the time of writing, has been a quiz obsessive since his teenage years. He was an almost nightly caller to Tony Delroy's after-midnight quiz on ABC radio and appeared on *The Rich List*, *The Einstein Factor*, *Who Wants To Be a Millionaire?* and *Millionaire Hot Seat* before *The Chase*. Ross is 68, values his privacy greatly and has had no interest in appearing on a television show since he was a long-haired teenager in the early

---

[1] The answer, by the way, to that question was anthropologist Carlos Castañeda.

1970s. Only within the past few years, since retiring from work, has Ross taken quizzing seriously.

Issa and Ross are friendly rivals, and COVID-19 has turned them into friendly teammates. Until 2020, they would see each other once a year when Issa flew from Brisbane to the WQC event in Ross's home town of Sydney. But lockdowns in 2020 led to a massive rise in the number of online quizzes, and not just casual pub-style trivia. Serious quizzing—the type that attracts WQC champions—moved online in a major way, using video apps such as Zoom to enable truly international competitions. Ross and Issa, who had never before teamed up, did so in tournaments such as the Quizzing World Cup, Champions League and the Asian Quiz League. In other competitions they remained opponents; they have played both with and against each other on the same day. In a Quizzing World Cup semi-final in early 2022, the four-person team of Issa, Ross, Michael Logue and David Regal achieved the unthinkable, defeating a British side featuring Kevin Ashman, Olav Bjortomt and Pat Gibson, who between them hold fourteen World Quizzing Championship titles. The Australians lost the final to an American team, but the semi-final win was a monumental victory.

You can never predict what an elite quizzer will or won't know. My *Chase* colleague Anne Hegerty, nicknamed The Governess, is in her sixties, and on the show she resembles a cross between a prison warder and Miss Trunchbull from Roald Dahl's *Matilda*. You wouldn't look at Anne and expect her to nail answers about modern rappers such as Doja Cat or Megan Thee Stallion, but she does, because she studies everything[1]. Likewise, Ross Evans pulls out answers that confound opponents and teammates. In a Champions League match, Ross, Issa and two youngish teammates who were good at pop culture were asked who recorded the 2016 album *A Place at the Table*. The young whippersnappers had no idea, but Ross confidently piped up: 'Solange Knowles'. Ross admits to having a 35-year chasm in his pop-culture knowledge, paying little attention from his mid-twenties until 2016, when he started studying. Solange's album was on a list of 2016 music that he compiled when quizzing became more obsession than hobby.

Ross stumbled into high-level quizzing through the happy accident of his regular pub trivia venue, the St George Leagues Club in Sydney, hosting the Australian leg of the WQC in 2008. The style of quizzing suited his knowledge base—strong in history and geography—and he kept coming back. Each year, Ross took the event more seriously. Now, he spends three or four hours a day, on average, studying, taking notes, filling folders of information that might come up in the WQC. Information sticks in his brain most effectively if he physically writes it down on paper; when I call him for an interview, he's adding notes to his folder on the periodic table. He studies not only to improve his quiz performances but because he enjoys it.

'I think anyone who does quizzing has an inquiring mind,' Ross says. 'And if you've got an inquiring mind, you want to

---

[1] You also wouldn't expect Anne Hegerty to swear as much as she does, which is a lot.

know stuff, you want to understand stuff. You want to know why this happened, or why someone did something, or how this works. I'm not a person who's any good at practical stuff like woodwork or home renovations, or even understanding how a television or a telephone works. That doesn't quite interest me so much. But knowing how the guy made the discovery, and then he did this, and the reason that happened is this—that's more fascinating to me.'

That sounds startlingly familiar. Recently, we had a handyman fix all manner of minor problems around the house, and I was in awe of the way he methodically solved each problem in its unique way. Sometimes he explained what he was doing, and he might as well have been speaking Icelandic. 'Oh, I'm just taking off the door handle to check the flobodob screw, give the jiggaflump a tighten, you can see it's click-clacked from all the nuzzlewanging. Too easy.'

▼

Like Ross, Issa Schultz finds that taking notes helps his recall. Like Barry Jones, Issa can visually recall the placement of information on a page, which helps him pinpoint answers. These answers could be in one of the many notebooks Issa has filled with random lists—I've seen inside one of them, and a list of video games and their creators is followed by Nobel Prize winners, which is followed by operations from wars. Issa always brings at least one of these notebooks to revise when filming *The Chase*. He studies every day, either facts that might come up on *The Chase* or else building his arsenal of arcane knowledge for the WQC. He might open a book, he might click a random Wikipedia tab, he might revise his own questions and notes.

Unlike Issa and Ross, none of my quiz study involves hand-written notes—although maybe it should, if I want to emulate the best. I work exclusively on screens, either studying information online or, if I'm reading a book, taking notes on my phone or computer to write questions on the topic later. I never have been a natural pen-and-paper quiz studier. Apart from my earliest jottings of famous birthdays, on a physical calendar or in a diary, most of my notes, even from childhood, have been on computer. I am notoriously disorganised when it comes to filing papers, and I like the fact that computerised lists can be sorted, filtered and easily searched. Random notebooks would do my head in.

Issa's love of quizzing emerged before he was a teenager, when the Schultz family lived in Cornwall, in England, where Issa was born. The third of four children, Issa spent the blisteringly cold Cornish winters rummaging through cupboards to find books that caught his interest or the original Trivial Pursuit game, which he read card by card. He would play board games with his siblings but they didn't share his passion for trivia, each finding other hobbies to occupy their time. In that regard, Issa says, he and his siblings were like opposite ends of a magnet. But Issa's late father John, who had worked in the Merchant Navy, ran quiz nights at the local Liberal Club in Cornwall. Issa would head to the club after his Boy Scout meetings and wait for his father to take him home, but in the meantime he had his eyes opened to the atmosphere of competitive quizzing.

'I was very fond of my father,' Issa says. 'He was a wonderfully read man. To see him asking the questions and giving the answers—he was the man of wisdom. And the whole to and fro of the questions and answers really appealed to me. When we moved to Australia, they dragged me out to trivia nights because we wanted to fit in; we were a new family in Australia, on the Sunshine Coast. We went to quiz nights and the quizzing illness grew from there, and I'm yet to find a cure.'

As a high school student, Issa obsessively played the Challenge quiz after midnight on ABC radio, but those were free phone calls. When *Who Wants To Be a Millionaire?* started and Issa was still living at home, his parents imposed a strict limit on how many times he could call the premium phone number to register as a contestant: their phone bill would have been through the roof otherwise. He appeared on the show at eighteen and, like Matt Parkinson and I had for *Sale of the Century*, had to buy a suit specifically for the occasion.

In hindsight, Issa knows he was too young to make it big on *Millionaire*. He recalls struggling in one early question to name the country that Robert Mugabe ruled[1]: he didn't have the worldly knowledge needed. He edged towards the $32,000 safe level, but used all his lifelines striving for it—and still got the question wrong. It asked which of *Heat*, *Goodfellas*, *Casino*

---

[1] Zimbabwe

and *The Age of Innocence* was not directed by Martin Scorsese[1]. Issa was so green that he called him 'Score-says' when talking to his phone-a-friend. He had a group of ten people together in a room for phone-a-friend duties—but none knew the answer. He locked in *The Age of Innocence* and crashed down to $1000.

'I was devastated,' Issa recalls. 'I went in thinking I was going to be the richest kid in town, thinking, "I'm going to win this." Especially because I'd seen episodes leading up to it where I'd known the half-million dollar answers. In the end, the money paid for the suit, and then I bought my first-ever mobile phone: a Nokia 3310. And then the money was gone. Twenty years later, I'm almost over it.'

The show that changed Issa's life was *The Rich List*; by this time he was 25 and had far more quizzing experience. The program suited his penchant for list-based learning. It required teams of two to compile long lists of answers to categories such as 'US state capitals' or 'Hugh Grant films'—which Issa and his partner Reuben nailed. In the two big-money rounds they played, Issa and Reuben correctly named twelve ranks in the Royal Australian Navy and fifteen (contestants were not allowed to list more than this) letters of the Greek alphabet, to share $400,000. Never a spendthrift, Issa saved the money to eventually buy an apartment, although he also took his father back to the UK so he could walk Issa's sister down the aisle at her wedding.

---

[1] *Heat*, which was directed by Michael Mann and is notable as the first film in which Robert De Niro and Al Pacino share a scene.

It was after his success on *The Rich List* that Issa first attempted the World Quizzing Championship in 2008. That was the second year that an organised Australian venue was included; in 2007, only a handful of people had sat the quiz at a church hall in the Sydney suburb of Banksia. Pub quiz operator Paula Morgan thought a couple of her smartest regular patrons might enjoy the event, but everyone was surprised at how difficult the questions were. In 2008, ten people attempted the quiz at the St George Leagues Club: Issa finished in second place, one point ahead of fellow debutant Ross Evans. The Australian champion was Trevor Evans—no relation to Ross.

'It's been an uphill climb ever since,' Issa says. 'It's a continual slog, and I've never got tired of it.'

Issa has even travelled to the other side of the world to the European Quizzing Championships (EQC), an annual event that brings together most of the world's leading quizzers. Anyone can enter, and when the event was held in Liverpool in 2013, Issa decided to build a holiday around the EQC. The championship was held at a cathedral, and as Issa waited for the event to begin he was soon star-struck. Kevin Ashman, widely regarded as the world's best quizzer, an unassuming bespectacled former civil servant, walked past, and Issa was in heaven. He couldn't bring himself to say hello to Kevin, nor to Anne Hegerty, The Governess, who in 2015 joined the inaugural cast of *The Chase Australia*, having starred on the UK version for several years.

'I was terrified,' Issa says. 'I didn't go anywhere near Anne. She sat down the front with Barry from *Eggheads*, and I sat well up the back. It was just bizarre, not knowing that less than two years later I would be working with her.'

Like Issa, Ross Evans has also flown around the world for quizzing. In 2016, an inaugural 'Quiz Olympiad' was held in Athens, and Quizzing Australia, a small organisation formed in 2011 to run the local WQC leg and other events such as state championships, selected two four-person teams. Ross Evans was in charge of Australia's 'A' team, and thus is one of the few individuals who can claim to have captained Australia at something.

▼

The international quizzing scene is relatively new. The World Quizzing Championship first ran in 2003 at just one venue in Birmingham, England, where 44 competitors took part. Then the International Quizzing Association was formed, and the event grew with each year. A centre of much of this quizzing growth has been the UK, where pub quizzes and leagues are ingrained in the national culture and 'serious' quiz shows such as *Mastermind* and *University Challenge* have long and respected histories. Elsewhere in Europe, the quizzing culture is just as strong. The same is true of India: in 2014, the late Vikram Joshi became the first person not from England to win the WQC.

Quizzing also has a strong history in the United States, where 'quiz bowl' tournaments for high school and college students have a long history. In quiz bowl, students travel the country competing in organised events that resemble *University Challenge*. Many *Jeopardy!* champions started in quiz bowl, including Ken

Jennings, who won 74 consecutive games on *Jeopardy!* and is widely considered the show's greatest player.

But even trivia legends like Ken Jennings find international quizzing a step up. In 2007, Ken, together with other American quiz show champions David Legler, Ed Toutant and Bob Harris, formed a Team USA to compete at the European Quiz Championships in Blackpool, England. At the time, the team style was new to the Americans, pub trivia having only taken off in the USA since then.

'We got smoked by Belgium so hard that we could only laugh,' Bob Harris, who moved to Australia a few years ago, tells me. 'They were all constantly in pub trivia, I learnt, and it seems to have sharpened them the way constant training does athletes. One question was about naming "this famous American beekeeper[1]" and Ken and I are looking at each other like "Whaaaaat?" while the Belgians are already scribbling their answer and ordering another beer. There was also a truly psychotic question about— and I'm paraphrasing, but this is surely close—which relative of the mongoose is known to attract mates by performing hand-stands in the Balearic Islands. Here I thought I knew a lot of trivia, and suddenly there's this sentence with a string of random

[1]   The answer was likely the Reverend Lorenzo Lorraine Langstroth, who sounds like a character from a Coen Brothers movie but was a nineteenth-century figure known as the 'father of American beekeeping'. And to highlight Wikipedia's depth, if you click the 'American beekeepers' category link on Langstroth's page there are 33—*thirty-three!*—entries.

nouns that I had no idea could even combine in the same sentence. It was like a question made out of refrigerator magnets.[1]'

I know the feeling. That's how the Don Juan Matus WQC question seemed to me. Australians have loved television and radio quiz shows for nearly a century but, when it comes to range and depth of quizzing options, we have been a laggard. Fortunately, that's starting to change. Quizzing Australia remains a small organisation but it runs championships in most Australian states plus the ACT. Monthly international written quizzes with names like Squizzed and the Hot 100 can also be sat around Australia, allowing you to compare your scores to the world's best, and a growing community of quiz lovers has started to build.

For me, quizzing is still primarily about fun. Yes, I enjoy showing off my obscure knowledge on *The Chase*, just as any pub trivia player wants to impress their friends by nailing a tricky answer. But what I love more is working out an answer. As Trivial Pursuit writer Bruce Elder said, the great joy in trivia is in *almost* knowing something.

When we filmed *Beat the Chasers* in 2020, as Matt Parkinson, Issa Schultz, Cheryl Toh and I paced the floor behind our seats waiting for the next contestant, Matt asked us a trivia question that he'd read in the newspaper and that had been bugging him.

---

[1] Bob thinks the answer was the genet, which is not a particularly close relative of the mongoose, but I did find a website that explained how male genets perform handstands while spraying anal secretions on vertical surfaces. Or was that a set of refrigerator magnets?

What were the only three songs that hit No. 1 in Australia in the 1980s that had the word 'girl' or 'girls' in their titles? Together, the chasers pondered this piece of trivia, and it got its hooks into us. I suggested 'Rich Girl' by Hall and Oates, but Matt was sure that was from the 1970s. We quickly landed on 'Girls Just Want to Have Fun' by Cyndi Lauper and 'Jessie's Girl' by Rick Springfield. But what was the third? And then, as a Billy Joel fan, it hit me.

'Uptown Girl!' I said, and Matt smiled and pointed at me in congratulation. He checked the answers in his newspaper: 'Girls Just Want to Have Fun', 'Jessie's Girl', 'Uptown Girl'. We were about to play against a contestant for up to $100,000, but that tantalising piece of worthless music minutiae could still grab our attention. That's what good trivia does: it makes you think 'I *should* know this.' It also brings out the competitive juices—everyone wants to be the one who *does* come up with the answer first. And let me tell you, standing next to three of Australia's finest quizzers, it felt damn good.

EPILOGUE

ONE OF THE MOST MEMORABLE SLEDGES IN CRICKET HISTORY WAS delivered by a little-remembered England bowler named James Ormond, who strode to the crease to bat against Australia on his Test debut at The Oval in 2001. As Ormond arrived at the wicket, Mark Waugh, whose brother Steve was the Australian captain, got stuck into him, wondering out loud how this bloke was good enough to play for England. Ormond's legendary retort even got a laugh out of the Aussies: 'At least I'm the best player in my family.'

I was reminded of this line at the 2019 Victorian Quiz Championship, when I was defending the title I had won the previous year. I dragged my older brother Chris along to the Kensington Town Hall to bolster the low numbers—and he

bloody won the thing[1]. I couldn't feel too bad about it: Chris is a
highly intelligent person and has always been terrific at quizzes.
Later that year, he and I played together in the Australian Pairs
Championship, which runs on the same day as the WQC. Almost
always, the pairs title is claimed by Issa Schultz and his partner
Michael Logue, so I was pretty chuffed that Chris and I won it
in 2019. The turnout at these events may not be huge, but my
brother and I can say we've each won a state title and together
won a national title.

I know my parents are proud. I suspect my mother was a
little concerned when *The Chase* started, worried that her son
might be shown as a big meanie on national television. But she
quickly realised that the game was all about fun. I have much
to thank her for. She instilled in me a love of books, of reading
and of learning. My father wears his pride without subtlety.
Dad has a remarkable ability to mention *The Chase* to anyone,
random strangers included. I get the feeling he doesn't so much
shoehorn it into the conversation as bludgeon it in with a mallet
('Sorry, no, I don't know where the post office is, but listen, do
you watch *The Chase*?'), although he disputes this. Either way,
I don't mind. There's a lot of my father in me, and I'm all the
better for it.

I never expected quizzing to change my life. I was obsessed
with *Sale of the Century* as a child, and at nineteen achieved my

---

[1] To be specific, he tied for the title with Louise Williams, who had won the cash
jackpot and all the prizes on *Sale of the Century* in 2001.

goal of competing on the show. But after that, why did I keep coming back to quiz and game shows again and again? It was addictive, an adrenaline rush, and enormously fun. Mostly, I just looked at all these shows and thought, why not? I loved playing games and liked the look of the prizes—so why shouldn't it be me who tries to win them? After I won $32,000 on *Who Wants To Be a Millionaire?*, someone at work referred to me as 'lucky'. Yes, there had been elements of luck in some of my game show wins, but true luck is winning the lottery. I had applied for these shows and used skill and tactics to give myself the best chance at success. And yet I was also aware that I *was* lucky—lucky to have been born to loving parents who nurtured my education, allowed me the freedom to pursue my passions and supported me all the way. Many people don't have that privilege. Winning the lottery of life allowed me to use my skills to achieve what I have.

Quizzing might even have helped me land my wonderful Zoe. On our second date, she expertly steered the conversation to game shows, having googled me after our first date and found a reference to me having been on quiz shows when I was younger. Of course, I didn't know that, or that Zoe had herself once auditioned for *Wheel of Fortune*. She was not a game show junkie, but the whole thing fascinated her. In 2012, we tried out together for *Deal or No Deal*, hoping that our story—wanting to win money for our wedding—would get us on the show. It did, but only as a couple of briefcase openers.

If you had stood up at a Camperdown College school assembly in the 1990s and said that one of these hundreds of students would become a television personality, nobody would have predicted it would be me. *I* wouldn't have predicted it would be me. I was studious and introverted and never the class clown. But I always loved quizzes, and through that passion I have stumbled into the world of television. It is a world so bizarre that I once found myself bundled onto a stage in Perth beside pop singers and *Home and Away* stars, singing alongside Daryl Braithwaite as he belted out 'The Horses' to close Telethon.

But the most surprising and meaningful experience came in 2017, when I was invited back to Camperdown College in rural Victoria to participate in the 'Principal for a Day' program. I was to tour the school, say a few words to the senior students and give something back to the community. But the school had something else in mind: a *This Is Your Life* event, which brought back many of my former teachers from Prep to Year 12, as well as several of my ex-classmates. It was an overwhelmingly emotional experience as, one by one, each familiar face came out and surprised me.

There was my Prep teacher, Karen Jeffs, who recalled that I could read and write before I started school, but that I was reluctant to show off in front of the other students. There was my Grade 6 teacher, Rob Baker, who tested us with regular quizzes on capital cities and times tables and current events. I was pleased to discover that, despite being in his seventies, Rob was still teaching and still gave his students these regular quizzes. There was Philip Bool, who taught me Indonesian in high school and was my favourite teacher because his lessons often became wide-ranging discussions about world culture, politics and what made a fair society. His classes helped shape my view of the big wide world that existed outside Camperdown.

Afterwards, one teacher told me it was fantastic to have a former student come back to the school who was known for using their brains, 'not just another sportsperson'. I love sport and have great respect for those who have the discipline to reach its elite level. But I understood the sentiment. Our society puts sports-people on a pedestal—but not every child wants to be a footy player or cricketer. We need role models of all sorts—doctors, scientists, authors, artists, environmentalists, thinkers—to remind children of what they can achieve, the difference they can make. I don't put myself in that category at all: I'm a quizzer, I remember and recite facts. I'm not Barry Jones, connecting all of those facts at a high level to solve the problems of the world. Still, my curiosity does shape my views, and if there's one thing the past few years have taught us, it is this: facts matter. In a modern world of opinion, hot takes and fake news, quizzing is a little desert island where facts are still respected. Quiz questions have right answers and wrong answers, and no amount of ideology or spin can change that.

At its most fundamental level, quizzing is driven by the same thing that has inspired explorers, scientists, writers and philoso-phers throughout history: curiosity. We can take that curiosity in any direction and take it as seriously or as flippantly as we choose. Trivia is no more an inane branch of esotericism than any other hobby. We can and do obsess over it. We can and do have fun with it. We shouldn't equate it with being smart, but neither does a passion for trivia mean we're *not* smart. Is it worth a million dollars? Maybe; maybe not. But one thing is certain: dictionaries are wrong. Trivia is worth *something*. And that's good enough for me.

ACKNOWLEDGEMENTS

I LOVED EVERY MINUTE OF WRITING THIS BOOK: RELIVING MY OWN DAYS as a quiz show hopeful; uncovering the fascinating stories of champion contestants, question writers, hosts, producers and more; and looking back nostalgically at game shows from past eras. My passion for trivia is born of curiosity, and writing this book gave me carte blanche to satisfy my curiosity about all things quiz. For more than 80 years, Australians have enjoyed quizzes in one form or another—on radio, on television, at a trivia night, in a board game, in the newspaper, under beer bottle caps—and I couldn't believe nobody had written a book that delved into this culture. I feel honoured to be the one to explore it. I can only hope you have enjoyed the reading as much as I enjoyed the writing.

Of course, writing a book through long COVID-19 lockdowns, with three small children at home virtually all the time, had its challenges. That it happened at all is testament to my incredible wife Zoe, who inspires me every day with her zest for life. I have dreamed for years of writing this book and Zoe has encouraged and enabled me every step of the way. While I shut myself in the study for long days of writing, she took on the countless and relentless and selfless tasks required to keep our family functioning. And then, late at night, she would act as my first editor, reading my work and making astute suggestions and corrections. This book is infinitely better for her attention to detail and candid feedback. I am a very lucky man to have Zoe in my life, and if you enjoyed this book then you too are very fortunate that I have Zoe in my life.

To my children, Heidi, Fletcher and Avery, it fills me with pride that I can already see in you all a burning curiosity about the world around you and a desire to learn and ask questions. I'll always do my best to foster that. And you would be surprised how much your interests help me to learn: when you play a new game, sing a new song, watch a new movie or TV show or read a new book, you are taking in all that new information, but so am I. Seeing the world through your eyes makes me a better person (and a better quizzer).

Thanks also to the rest of my family—my parents David and Valerie, my sisters Lindy and Judi, my brother Chris—for helping to instil in me a love of learning and a passion for games and trivia. All those competitive games of Trivial Pursuit and

Sale of the Century as a child set me on the path to where I am today. I am forever grateful to my parents for their support and encouragement to pursue whatever goals I wanted to in life. And, for the writing of this book, my mum's habit of keeping a daily diary for more than thirty years proved invaluable for checking dates and recalling long-forgotten details. Thanks also to my brother-in-law Paul for his recollections of training as a prospective *Sale* contestant more than twenty years ago, and for being my *Millionaire* phone-a-friend.

I am greatly indebted to Malcolm Knox for his support and advice, and for championing this project and seeing its potential. Malcolm is one of Australia's finest writers, and I have also discovered he's an outstanding editor as well. To have him in my corner was invaluable. At Allen & Unwin, thanks to Tom Gilliatt for his support and encouraging feedback, and to Courtney Lick and Rebecca Kaiser for their hard work on making the manuscript as sharp as it could be. Special thanks to copyeditor Susan Keogh, who, as one of the best in the business and as a former quiz show contestant herself, had uniquely valuable insights and suggestions.

Although this book traces my own journey in quizzing, it was never intended to be a memoir. My vision was always to tell the stories of others involved in every part of the quiz world, and I thank each and every person who agreed to be interviewed. The process began back in 2017, when I had no publisher and no firm plan. But what I did know was that I one day wanted to write a book about quizzing, and I sought out Cary and Lyn Young for my first interview. They warmly welcomed me into their home, told me their story and, without knowing it, confirmed my belief that there was an interesting book in all of these quizzing tales. A heartfelt thanks to everyone else whom I interviewed: Tony Delroy, David Poltorak, Deb Stewart, Larry Emdur, Mark Humphries, Simon Hoffman, Leon Fent, Martin and Robyn Flood, Bruce Elder, David Astle, Lisa Paton, Jennifer Ong, Scott O'Keefe, Sally Gridley, William Laing, Caron Wasserfall, Ross Evans and Bob Harris. A special thankyou to my fellow Australian chasers, Issa Schultz, Matt Parkinson and Cheryl Toh, not only for their interviews but for being such wonderful friends and colleagues on the show.

Thank you also to everyone who assisted by answering my random queries about various aspects of the quiz world: Anthony Watt, Michael Mawson, Dave Warneke, David Morgan, David Regal, Miles Glaspole, Eve Levens, Pete Curry, Christian Kelly and Paula Morgan. Christian and Paula run Quizzing Australia, and if you like the idea of having a go at the state or national quizzing championships, or the regular international quizzes they facilitate, visit https://www.quizzingaustralia.org. A special thankyou to the Bolger family—Rhona, Clay, Alyssa and Lachlan—for being such loyal fans of *The Chase Australia* and friends of the chasers, and for describing the scene in the Bolger house when the show is on.

I am indebted to filmmaker Ronen Becker for allowing me to source and quote information from his outstanding documentary *The Trivialist*. I encourage anyone interested in that story to seek out the film. Thank you to Shayne Bushfield for permitting me to quote questions from his excellent and addictive Learned League online trivia competition. Also to Jane Allen at the International Quizzing Association for allowing me to reprint questions from the World Quizzing Championships. And to Stephen Hall, who permitted me to use a paragraph from his insightful blog 'How To Win Game Shows', which I heartily recommend to any readers interested in more interviews and behind-the-scenes stories from the Australian game-show industry. Other quiz-related works that may be of interest to readers include William Laing's *How to Win a Million*, about his successful run on *Who Wants To Be a Millionaire?*; *Quiz: The Consortium The Truth* by Paddy Spooner and Keith Burgess, which outlines how they mastered *Millionaire* in the UK; Tony Barber's memoir *Who Am I?*, which tells of his time on *The Great Temptation*, *Sale of the Century* and *Jeopardy!*; *A Thinking Reed* by Barry Jones, which includes a detailed section on his *Pick a Box* years; and other general books on international quizzing such as *Prisoner of Trebekistan* by Bob Harris and *Brainiac* by Ken Jennings in the USA, and Alan Connor's *The Joy of Quiz*, Marcus Berkmann's *Brain Men* and Mark Mason's *Question Time* in the UK.

Finally, thank you to all the loyal viewers of *The Chase Australia* and to everyone who enjoys quizzing in any form, for making it such an enjoyable, quirky world of which to be a part. May our curiosity never die.

INDEX